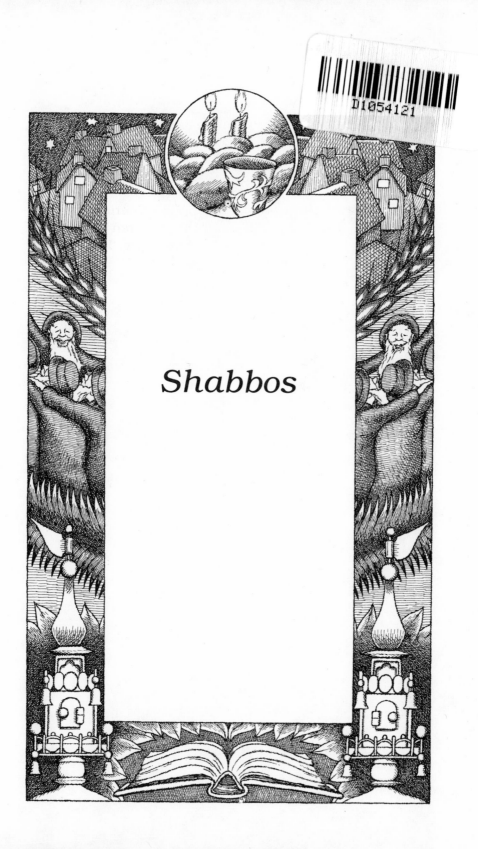

Shabbos

Shabbos is the foundation of Jewish life. The observance of *Shabbos* is the secret of the existence of the Jewish people.

Everything in this world was created in pairs: male and female, Sunday and Monday, Tuesday and Wednesday, Thursday and Friday, *Shabbos* and the Jewish people.

The Almighty said to the Jewish people, "I have a precious gift in My Treasure House and *Shabbos* is her name."[1]

Shabbos, the seventh day of the week, commemorates the creation of the world, reminds us of the day the *Torah* was given on Mount Sinai, and provides a taste of eternity.

In the Friday evening prayer service, *Shabbos* is referred to as *Shabbat Hamalkah*, the Sabbath Queen. As befitting royalty, we welcome her with special rituals that create a majestic environment of peacefulness and serenity.

Kindling the *Shabbos* candles and *kiddush* (sanctification of the wine) signal her arrival. *Challos*—twisted loaves of freshly baked bread—add a special zest to the three *Shabbos* meals. The twenty-five hours of the Sabbath are spent in prayer, study of *Torah*, and song.

Cessation from work, defined as man's mastery over creative energy, allows for *Shabbos* rest.

The *havdalah* ceremony—using wine, fragrant spices, and the glowing light of a twisted, double-wicked candle—accompanies the *Shabbos* Queen upon her departure.

[1]Talmud, *Shabbos* 12b.

Torah Thoughts

Shabbos, A Taste of Eternity

How can we, living in this world, experience eternity? From the moment that *Shabbos* begins, an aura of peace descends upon the home. "Peace spreads itself throughout the world on the eve of *Shabbos*."[1]

On *Shabbos*, we experience this peacefulness as a taste of eternity.

Elevation into the spiritual universe, the creation of a *Shabbos* environment, is achieved by the combination of a *Torah* precept and by the greetings, the prayers, the songs, and the meals.

First, the *Torah* instructs us with a negative precept: "Do not burn fire in your dwelling places on *Shabbos*."[2] Besides actually burning fire, this precept could mean the prohibition against rage, since it is equated with the burning of fire. Therefore, *Shabbos* should be free of provocation, quarreling, and disputes.[3]

[1]*Zohar*, Deuteronomy 15:2.
[2]Exodus 35:3.
[3]*Zohar*, Exodus 85a.

Two greetings exchanged on this day set the mood: "Good Shabbos" and "*Shabbat shalom u'm'vorach*," a *Shabbos* of blessed peace.

Just before reciting the *Amidah*, the "silent prayer," during the Friday evening prayer service, we recite, "Spread over us the shelter of Your Peace. Blessed are You, Who spreads His shelter of peace upon us, upon all of His people Israel, and upon Jerusalem."

This blessing describes the peace and tranquility that fill the Jewish home on the *Shabbos*, for it is not recited on weekdays.

During the *Shabbos* afternoon prayer, the concept of tranquility, of a spiritual universe, is repeated: "A rest of peace, serenity, tranquility, and security, a perfect rest. . . ."

Many of the *Shabbos* songs include the theme of peace. Among the most well-known is the hymn *Shalom Aleichem*:

> Peace unto you, angels of peace, messengers of the Holy
>   One, the King of Kings, Blessed be He.
> Come in peace, messengers of peace. . . .
> Bless me (us) with peace. . . .
> Before you depart, messengers of peace, bestow your bless-
>   ings of peace upon me (us).

Implied in the verse "And you shall call *Shabbos* a delight"[4] are the three meals on the Sabbath, prepared and shared to honor the presence of the King. It is as if we are guests at the royal table during *Shabbos*. On this day of peace and tranquility, we are granted a glimpse of His eternal world.[5] The peace and tranquility of *Shabbos* provide a taste of "an eternal world."[6] May the Merciful One grant us a day that is completely peaceful, a day in which we can experience a taste of eternity.

---

[4]Isaiah 58:13.
[5]*Zohar*, Leviticus 49b.
[6]*Zohar*, Genesis 1:48a.

Good *Shabbos*

Normally, we take for granted those expressions that are part of our everyday vocabulary and those habits that are part of our daily routine.

Did you ever wonder why we greet friends with "Good evening," "Good night," "Good morning," or "Good afternoon," depending on the time of day, but our greeting on *Shabbos* has no reference to time? We simply say "Good *Shabbos*" during the twenty-five hours of the day of rest.

Three biblical verses provide us with a clue as to why no reference is made to any particular time on *Shabbos.*

"And on the seventh *day* God finished His work."

"He rested on the seventh *day* from all His work which He created."

"And God blessed the seventh *day* and made it holy."[1]

It is obvious from these verses that *Shabbos* is a twenty-five

---

[1]Genesis 2:2–3.

hour period which is all *day.* Day is symbolic of light, blessings, joy, peace, family togetherness, and rest.

There is no "night" in *Shabbos,* which means there is no darkness, no evil, no shadow, no fear, no pain.

Therefore, our greeting on the Sabbath is "Good *Shabbos.*"

Welcoming a *Shabbos* Guest

One of the most popular advertisements in Jewish magazines, newspapers, posters, storefront windows, and on bumper stickers proclaims, "Jewish women! Mothers and daughters . . . light *Shabbos* candles!"

Of all the rituals associated with the observance of *Shabbos*, lighting candles is considered the special *mitzvah* (commandment) for women.

The *Zohar* teaches that the *mitzvah* of kindling the lights was especially given to the "women of a holy people because their souls are attached to royalty."[1]

Women are considered to be daughters of "The King," whose majesty rules the world. Yet, they are described with a simple verse: "The honor of the daughter of the King is inward."[2] This verse describes the role of women in relationship to men as having the inside role: the wife, the homemaker, the mother, the

---

[1] *Zohar*, Deuteronomy 16:1.
[2] Psalms 45:14.

mistress in charge of the home, the most important (albeit, in this age of equality, many women function in multiple roles).

It is the women who are the creators of that environment called *Shabbos.* It is they who create a miniature sanctuary, a place where the Divine Presence is welcomed into the Jewish home each *Shabbos.*

How does the woman welcome the Divine Presence, who arrives as a special guest? She welcomes the Divine Presence by kindling the *Shabbos* lights, thereby lighting the way for the arrival of the royal visitor.

Women do today exactly what our matriarchs Sarah and Rebecca did 3,500 years ago.

"All the days that Sarah lived, the Divine Presence hovered over her tent and the flames of the *Shabbos* candles burned from one *Shabbos* eve to the next. When Sarah died, the flames were extinguished, until Rebecca continued in the footsteps of Sarah; and the flames of her candles once again sparkled from *Shabbos* to *Shabbos.*"[3]

[3]*Zohar*, Genesis 45:2.

Kiddush Hayom:
Sanctification of the Day

Most of us associate *kiddush,* sanctification, recited at the beginning of the *Shabbos* meal, with wine. The recitation of *kiddush*
signifies the separation between the weekday and the *Shabbos.*

Using wine for *kiddush* is a Rabbinic dictum. Our Rabbis
explained "Remember the *Shabbos* day to sanctify it"[1] to mean
"Remember it with wine."[2]

Why did our Rabbis specifically choose wine, an intoxicating beverage, with which to sanctify *Shabbos?*

So many people use intoxicants as an escape. Rather than
coping with life's myriad problems, they seek flight through
drink, hoping that the next day the problem will have vanished.
Intoxicating drink also suppresses the recognition of a Supreme
Creator, because it neglects the personal responsibility of choos-
ing right from wrong.

Each week, on the *Shabbos,* we set aside twenty-five hours
to contemplate Creator and Creation. Our inclination would nat-

[1]Exodus 20:5.
[2]Talmud, *Pesachim* 106a.

urally be to refrain from intoxicating beverages. But the *Torah* does not demand that we become ascetics, denying ourselves for religious purposes. Rather, the *Torah* wants to teach us to sublimate the mundane, to moderate the intoxicant, to elevate the *kiddush* for a higher purpose, namely, to recognize that the true purpose of life is the service of the Creator.

Lechem Mishnah

Whether we buy or bake *challos* for *Shabbos*, we automatically think in terms of two, for we have been taught that while the Jewish people sojourned in the desert, they received a single portion of manna daily and a double portion on Friday, for no manna fell on *Shabbos*.

"And on the sixth day, they gathered twice as much bread."[1] "See, because God has given you the *Shabbos*, therefore He gives you double bread on the sixth day, enough for two days."[2]

The biblical text itself clearly spells out the reason for *lechem mishnah* (the two *challos* that grace our *Shabbos* table). Many explanations for *lechem mishnah* go beyond the simple interpretation of the biblical text. The manna is introduced with a seemingly strange phrase: "Behold I will rain down upon you bread from the heaven."[3] We all recognize that bread is a

[1]Exodus 16:22.
[2]Exodus 16:29.
[3]Exodus 16:4.

product of the earth; it does not rain down from Heaven. The whole concept of the manna teaches us that when God rains down manna from Heaven, He will provide for all our needs.

When the Jewish people left Egypt, they took with them a small supply of *matzos*.[4] When this supply ended, the nations of the world mocked the Almighty. They said, "He took them from Egyptian bondage to starve them in the desert." The Almighty answered, "I will feed them heavenly food."

He gathered them under the protection of His Clouds of Glory, the seven clouds that surrounded the Jewish people throughout their sojourn in the desert, and fed them with the manna.

The nations of the world stared incredulously at the Jewish people, basking under the protection of His Clouds of Glory, praising Him for providing their daily sustenance. It was as if the Jewish people were sitting at tables in the Garden of Eden, laden with all varieties of delicacies.[5]

Through the daily flow of the manna from Heaven to earth, the Jewish people were taught that the Almighty would provide for their sustenance. Through the doubling of the portion of manna on Friday, the Jewish people were taught that on *Shabbos* it was not necessary to work because God provided for their needs.

Each *Shabbos*, the *lechem mishnah* remind us of the miracle of the manna in the desert. We become cognizant that we do not need to worry about our sustenance, that we do not need to work on *Shabbos*, that we can set aside one day each week to enjoy the holiness of *Shabbos*. We are blessed with a double portion on Friday, which provides for all our *Shabbos* needs.

[4]"The day of the encampment in the Sinai desert is specifically mentioned here because they finished the *matzos* which they had brought forth from Egypt (Rashi, Exodus 16:1).

[5]*Midrash Rabbah* Exodus 25:5.

A Holy Day and a Holy Land

Shabbos celebrates the sanctification of time (the day is holy), while *Eretz Yisrael* marks the sanctification of space (the land is holy). Our patriarchs, Abraham, Isaac, and Jacob, taught us that through the sanctification of space (*Eretz Yisrael*), we learn to sanctify time (*Shabbos*).

Abraham discovered the Almighty in the Diaspora (exile). He was commanded, "Go from your country and your birthplace and the house of your father to the land that I will show you."[1] By following God's command, Abraham paved the way out of the Diaspora to *Eretz Yisrael,* the Holy land.

There are three meals that we eat on *Shabbos,* each representing one of our patriarchs. When we eat the first meal of *Shabbos* on Friday night, we sever our ties with the Diaspora of the weekday, the cares, the problems, the pain, and commit ourselves to the sanctification of time. We sanctify time as Abraham sanctified space.

[1]Genesis 12:1.

Our patriarch Isaac was commanded never to leave *Eretz Yisrael:* "Live in this land and I will bless you."[2] Isaac lived only in *Eretz Yisrael,* far removed from any ties with the Diaspora. When we eat the second meal of *Shabbos,* we are surrounded only with *Shabbos.* The lunch meal is eaten when we are far removed from the Diaspora of time.

The third meal of *Shabbos* parallels the life of Jacob, who was born in *Eretz Yisrael* but forced to leave it for the Diaspora. Yet, the Almighty promised him, "Do not fear from going down to Egypt (leaving *Eretz Yisrael*) . . . I will go with you, and I will return with you (to *Eretz Yisrael*).[3] The third meal of *Shabbos* is eaten before the setting of the sun, after we have spent the majority of our time delighting in the holy day. Nevertheless, we must prepare once again to meet the Diaspora of time. We have experienced a day of complete *Shabbos* peace. As Jacob was forced to leave *Eretz Yisrael,* sanctified space for the Diaspora, so we leave sanctified time, *Shabbos,* for the Diaspora of the week, in anticipation of future *Shabbos* days.

[2]Genesis 26:3.
[3]Genesis 46:3–4.

The *Shabbos* Ladder

Aleksander was a *shtetl* located adjacent to Lodz, Poland, in the heart of the textile district. The *beis hamidrash* (study hall) opened its doors in 1866, and students studied and taught *chasidus* there until the years of the Holocaust.

The first rebbe of Aleksander, Rebbe Chanoch Henich Hakohen, taught:

> The weekdays are compared to a crooked ladder;
>> On *Shabbos* we ascend straight up.
> During the week we must work to achieve;
>> On *Shabbos* we receive Heaven's gifts.
> During the week we have half a soul, like the half a *shekel*
>> that was collected to count every Jew;
>> On *Shabbos* a little is added toward the completion of our souls.
> The weekdays are the body of mankind;
>> *Shabbos* is the soul that is restored and reinvigorated.

Havdalah

Commensurate with our love is the manner with which we say goodbye when we depart. So it is with *Shabbos,* the most beloved day of the week. We express this love in a farewell ritual ceremony called *havdalah. Havdalah* means dividing and separating holy and less holy, truthful and less truthful, peaceful and less peaceful. The purpose of the ritual ceremony of *havdalah* is to enable us to take some of the holiness, the truth, and the peace of *Shabbos,* experienced during the previous twenty-five hours, with us into the week. We use wine, a twisted, double-wicked candle, and fragrant spices for *havdalah.*

Wine is usually used as the symbol of sanctification in most of our rituals.[1] The light of the twisted, double-wicked candle symbolizes truth. The wicks are twisted because truth and deceit are easily twisted, often difficult to differentiate. The approaching weekday is filled with choices. We raise the candle and hold our fingers up to the reflection of its flame, as if grasping

---

[1]Talmud, *Pesachim* 106a.

at the truth, bringing it closer to our being. Because we love *Shabbos* so much, we want to take some of its light and the truth with us into our weekday activities.

The fragrant spices symbolize the "extra soul" we receive on *Shabbos*. After *havdalah*, the "extra soul" departs until the following *Shabbos*. Desiring to take part of the "extra soul" with us into the weekdays, we deeply inhale the fragrant spices, thereby absorbing their aroma into our being until we begin preparations for the next *Shabbos*.

Stories

Challos in the Holy Ark

During the years of the Spanish Inquisition, the fourteenth and fifteenth centuries, many Jews fled rather than chance arrest, trial, and torture under the direction of the infamous Thomas de Torquemada and the *auto-da-fé*. They resettled all over the Ottoman-Turkish Empire, whose borders extended as far north as Vienna, Austria, and included the entire Middle East.

Among the refugees were Jacobo and his wife Esperanza. They settled in Safed, the Galilean capital of the kabbalists, the mystics, along with many other refugees. Jacobo, Esperanza, and most of the refugees spoke Spanish. The natives of Safed spoke Hebrew. Often it was difficult for them to understand one another.

One *Shabbos* morning, in the little *shul* where Jacobo had gone to *daven*, he heard the 60-year-old rabbi speak about the showbread that was brought into the Holy Temple each week before *Shabbos*. The rabbi quoted the biblical verse, "It is on this table that the showbread (twelve rectangular loaves of *challah*, a cubit long by five handbreadths wide, fifteen by eighteen inches) shall be placed before Me at all times (shall cover the entire table).''[1]

Jacobo did not understand every word in the rabbi's speech, but after the prayer service ended, he ran home excitedly and said to Esperanza, "The old rabbi said that the *Dios* likes special *challah* for *Shabbos*. Since you bake the best *challos* in the world, I will bring you ingredients to bake twelve of them. I will take them to the *shul* and leave them for Him."

The following Thursday, Jacobo brought Esperanza flour and yeast. She lovingly mixed together the ingredients, formed the dough, and set it aside to rise overnight. Early the next morning, she shaped the dough into twelve loaves and baked them. The aroma of freshly baked *challos* filled their one-room cottage. When the *challos* cooled enough to touch, Jacobo wrapped them in a clean white tablecloth and ran with them to the *shul*.

He entered cautiously. Certain that no one watched, he placed the freshly baked *challos* in the Holy Ark, kissed the ark curtain and mumbled, "I hope you enjoy my Esperanza's *challos* . . . they are the best in the world. Tomorrow morning when they take out the *Torah*, I don't expect to find one crumb left. *Buen apetito*." Then he stepped backwards until he reached the door, walked outside, and ran home. Jacobo was a very happy man. He was sure that God was happy to have the very best *challos* in the world.

As Jacobo emerged from the back door of the *shul*, the *shamish* (beadle)[2] entered through the front door. He carried a broom in his hand to sweep the *shul* in preparation for *Shabbos*. He stopped in front of the Holy Ark and addressed God. "Master of the Universe! I have not been paid for seven weeks, yet every week I faithfully come to clean Your House. I don't want another

---

[1]Exodus 25:30.

[2]The root of the Hebrew word for beadle is *shimesh*, meaning "to serve or function within the Jewish community." The person who served in this capacity was called a *shamish*. Throughout Jewish history, his role varied: he was a messenger of the Jewish court, a scribe, a janitor in the synagogue, the caller who announced the start of the Sabbath from the marketplace, the runner who knocked on doors to awaken people for the morning prayer service.

job; I only want to serve You. But my wife and children are hungry. I know you make miracles happen. Make a miracle happen now so that I will know that you are listening to my prayer. I will open the curtain of the Holy Ark. I know I will find something inside to help me feed my family.''

The *shamish* drew the ark curtain open. Ecstatically, he began to shout, "You do answer prayers! You do make miracles happen! I knew you would not forsake me, my wife, my children. Thank you! Thank you!"

He counted the *challos*: there were twelve. Mentally, he divided the number so they would sustain his family for the entire week. They would use two *challos* for the Friday night meal, two for the *Shabbos* lunch, and two for the third meal of the *Shabbos* in the late afternoon. They would use the remaining six, one for each night of the week.

The *shamish* took the twelve *challos* and joyfully ran home.

On *Shabbos* morning, Jacobo and Esperanza went to *shul* to *daven*. As the *Torah* was removed from the Holy Ark, Jacobo stealthily crept beside the old rabbi, peered inside, saw that every crumb was gone, winked to his wife, whispered "Blessed God, I'm so glad He enjoyed the *challos,*" and returned to his seat.

During the following week, Esperanza watched the merchants in the marketplace. When she spotted a wheat merchant, a yeast merchant, and an oil merchant, she purchased the best of their products. On Thursday, she once again mixed together the ingredients. Lovingly, she kneaded the dough and set it aside to rise overnight. Early Friday morning, she shaped the dough into twelve loaves and baked them. When the *challos* cooled enough to touch, Jacobo wrapped them in a clean white tablecloth and ran with them to the *shul*. He placed the freshly baked *challos* in the Holy Ark and returned home.

Soon after Jacobo emerged from the *shul*, the *shamish* entered, walked over to the Holy Ark, smelled the aroma of the freshly baked *challos*, picked them up, as was his custom, and went home.

Esperanza baked *challos* every Friday for thirty years. The *shamish* picked up the *challos* from the Holy Ark every Friday for thirty years.

Then, one Friday morning, as Jacobo delivered the *challos*, he tarried a bit longer than usual in the *shul*. He stopped to offer a special prayer for his aging wife, who was finding it more and more difficult to knead the dough. Jacobo prayed, "*Mi Dios!* I know You enjoy Esperanza's *challos* because You eat them every week. But I see that the *challah* is a little lumpy these days. It is very hard for Esperanza to knead the dough smoothly. If you want Your *challos* to be smooth again, please heal Esperanza. Meantime, until she gets better, enjoy Your bread."

Jacobo stepped backwards to leave the *shul*. Suddenly, he felt a long, bony hand grab him around the neck. He struggled to turn to see his attacker and saw that he was standing face to face with the aged rabbi.

"What have you done?" yelled the rabbi angrily.

Jacobo answered meekly, "I brought the *Dios* His weekly *challos*. I've been doing it every week for the past thirty years, ever since I heard you explain that the 'showbread shall be placed before Me at all times.'"[3]

The aged rabbi was aghast. He continued screaming. "Are you crazy? God does not eat!"

Jacobo answered, "You are wrong! He does eat. In all these thirty years, there has never been a crumb left in the Holy Ark."

The rabbi did not know how to answer Jacobo's challenge. He said, "Let's wait in the back of the *shul* and see what happens."

They did not have to wait more than a few minutes. Humming a joyful *Shabbos* melody, the *shamish* ambled into the *shul*, his broom in one hand, a cane in the other. He opened the Holy Ark, removed his *challos*, and slowly walked away.

The rabbi stepped forward from his hiding place in the back of the *shul* and shouted at the top of his voice, "Who do you think you are? On account of you, this man has been misled into believing that the Almighty has anthropomorphic qualities!"

[3]Exodus 25:30.

The *shamish* was not ruffled by the rabbi's outburst. "Listen," he said, "I have not been paid for my work here for thirty years. This is my livelihood. Every week the Almighty makes a miracle for me that I might sustain my family!"

Then the *shamish* started to howl. He knew he would have no more *challos* to sustain his family. The rabbi cried because his speech had been misinterpreted. Jacobo wailed louder than both of them; he had only wanted to perform a *mitzvah*.

The mournful sounds carried out into the street, to the study hall of Rabbi Yitzchak Luria, the Arizal, the master kabbalist. He sent his disciple, Rabbi Chayim Vital, to find out the problem.

Rabbi Chayim Vital said, "My master, Rabbi Yitzchak, wants all of you to come to him now!"

The three men followed him across the street. They stood facing Rabbi Yitzchak, and he spoke to each one individually, beginning with the aged rabbi. "Do you know why you were blessed with such long life?" he asked. "Since the destruction of the second Holy Temple, no one has fulfilled the *mitzvah* of showbread with such sincere and honest devotion as this man Jacobo. Because your speech inspired him, you were blessed with years. Now that the truth has been revealed, you shall die. Go home and prepare your will."

Then he turned to Jacobo and said quietly, "Now you know the truth. The *shamish* has been using the *challos* that your wife baked to sustain himself and his family. It might not be so easy for your wife to continue baking, now that she knows the truth. I want to assure you, however, that the deed that she did was pleasing to the Almighty. I hope she continues to bake *challos*. Give them directly to the *shamish* instead of placing them in the Holy Ark."

Chazkele L'Koved Shabbos

Chazkele was a porter. Every day he sat near the stalls in the marketplace, either assisting merchants to shift around their merchandise or delivering purchases to shoppers' houses. Chazkele shlepped everything: heavy cartons, loaded baskets, cumbersome boxes, and full sacks of potatoes.

Since he was dependent upon tips, he barely eked out a living. Yet he was always joyful. As he shlepped after the people for whom he carried packages, he chattered incessantly about the beauty of the world, the kindness of the Creator, the holiness of *Shabbos.* The people of the town called him "Chazkele L'Koved Shabbos"—Chazkele in honor of *Shabbos*—because the subject of his chattering was always *Shabbos.*

He was not called that nickname with respect, for the people of the town resented Chazkele's constantly reminding them of the sanctity of *Shabbos.* They mocked him when he told them the potatoes they had just purchased would be perfect for a *kugel l'koved Shabbos,* or that the flour was the major ingredient for baking fragrant, delectable *challos l'koved Shabbos.* They scoffed at him!

"Who is he, that ignorant, illiterate *shlepper,*" they demanded to know, "who dares to tell us how to prepare for *Shabbos?*"

"Food," they thundered, "is for eating, not *l'koved Shabbos.*" Sneering at Chazkele, they muttered, "You do what you want with the money we pay you, but don't preach to us!"

Chazkele never became discouraged. He continued chattering about *Shabbos* with all his customers. Sometimes, besides paying him for his labor, a kind customer would open the carton, basket, box, or sack in Chazkele's presence and give him a small portion of the contents in addition to the tip.

Chazkele saved all the tidbits of food. He stored eggs, noodles, potatoes, onions, chicken, fish, everything until Friday. Then he took inventory and planned a menu for his own personal *Shabbos* feasts.

Many years passed. Chazkele L'Koved Shabbos talked lovingly about *Shabbos,* but most people in the town harassed him. Gradually, he became more and more unhappy. He wondered how long the people of the town would scoff at him. He yearned to be able to go someplace where he could study the *Torah* with all its secrets and mysteries. He dreamed of sitting at a *Shabbos* table, tasting the flavor of an eternal world! All week, as he shlepped around the marketplace, he searched for a rebbe who would show him the way.

One Friday night, a special guest appeared in the *shul.* He had the appearance of a great rebbe. The townspeople treated him with great respect. Chazkele L'Koved Shabbos watched the guest from his corner in back of the *shul* throughout the whole prayer service. Maybe, he thought, this special guest is the rebbe for whom I have been searching.

At one point their eyes met. After the conclusion of the prayer service, people wished each other "Good *Shabbos*" and left. Only the rebbe and his host remained.

The rebbe walked slowly over to the bench where Chazkele sat. He stretched out his hands, grabbed Chazkele's hands in his, and said softly, "Good *Shabbos.*" Chazkele could not move for a long while. Then, timidly, he rose and said, "Good *Shabbos,* rebbe." The rebbe continued, "Your hands are very calloused. You must work very hard. Who are you?"

Chazkele trembled. "My name," he said, "is Chazkele L'Koved Shabbos. The people of this town call me by this name because I talk about *Shabbos* all the time."

As Chazkele spoke, tears welled up in his eyes. He swayed. The tears rolled down his cheeks. He closed his eyes. The rebbe prompted Chazkele to continue telling his story.

"I was orphaned at a very young age. I've lived all my life in this town. I've had very little schooling. I know very little about the Jewish people. I only know that we had three patriarchs and four matriarchs, Abraham and Sarah, Isaac and Rebecca, and Jacob and Rachel and Leah. I know that my people were enslaved in Egypt, and the Almighty redeemed us and gave us His *Torah* on Mount Sinai. We returned to *Eretz Yisrael*, the promised land, the land of our patriarchs and matriarchs. We built a Holy Temple in Jerusalem where we worshipped our Creator. It was destroyed, but we rebuilt it. Then it was destroyed again. Now we are without a Holy Temple, without a homeland. We have been in exile for so long. I know that *Shabbos* is the only reason that we survive. I know little else about being a Jew. I would very much like to learn what it is all about."

The rebbe lifted Chazkele's hands to his cheeks. Until he opened his eyes, he thought he was dreaming. Then he realized he had found his rebbe.

"Chazkele," he said softly, "I wish I knew as much about being a Jew as you do."

After *Shabbos*, the rebbe said, "Please come with me to teach the world the real meaning of *Shabbos.* Until I met you, I never really understood it myself."

The rebbe and Chazkele spent the rest of their lives traveling, teaching the world everything, *l'koved Shabbos.*

A Song in Honor of the *Shabbos*

The Maharal (Rabbi Yehuda Lev ben Bezalel Loew), the six-teenth-century leader of Prague Jewry, had already gone to the Altneuschul[1] for the *Shabbos* eve prayer service.

His wife was busy making last-minute preparations for the *Shabbos*. As she rushed around her kitchen, she realized that she had neglected to fill the water urns. She did not have enough time before *Shabbos* to go to the town well herself, so she called the Golem, the clay robot that the Maharal had created to save the Jewish community from a blood libel,[2] and commanded him to bring water.

[1] The Altneuschul is the oldest standing synagogue in Europe today. It is located in the medieval Jewish ghetto section in Prague, Czechoslovakia. The exact date of the original building is unknown, but records, dating 1142–1171, describe its refurbishment; therefore it is called *altneuschul*, the old new synagogue. Another interpretation of the name has its roots in the Hebrew *al tenai*, meaning "on the condition." According to historical tradition, the Jews of Prague prayed in the Altneuschul on the condition that when the Messiah arrived, they would all return to *Eretz Yisrael*.

[2] A blood libel was the common belief that Jews killed Christian children and used their blood to bake *matzos* for *Pesach*. If a Christian child was found dead in a field around the Passover season, a pogrom against the entire community usually followed. The majority of the peasants, exhorted by their leaders to believe this false accusation, used this opportunity to wreak vengeance upon the Jews. The usual result of a blood libel was the expulsion of the Jews from their homes or the massacre of the entire Jewish community.

It did not take long for the Golem to fulfill her command. The urns were filled, but he continued to run back and forth between the well and the house. The water poured out over the tops of the urns onto the floor, but the Golem did not stop. The house was gradually being flooded. The wife of the Maharal did not know how to control the Golem, how to command him to stop bringing water, so she ran to the Altneuschul to fetch her husband.

Hurriedly, he left the *shul*. He found the Golem between the house and the well, lugging two pails of water. "Stop!" he shouted. The Golem froze in his footsteps. The Maharal removed from the Golem's mouth the parchment that had been inscribed with the four letters of the Holy Name. Then the Golem collapsed in front of the Maharal, who carried the Golem back to his place in the house.

Meanwhile, the congregation had reached that part of the prayer service where the *kaddish* was recited, right after the Psalm, "A song in honor of *Shabbos*." The worshippers did not want the Maharal to miss the remainder of the service, so they recited the *kaddish* and waited for him to return.

When he returned to the Altneuschul after quieting the Golem, they repeated the *kaddish*, as if to signal that the service had begun again.

That *Shabbos* eve, the worshippers in the Altneuschul recited the *kaddish* twice. The custom has remained part of the *Shabbos* service in the Altneuschul for the past four centuries.

One of the most infamous blood libels took place in the Prague ghetto. There, the Maharal is said to have created a Golem, a clay-shaped human form, that reacted to his command upon the insertion in its mouth of a piece of parchment inscribed with the Holy Letters of the Almighty's Name. The Maharal commanded the Golem to find the "murderer." His mission accomplished, the Jewish community was saved from destruction. According to tradition, the remains of the Golem were hidden in the attic of the Altneuschul, where an aura of mysterious holiness still envelops it.

Authors' note: This story was told to us by one of the young men who regularly attends the *Shabbos* service in the Altneuschul. He volunteered the information because we were surprised at the double recitation of the *kaddish*, something not done in synagogues in other parts of the world. We visited Prague in the summer of 1982.

The Coppersmith

Yisrael, a talented craftsman, worked as a coppersmith. He smelted, hammered, pounded, and shaped sheets of copper into lustrous *Chanukah menorahs, Shabbos* candelabra, *kiddush* cups, *Torah* ornaments, and lanterns that displayed the eternal light adorning the Holy Ark in the *shul.* As he worked, Yisrael hummed. Normally, he hummed *Shabbos* melodies. However, if he was crafting a special container for the *esrog,*[1] he hummed *Sukkos* melodies, and if he was crafting a *seder* plate, he hummed *Pesach* melodies. Yisrael imagined that the Heavenly Angels accompanied his song in chorus. Sometimes he was so carried away with the response of the Heavenly chorus that his humming reverberated to the street outside his little shop. For Yisrael, these were moments of ecstasy.

He had only one problem; the fruits of his labor yielded a very meager income. Most of the time, Yisrael earned just

[1]An *esrog* is a yellow, thick-skinned fruit resembling a lemon but having a knobbed end at its base. Together with the palm branch, the willows, and the myrtles, the *esrog* is one of the four species that enhance the beauty of the *Sukkos* festival.

enough to sustain himself and his wife, but one particular week, no customers crossed the threshold of his little shop. Towards the end of that week, he realized that he had no money to provide food for *Shabbos*. As he looked around his shop, he saw samples of his beautiful handiwork resting on the shelves of his shop. But the candelabra had not been filled with candles, the *esrog* box had not been filled with an *esrog*, the *Chanukah menorah* had not been filled with oil, the *seder* plate had no roasted egg.

He sat down on his stool, lowered his head into his hands, and hummed a melody:

> *L'koved Shabbos, bim,*
> *L'koved Shabbos, bam,*
> *L'koved dem heilige Shabbos* (the holy Sabbath).

He was in a quandary. He did not know how to obtain money to buy food for *Shabbos*. Despondently, he closed his little shop and shuffled homeward. He walked in the shadows of the other shops, not knowing how to face his wife. As he walked, he thought he noticed a light in the distance. At first, he thought it was the glow of the setting sun. As he drew closer, he realized that some new coins were laying in the gutter. Excitedly, he picked them up and ran home to his wife. "Look," he exclaimed, "look what I found! We have enough money to purchase the best for *Shabbos*."

When Yisrael and his wife welcomed *Shabbat Hamalkah* (the Sabbath Queen) to their humble cottage that week, serenity hovered over them. The house sparkled from the *Shabbos* candles, the fragrance of special *Shabbos* food filled the air, and the joyful sound of Yisrael's *Shabbos* melodies rang out.

A week passed. Yisrael and his wife relished the taste of that special *Shabbos*.

On Thursday afternoon, a police constable walked into Yisrael's shop. He poked around the corners and moved the merchandise back and forth on the shelves. Clearly, he was searching for something that he could not find. Finally he said, "Someone has informed me that you celebrated your *Shabbos* in a most extraordinary way last week. From the merchandise I see in this shop, it is impossible for you to have had that much money to spend for *Shabbos*. I am arresting you until I have a chance to complete my investigation.''

Yisrael could not protest his innocence. Before he knew it, his hands were shackled, and he was dragged off to prison.

Rumor spread quickly. Yisrael's wife, hearing that he had been imprisoned, ran to plead with the constable, trying to convince him of her husband's innocence. He refused to see her.

Yisrael's wife returned to their humble cottage. She was completely and utterly alone. She had no idea how she would survive. She looked around at her meager possessions. There was not one thing valuable enough to pawn that would provide her with mere sustenance or with candles and food for the coming Sabbath. She did not know how long her husband would be incarcerated. The burden of her pain was more than she could bear. She paced the floor and began to cry. Helplessly, she raised her hands in prayer. "Almighty, what have You done? We only used the money Yisrael found to honor the *Shabbos*. Didn't You command us to honor the *Shabbos*? Didn't Your prophets instruct us to observe it in a spirit of joy and cheerfulness? We have followed Your teachings. Yet, my husband is in jail, and I am utterly alone.''

She stopped pacing and sat down on the floor, still sobbing, still burdened with pain.

It seemed that a long time passed before she heard the knock on the door. Blinded by her tears, her shoulders sagging from her painful burden, she ran to open the door. She found an old man, preparing to raise his cane to knock on her door again.

"Is this the house of Yisrael the coppersmith?" he queried.

As she lifted her head to answer his question, she saw that the old man had a long, flowing beard and sparkling eyes. His voice sounded as sweet as the voice of the man who read the *Torah* each *Shabbos* in the *shul* where they davened. The old man continued softly, "Your husband sent me to give you these seven coins so you will be able to purchase candles, wine, *challos*, fish, and chicken for *Shabbos*.'' He placed the coins in her hand, turned his back to her, walked down the path, and disappeared.

She dried her eyes, took the coins, and started for the marketplace, where she purchased what she needed and returned home.

The police investigation into Yisrael's case dragged on for many weeks. Each Friday morning, as long as Yisrael the coppersmith was incarcerated, the old man came to the humble cottage and gave his wife seven coins to purchase whatever she needed for *Shabbos*. He always told her that the coins were from her husband. She never asked him who he was.

The government finally finished its investigation of the charges against Yisrael many months later. It could not prove him guilty of anything, since it had no evidence. He was released from prison.

Yisrael the coppersmith was reunited with his wife. Their joy was unbounded. In passing, Yisrael asked his wife how she had managed to obtain money for *Shabbos*. She answered, "All week I struggled. Once I sold a pair of candlesticks from your shop. The money lasted a few weeks. Every other Friday morning, a messenger appeared on our doorstep bringing me seven coins from you." Yisrael was astounded; he did not have the vaguest idea what she was talking about.

He pressed her to repeat the story. "Are you sure the messenger told you that it was I who was sending the coins?" he asked.

Yisrael's wife was certain. He said, "I don't know who the messenger was. You don't know who the messenger was. Maybe we will never be able to unravel the mystery. Maybe it was Elyahu Hanavi. Maybe it doesn't matter. What really matters is that we are together again. What really matters is that we can celebrate *Shabbos* together again!"

The Wheel of Fortune

A long time ago, before railroads, highways, and delivery services, merchants traveled to various factories to pick up the merchandise they had ordered. After their purchases were loaded onto their wagons, they paid their bills with the gold coins they carried in locked strongboxes.

Yankel, a Jewish merchant, a skillful businessman, sold exceptionally beautiful fabric, farm tools, oversized cookware utensils, household supplies, and exotic spices.

He controlled a large, exclusive market, distributing his unique merchandise to small shopkeepers within a radius of a few hundred miles. Yankel became very wealthy. In order to expand his business dealings over an even larger area, he persuaded his friend Berel to invest with him, and they became partners. Their partnership agreement stated that Yankel would continue to make the business decisions and that they would travel together on buying trips. When it was necessary to deliver merchandise to widespread areas, they would work separately so as to service their customers more efficiently. The agreement pleased both partners and they prospered.

It happened that Yankel and Berel were on their way to pick up a load of household supplies at the factory. The road upon which they traveled crossed through a clearing in the forest. Nearby, they heard the trickle of a brook. They decided to stop to refresh themselves for a while. They unhitched the horses from the wagon and tied them to a tree, washed their hands and faces in the brook, and lay down on the ground to snooze. Carrying his strongbox with him, Yankel used it to prop his head. Both slept soundly.

They awoke, startled at the lateness of the hour, for the sun had begun its descent. Worried that they could not reach their destination before dark, they hurriedly ran to the tree, untied the horses, hitched them to the wagon, jumped in, and took off.

They reached the inn near the factory after dark, and Berel made arrangements for them to spend the night.

The next morning, Yankel and Berel set out for the factory. The merchandise they had ordered was loaded in their wagon. When Yankel went to pay for the merchandise, he could not find his strongbox.

Anxiously, he ran to the owner of the factory and blurted out, "I can't pay for this merchandise. My strongbox, with all my money, has disappeared! I haven't one ruble in my pocket!"

"Calm down," the owner of the factory said soothingly. "Where did you spend the night?"

"I spent the night at the inn down the road," wailed Yankel.

"Go back there. Maybe you left your strongbox in the inn," suggested the owner of the factory.

Yankel ran back to the inn, searched the room where he had stayed, even asked the innkeeper if he had found the strongbox, but the innkeeper had not seen it.

Yankel returned to the factory shamefacedly.

"I'm afraid I will have to cancel my order since I can't pay for it. Please have the wagon unloaded," Yankel muttered.

The owner of the factory tried to convince Yankel to keep the merchandise. "Listen to me! I know you are an honest businessman. We have done business together for a long time. Take the merchandise on credit. You will pay me on your next buying trip!"

But Yankel shook his head. "No," he said. "I can't do that. I can't owe you money. Please ask one of your workers to unload my wagon."

Reluctantly, the factory owner agreed to the request. Yankel and Berel stood idly by while the merchandise was unloaded. Then they jumped into the empty wagon, turned the horses around, and started homeward.

Yankel guided the horses back along the same road they had come. He hoped that, by retracing his steps, he would locate his strongbox somewhere along the way. The road crossed the clearing in the forest; they heard the trickle of the brook. Only a few days before, they had snoozed in the clearing. Only a few days before, they were rich businessmen. Yankel stopped the horses, jumped off the wagon, and ran around the clearing, searching, hoping to find his strongbox. To his amazement, it was on the exact spot where it had supported his head a few days before. He sat down on the ground and cried.

Berel couldn't understand Yankel's actions. He thought that his partner would be overjoyed, but Yankel beckoned to him after he gained control of himself.

"Listen," he said, "I have to break up our partnership. I want you to count every coin in this strongbox and divide it equally between us. You take your half. We will return to our town together, but then we must go our separate ways. Please do as I say. Don't ask me to explain."

Berel could not believe his ears, but he did as Yankel requested. The former partners returned silently to town and went their separate ways.

Berel invested his share of the money in another business and continued to prosper. Eventually, he moved to the big city.

Yankel, on the other hand, miscalculated each opportunity that presented itself. Suddenly, there was no market for silk fabrics, farm tools, oversized cookware, and household supplies. Yankel's fortune dwindled away slowly. In time he became very poor. He was forced to beg in order to sustain himself.

He felt uncomfortable in his own town, for people stared at the former rich man who had become poor, so he decided to join the cadre of beggars who traveled from town to town. When they arrived in the big city, the leader of the beggars said, "Let's divide up. Each one of us can knock on doors for two blocks. When we finish our work, we will meet at the outskirts of the city and divide the money." All the beggars agreed.

Yankel knocked on the door of a mansion. The owner opened the door. He stared at Yankel for a long while and then, remembering his manners, asked him if he would like a drink. Yankel said, "Yes, please. I am very thirsty. I've been knocking on doors for a long time."

The homeowner brought him a drink and watched while Yankel gulped it down. "Maybe you are hungry," suggested the homeowner. "Please come in. I will give you some cake with the drink. If you wait, I will ask my servant to prepare a meal for you."

Yankel was overwhelmed with the man's hospitality. After he had eaten and drunk his fill, the man handed him a ruble and said, "If you stay in this town for a few days, please return at lunchtime and I will be happy to provide you with a meal. If you are still here for *Shabbos*, please stay as my guest."

Yankel could not believe his good fortune. Day after day he ate in the mansion, and each day after lunch, the homeowner gave Yankel a ruble.

Yankel shared his good fortune with his beggar friends, who were very jealous of his success. The beggars decided that Yankel was hiding more than one ruble from them, so they planned to steal his money while he slept. Each night, his friends searched his clothing, but the rubles were not there. The beggars decided to try again on the eve of *Shabbos*, when Yankel was in the bath house. They would take his money from his clothes while he bathed.

The beggars waited patiently for the days to pass. Finally, it was the eve of *Shabbos*. Yankel entered the anteroom of the bath house, disrobed, and went to bathe. The beggars pounced on his clothing and tore his garments apart. They were furious when they did not find the hidden rubles, so they decided to play a trick on Yankel. They took his clothes and scattered them behind the trees that grew beside the road leading to the riverbank.

When Yankel emerged from the water, he went into the anteroom to dress. He never suspected foul play. To his surprise, his clothes were gone. He jumped out the window and ran behind the trees to hide. He did not know what to do.

Meantime, his host was expecting him. He was disappointed that his guest had not shown up in his synagogue for the *Shabbos* evening prayer service, but he thought that he had gone to a different one, so he walked home alone. But Yankel was not in the mansion. The rich man waited and waited. He was anxious to begin the *Shabbos* meal with the *kiddush*, but his guest had not arrived. Worriedly, he sent his servant to search the town for Yankel.

The servant searched in all the synagogues. No one had seen or heard of Yankel the beggar. He went to the bath house. Three or four beggars were still sitting on the steps. When the servant asked if they had seen Yankel, they jeered, "We saw him a while ago around here, but no one is inside now."

They giggled, reveling at their prank.

The servant walked away in disgust. He was sad that he could not find his master's *Shabbos* guest. Suddenly, he heard screams, shouts, and song coming from behind the trees. He ran to see the sight of Yankel, stark naked, shouting, "Please help me, help me!"

The servant stood on the spot, dumbfounded. Finally, he spoke. "Why did you not come for *Shabbos*? My master is expecting you."

"How can I come like this? My clothes were stolen from the bath house. I've been hiding here for hours, hoping someone would come along to help me."

The servant ran back to the mansion and told his master how he had found the *Shabbos* guest. The master bade his servant, "Quickly, take this clothing for our *Shabbos* guest. Help him dress and bring him here."

Yankel spent the entire *Shabbos* in the mansion with the rich man.

After *havdalah*, he prepared to leave.

"Wait," said the rich man. "Don't leave yet, I want to talk with you. Don't you recognize me?"

This time Yankel stared at his host. He could not believe his eyes. He hesitated for a moment and then sputtered, "Berel, Berel, is it really you, Berel?"

The two former partners embraced. Tears streamed down their cheeks.

"I'm so happy I found you, Yankel," Berel gasped. "It has been so many years. Let me tell you what has happened to me since we parted ways. You see all this," he said, pointing his hand around his magnificent mansion. "God has blessed me. When you told me to leave you, I was heartbroken. I didn't understand. I took my share of the money and came to this city. I married and raised a family. I invested in some great businesses, and I have prospered more than I dreamed possible. When I saw you begging for money from door to door, I was puzzled. I decided to befriend you until I could gain your confidence and have the opportunity to talk to you. I am prepared to give you a large sum of money, so you can go into business again."

Berel paused, then continued slowly, "Please answer two or three questions for me. Why did you break up our partnership? We were doing so well! Why, when you located your strongbox in the clearing in the forest, did you cry rather than laugh? Why, when my servant found you barefoot and naked, hiding behind the trees, were you singing, screaming, and dancing?"

Yankel had to organize his thoughts. So many years had passed since he had broken up his partnership with Berel. He began to speak.

"I want you to know that I honestly believe that life is like a spinning wheel of fortune. One never knows if he will have the winning or losing number. When we were partners, we were on top of the world. I feared it would not last. It was like a self-fulfilling prophecy. When I lost the strongbox in a clearing in the forest, and no one claimed it as their own—in spite of the fact that it had been there for two days—then I thought something was wrong. I felt I was being given a message. I had the gut feeling that my wheel of fortune had reached its peak. I had no place else to go but down. I did not want you to get hurt. I did not want to drag you down with me, so I dissolved the partnership. That's why I was so sad. My premonition became a reality. When I returned home, every business investment turned sour, until I was reduced to begging for sustenance. The reason I danced and sang yesterday in the forest was because I believed that my wheel of fortune was about to turn upward again. I did not know what opportunity would present itself. I only knew that I had fallen to the lowest depths a human being could fall."

Berel was overcome with joy at finding his former partner. "Please, let me help you get started again," he said softly. "It will give me the chance to say thank you for all the favors you did for me." He glanced at Yankel. Tears were streaming down his cheeks.

The next morning, Yankel took the money that Berel offered and started for his home. Knowing that his wheel of fortune was on the upswing, he invested the money carefully. He reinvested the profits and prospered, eventually becoming a rich man again.

The Seven Golden Buttons

It was unbelievable! It was impossible! The people sitting at the *Shabbos* table glanced at each other, not knowing whether to join in the laughter or not. It is true that the Baal Shem Tov introduced the concept of serving the Almighty with joy, that he raised the hopes of the downtrodden and the helpless, but laughing mirthfully at the *Shabbos* table was unheard of!

Why was the Baal Shem Tov laughing?

The Baal Shem Tov was chanting a *Shabbos niggun,* a melody. He sang a little and chuckled a little. The people sitting around the table joined the singing. The sound of *Shabbos* joy became more intense. Then the Baal Shem Tov stopped abruptly and chuckled again. The people exchanged glances, puzzled. Why was the Baal Shem Tov laughing? Who would dare ask the rebbe to explain the reason for his laughter?

The *kiddush* was interrupted by strange, exhilarating sounds, smiles, and the hand clapping of the Baal Shem Tov. This had clearly never occurred in Medziboz before. The *Shabbos* meal commenced with the ritual washing of the hands. As the Baal Shem Tov washed and dried his hands, he lifted his feet to the inaudible rhythm of a frisky dance step, and he jumped and pranced all the way back to his place at the head of the table.

His exultation continued throughout the *Shabbos* meal. His mysterious behavior puzzled his guests.

Afterwards, two students from among the guests volunteered to ask the rebbe why he laughed at the *Shabbos* table. They decided, however, to wait until after *Shabbos.*

Three stars appeared in the darkened sky. The Baal Shem Tov was chanting *havdalah,* dividing *Shabbos* from the weekday with wine, twisted double-wicked candle, and fragrant spices. Not wanting to rush away the *Shabbos* Queen, he concluded the ceremony with a soft tune. People flocked around him in the *shul.* One reflected upon his fingernails in the shadow of the candlelight. Another dipped his fingers in the wine and touched his eyelids. The two students pushed through the crowd. "Rebbe," they said, "we want to know why you laughed last night."

The Baal Shem Tov replied, "I cannot answer your question. However, if you wish to join me for a ride in the wagon, I will show you why I laughed."

Excitedly, the two volunteers motioned to some of their friends to follow them. They ran to the barn, told Alexy the wagon driver to hitch up the horses, piled in, and returned to the *shul* to fetch the Baal Shem Tov. He guided the horses to the outskirts of Medziboz, and they took off for a neighboring village.

The Baal Shem Tov directed Alexy to stop the wagon in front of the dilapidated hut of Shabtai the bookbinder. He motioned his students out of the wagon.

Quietly, they walked up the weed-strewn path toward the door. Answering the Baal Shem Tov's knock, a surprised Shabtai and his sleepy-eyed wife answered the door. "Rebbe," he stammered, "what are you doing here? It is past midnight. Won't you come in?"

The Baal Shem Tov and his students entered the barren hut. They sat down on the floor.

"Shabtai," began the Baal Shem Tov, "we came to find out why you were laughing last night."

The bookbinder stuttered. "I did nothing wrong. My wife and I were only celebrating *Shabbos.* You see, I am a very poor man," Shabtai muttered, "but somehow, from the money I earn I manage to save a few kopeks each day for *Shabbos.* This past week, I had very little work, so I was unable to save any money. On Friday, I had nothing to give my wife to buy food for *Shabbos.* I pleaded with her not to borrow from the neighbors. In my misery, I went to the *shul,* and I sat there all day, studying, expecting to come home to a dark house, with no *Shabbos* food. However, as I approached my house, I noticed the warm glow of candlelight streaming from the window. I drew closer, smelling the intense fragrance of *Shabbos* food. Anger seethed in me, for I had begged my wife not to borrow from the neighbors. Much to my surprise, I opened the door and found her smiling, wearing a new dress. A new coat hung on the back of my chair, the fragrance of *Shabbos* food filled my humble abode, and candles sparkled in every corner. I was truly dumbfounded."

Shabtai's wife had not said one word since he began his explanation. Now she interrupted his narrative. "Let me continue," she said. "Usually, I am very busy on Friday, preparing for *Shabbos.* I shop early in the morning, then clean this hut. When I finish cleaning, I cook for *Shabbos.* Yesterday, I could not go shopping because I had no money, so I decided to clean twice as much as I usually do. I wanted to do something special in honor of *Shabbos.* You see that old chest in the corner? I haven't paid attention to it for a long time. Since I had extra time, I decided to empty it. I was curious to see what had accumulated in all these years. Much to my surprise, my wedding dress was neatly folded on the top of the chest. It had seven golden buttons. I snipped the buttons and ran with them to the pawnbroker. He gave me enough money to buy food and candles for *Shabbos.* I had money left over to buy a new dress for myself and a new coat for my husband. As soon as I finished shopping, I ran home and started cooking. I finished my preparations just in time to light the *Shabbos* candles. Then I sat down and waited for Shabtai. When he came home from *shul,* I explained to him what had happened. His anger turned to joy. He began to chant a *Shabbos* melody. He grabbed my hands, and we danced around the table. He chanted the *kiddush,* and we danced and sang. Our hearts were overflowing. He commenced the meal I had prepared with the ritual hand washing, and we danced and sang and laughed." Her voice trailed off. She remembered every moment of that *Shabbos* joy as if it were a dream.

The Baal Shem Tov turned to his students. "Now you understand why I could not answer your question. I had to *show* you. When Shabtai and his wife danced, I danced, when they sang, I sang, when they laughed, I laughed. I was simply joining with them as they celebrated *Shabbos.*"

Who Will Be My Partner?

He never hastened to make *havdalah* as the last moments of *Shabbos* ebbed away. Rather, he sat with a small group of disciples and friends around a table, nibbling bits of *challah*, crunching a few nuts and raisins between his teeth, munching morsels of leftover gefilte fish, sipping a capful of whiskey, chanting soft melodies, exchanging *Torah* thoughts, clinging to the sparks of the Divine Presence that hovered over the house. This was *sholosh seudos*, the third meal of *Shabbos.* The sun had almost sunk below the horizon, but Rebbe Shlomo Layb lingered. The tone of the melody he chanted intensified. These last moments of *Shabbos* peace were precious. There was no need to rush into the weekday. Clearly, Rebbe Shlomo Layb was master of time. Clearly, he understood the true meaning of deep joy. One of his favorite expressions, which he learned from his teacher, the Baal Shem Tov, was, "When joy reigns in the body of an individual, it also brings joy to the soul. For sadness is the greatest impediment to one's service of his Creator."

Rebbe Shlomo Layb's disciples and friends were used to a

lengthy *sholosh seudos,* so they were not surprised when he began to tell a story.

Elyahu Hanavi once revealed himself to my teacher, the Baal Shem Tov. "Please show me," he pleaded, "the place in Paradise that is reserved for those who observed the *Shabbos.*" Elyahu showed him two chairs, higher than all the rest. "That one is reserved for you," he said, pointing to the chair on the right. "The other is reserved for someone else."

Elyahu disappeared. The Baal Shem Tov was determined to find his partner in Paradise. He ordered Alexy, his wagon driver, to harness the horses to the wagon and prepare for a long journey. When all was ready, the Baal Shem Tov took his accustomed place in the wagon. Alexy sat facing his master, his back opposite the horses. The horses raced down the open road, and it seemed as if they pranced undirected.

They traveled all that day and night. Early the next morning, they arrived at the outskirts of a big city. As the horses continued racing down the road, they noticed large spacious homes interspersed with well-tended gardens dotting the roadside. The spires of Gothic churches pointed skyward. In the center of the city—the marketplace—people hurried to and fro, exchanging greetings. Listening closely to the sound of their words, the Baal Shem Tov realized that the spoken language was not Yiddish, the vernacular of the Jewish people.

It was obvious that they were traveling through a non-Jewish city. However, the horses did not halt in the center of the city. They continued racing down the road until they stopped in front of a small cottage at the edge.

The Baal Shem Tov and Alexy alighted from the wagon and looked around. They walked up the path and knocked at the door. A man with long, braided hair and no head covering opened the door. He spoke the language of the city people.

The Baal Shem Tov asked him for lodging for a few days. He readily agreed, making his guests as comfortable as possible. Each day, the Baal Shem Tov noticed that his host neglected to pray three times a day. He ate his meals without ritual hand washing or grace. When he emerged from his house into the street, he walked straight down the path, for there was no *mezuzah*[1] on his doorpost to stop and kiss. So when *Shabbos* arrived, he was not surprised with his host's actions. Friends from the neighborhood arrived shortly after sundown. They drank, smoked, sang, danced, and joked.

The Baal Shem Tov grieved over his lot when he recognized that his partner in Paradise was a man who desecrated the *Shabbos.*

He questioned the judgment of The Judge. "Maybe," he thought, "I don't understand what my partner is doing. Maybe he is one of the thirty-six hidden *tzadikim* (righteous men) who sustain the world by the merit of their deeds. Maybe he acts this way to hide his Jewishness from his neighbors. I will question him tomorrow morning."

The Baal Shem Tov lay down to sleep, deeply troubled. In the morning he gently approached his host and asked him why he celebrated *Shabbos* in the manner he did.

The host answered, "Rebbe, please remember always that I am a Jew. I was kidnapped from my father's house at a very young age. I must have been only five or six years old. My captors released me on the condition that I remain in this city. I am the only Jew in this area. I remember nothing about Judaism from my father's house except that *Shabbos* is a day of pleasure. Therefore, I live frugally all week—I smoke cheap tobacco, I drink water instead of wine, I accumulate money for my *Shabbos* feast. Then I invite my friends to celebrate with me every Friday night."

The Baal Shem Tov understood why his host celebrated *Shabbos* the way he did. He thought he understood the judgment of The Judge, namely that his place in Heaven would be shared with someone who truly knew the joy of *Shabbos.* After *Shab-*

[1]A *mezuzah* is the parchment scroll affixed to the doorposts of Jewish homes. It is inscribed with the first two paragraphs of the *Sh'ma,* found in the *Torah* (Deuteronomy 6:4–8, 11:13–21).

bos, he ordered Alexy to prepare the wagon for their return trip home.

On another occasion, Elyahu revealed himself to my teacher. This time, my teacher asked him to reveal the place that is reserved for those people who desecrated the *Shabbos* publicly.

Elyahu answered, "I cannot show you that place, but I will show you a similar place that is reserved for people who fear Heaven and dread sin."

The Baal Shem Tov saw two large, bubbling kettles, filled with boiling gold. The vision frightened my teacher. He asked Elyahu, "For whom are these kettles?" He answered, "These kettles are prepared for you and for someone else."

Elyahu disappeared again. The Baal Shem Tov was determined to find the "someone else," so he ordered Alexy to harness the horses to the wagons and prepare for another long journey.

When all was ready, the Baal Shem Tov took his accustomed place in the wagon, but strangely, Alexy sat with his back opposite his master. They traveled all that day and night. They crossed plains and valleys, forests and streams. Early the next morning, they arrived in the outskirts of a *shtetl*. As the horses raced down the road, it was obvious that Jews were the majority of the inhabitants in this town. The small, neat houses had big *mezuzos* on the doors. Every yard had a *sukkah*. The people who emerged from their houses and walked toward the marketplace were not dressed in the fashion of the times. Rather, the men wore long black coats and large fur hats. The women wore long-sleeved, floor-length, high-necked dresses, and shawls covered their heads.

The Baal Shem Tov, weary from a long journey, sought a place to rest, but all the public buildings were *shuls* or study halls. He asked a passerby where he could find the *rosh yeshivah* (the dean of the *yeshivah*), and the passerby absentmindedly pointed his finger straight ahead of him. Finally, the Baal Shem Tov found the study hall. He entered, Alexy following him. He approached the *rosh yeshivah* and asked him for room and board. The *rosh yeshivah* nodded his head, intimating that when he finished studying that passage of the Talmud, he would help them, but the day dragged on, and he did not move from his seat.

The Baal Shem Tov sat in the study hall for days, waiting for the *rosh yeshivah* to pay attention to him. When *Shabbos* approached, the *rosh yeshivah* closed his volume of the Talmud. He wanted to bathe and change his clothes. Only then did he realize that the visitors had no place to spend *Shabbos,* so he invited them to his home. The Baal Shem Tov and Alexy followed him. Considering that he was such a great scholar, they thought they would learn a lot about the observance of *Shabbos* from their host.

To their surprise, the *rosh yeshivah* lit candles that were one-third the height of normal *Shabbos* candles. When the Baal Shem Tov asked him to explain why he used such small candles, he said, "I am afraid that if they last longer, I will be tempted to blow them out."

The whole day of *Shabbos,* the *rosh yeshivah* sat on a chair. He did not move a limb. When the Baal Shem Tov asked him why he did not move from his chair, he answered, "There are so many restrictions on *Shabbos.* I am afraid that if I walk outdoors, my footsteps will create a hole in the sand, or I will step on a worm, or my shoes will squeak. I am always depressed on *Shabbos.* How can I be happy?"

The Baal Shem Tov grieved for the *rosh yeshivah* because he neither understood nor felt the joy of *Shabbos.* He compared both of his experiences and concluded that the only way to serve the Creator was with joy.

Rebbe Shlomo Layb concluded his story. Then he added a word of explanation to his friends and disciples. "You see," he said, "it is very important that every *mitzvah* you do be done with joy. *Torah* study and good deeds are important, but they should be done with joy."

Then Rebbe Shlomo Layb prepared for *havdalah.* His friends and disciples chanted soft, farewell melodies to accompany the departing Sabbath Queen.

Wine Drops on the Eyelids

Yossele was a *yoshev* (perpetual student) of the Baal Shem Tov. He sat and studied *Torah* day and night. In order to earn a livelihood for his family, he received a meager stipend as compensation.

Each Tuesday, the Baal Shem Tov distributed the weekly stipends, and Yossele waited his turn in line with the other *yoshvim* (plural of *yoshev*). The Baal Shem Tov called each student by name. One by one each entered the Baal Shem Tov's private room in order to receive the money he would use for food and supplies for the week.

One Tuesday, Yossele was waiting patiently in line for his turn, but his name was not called. All the other *yoshvim* received their stipends and left. Yossele remained till the very end, but his name was not called. He thought that the Baal Shem Tov inadvertently forgot him. He went home empty-handed.

His poor wife was disappointed. She did not know how the family would survive during the coming week, but she, too, thought that the omission was inadvertent. "It's all right," she said comfortingly. "I will pawn our pillows and use the money to buy food for our family for the coming week."

The following Tuesday, Yossele again waited in line for his stipend, and again the Baal Shem Tov omitted his name from the roll call. Yossele returned home crushed. His wife was disgruntled. She did not know how the family would survive in the coming week. Looking around the barren room, she noticed her Sabbath candlesticks on the ledge above the fireplace. Although she was heartbroken over the prospect of pawning her one cherished possession, she realized that she had no choice.

The following Tuesday, Yossele's wife insisted on accompanying him to the Baal Shem Tov. She wanted to make certain that her Yossele would not inadvertently be omitted again this week. Together they waited as the line of *yoshvim* grew smaller and smaller. Finally, there was no one else in line except them, but the Baal Shem Tov didn't call Yossele's name.

Yossele's wife was angry. She knew that her husband studied well during the week. She barged into the Baal Shem Tov's study and demanded Yossele's weekly stipend in order to be able to feed her hungry children.

The Baal Shem Tov simply said, "I bless you with prosperity."

Yossele's wife answered the Baal Shem Tov. "Are you telling me that Yossele is no longer considered a *yoshev* of the Baal Shem Tov?

The Baal Shem Tov reiterated, "I bless you with prosperity."

Yossele and his wife left the Baal Shem Tov, sadly making their way home. When they reached home, they noticed that their hen had laid double the amount of eggs she normally lays. They saved the extra eggs. The next day, the hen laid double the amount of eggs again. They also saved these extra eggs. The hen continued to double her outlay of eggs for a week. Yossele's wife continued to save the extra eggs. At the end of the week, Yossele took all the extra eggs to the marketplace and bartered them for a goat. The goat gave an enormous amount of milk. Yossele's wife made butter and cheese, and soon they had a prosperous dairy business. With the profits, Yossele and his wife bought fabrics and housewares. Soon, Yossele found it necessary to travel to the twice-yearly fair in Lublin to purchase merchandise.

At the fair in Lublin, Yossele met a wealthy merchant from Berlin. The merchant convinced Yossele to go to Berlin to shop for new merchandise. Yossele thought about all the possibilities of bringing modern merchandise to his little village, so he decided to skip the next fair in Lublin and go directly to Berlin. In Berlin, Yossele purchased a variety of exquisite, ready-made fashions. While there, he investigated the possibility of buying and selling precious stones. A merchant told him that the diamond center was in Amsterdam.

Yossele returned home but decided to go to Amsterdam the next time he needed merchandise for his business. A few months later, Yossele arrived in Amsterdam. He was informed that the source of all diamonds was South Africa, so Yossele bought passage on a ship sailing for South Africa immediately. He did not return home.

The boat sailed from Amsterdam on a clear, spring day. Five days later, a violent sea storm threatened the safety of the boat. The boat was tossed back and forth in four-foot-high waves as thunder and lightning spread for miles across the sky. Suddenly an ear-splitting thunder bolt, followed by fierce lightning, broke across the dark sky and struck the boat. The boat was shattered. Most of the people grabbed on to the sails and planks of the boat and floated toward a distant coastline, barely visible in the storm. Strangely, Yossele was propelled along the crest of the waves toward an island that seemed to appear out of nowhere.

Yossele swam toward the island and pulled himself out of the water. He saw a neat arrangement of cottages and gardens equally spaced over the entire island. He searched for people but didn't find anyone anywhere. He figured that the people were working on another part of the island and would return to their homes at dusk. Yossele entered one house and noticed a large cauldron of soup bubbling on the fire in the fireplace, a bottle of *schnapps* (whiskey), and a large honey cake on the table. He also noticed a volume of the Talmud lying open on the table turned to the same page he had finished studying when he was a *yoshev* of the Baal Shem Tov. Next to the volume of the Talmud lay *tefillin* (phylacteries) and a *siddur* (prayerbook). While he was waiting, he wrapped himself in the *tefillin* and recited his morning prayers. When he finished praying, he helped himself to a little *schnapps* and a piece of honey cake. Then he sat down at the table in front of the open volume of the Talmud and began to study.

The day passed. Yossele was very hungry, but he decided to wait until the owners returned from work. As it grew dark, Yossele began to think that no one would come, so he helped himself to some soup, stretched out on a cot, and fell asleep.

Yossele awoke the next morning refreshed, hoping to see a human being, but the cottage was empty. He noticed, however, that fresh soup was simmering in the cauldron, and the honey cake and *schnapps* had been replenished.

Yossele was puzzled by this strange phenomenon, but since he was so happy to be alive, he prepared to recite his morning prayers. When he was finished, he helped himself to a little *schnapps* and a piece of honey cake. Then he sat down at the table to continue his studies. The day passed.

Towards dusk, Yossele served himself some soup. When he was done, he made himself comfortable on the cot and retired for the night.

The next day was a repetition of the previous day. On the third day, however, Yossele awoke amid tremendous commotion. He jumped from the cot, ran toward the door of the cottage, and observed people running helter-skelter. From some cottages he smelled the aroma of baking *challos*, from some he sniffed the pungent flavor of gefilte fish, and from some cottages emanated the garlic flavor of roasting chickens.

People were chopping wood, drawing water, washing clothes, plucking flowers, and gathering vegetables. It was as if they were rushing to complete preparations for an honored guest.

Yossele joined the people in their activities. He performed whatever task he was asked to perform. As the day began to wane, Yossele noticed that all the people bathed in the ocean, returned to their cottages, donned white clothing, and rushed toward the center of the island. He followed the crowd and found himself in a small synagogue. Yossele sat down among the worshippers. When the prayers began, Yossele thought he was sitting in the synagogue of the Baal Shem Tov, back in Medziboz, because the melodies that the prayer leader chanted were exactly the same *Shabbos* melodies he remembered from his hometown.

After the prayers, the rabbi invited Yossele to share the *Shabbos* meal in his cottage. With other invited guests, Yossele accepted the invitation. As he sat at the table with the rabbi, he listened to the *Shabbos* melodies, which were reminiscent of the melodies sung at the table of the Baal Shem Tov. The meal was followed by a discourse on the weekly *Torah* reading. Then the guests departed.

When Yossele awakened the following morning, he saw that some people were returning from bathing in the ocean while others were already walking toward the synagogue. Yossele joined the worshippers. The melodies again stirred up memories of his hometown. After the prayers, he returned to the rabbi's cottage for the second *Shabbos* meal. The meal, the singing, and the *Torah* discourses continued until it was time to partake of *sholosh seudos,* the third meal of *Shabbos.*

All the people gathered in the synagogue as darkness descended on the island. The people were preparing to say farewell to *Shabbos.* The rabbi made *havdalah,* holding high a lighted candle in one hand, a spice box and an overflowing cup of wine on a tray in the other hand. At the conclusion of the ceremony, the rabbi placed the tray on the table. One by one, the people approached the table, dipped their index fingers into the spilt wine, touched their eyelids, and instantly disappeared.

Yossele watched the scene, but he was so confused that he couldn't react. Soon, all the people had vanished. Then the rabbi dipped his fingers into the wine, touched his eyelids, blew out the candle, and disappeared.

Yossele was alone on the deserted island. He walked slowly

back to the cottage and retired for the night. As he dropped off into a deep sleep, he tried to recall each aspect of the beautiful *Shabbos* he experienced.

Yossele awakened Sunday morning and found the bubbling cauldron of soup, the *schnapps,* the honey cake, the *tefillin,* and the open volume of the Talmud in their usual places. He realized that he had a long week of loneliness ahead of him. The days passed slowly. Yossele calculated when the people would return to the deserted island to celebrate *Shabbos* again.

His assumptions were correct. The following Friday morning, Yossele awakened to tremendous excitement. The people had returned to the island, and they were in the midst of preparing for *Shabbos.* Yossele tried to make conversation with the people. He wanted an explanation for his being alone during the week. He wanted to know why the people only appeared on the island for *Shabbos* and vanished afterwards. The people were too busy to answer Yossele's questions.

Yossele experienced a very holy *Shabbos* on the deserted island. Much of the observances were reminiscent of the rituals of the Baal Shem Tov. However, when *Shabbos* ended, he had no more information about these strange people and their customs than he did before. The rabbi made *havdalah.* The people dipped their fingers into the wine, touched their eyelids, and vanished one by one. Yossele tried to stop the people from disappearing, but he could not.

On the third *Shabbos,* Yossele was determined to find a way to stop the rabbi from vanishing. He planned to *daven* the evening prayer a few minutes before everyone else. He stationed himself behind the rabbi, and as the rabbi dipped his fingers in the wine, Yossele grabbed his arms and yelled, "Stop! Before you leave, please explain to me who you are and why you come here each week."

The rabbi said, "I was hoping you wouldn't ask, but now that you did, this is our story. We lived when the first Holy Temple stood in Jerusalem, but we were unhappy because so many Jews had adopted pagan practices. We asked Elyahu Hanavi if we could live someplace other than *Eretz Yisrael.* He granted our request, blessed us with success, taught us the secret of *kefitzas haderech* (the shortening of the way), and pointed us in the direction of this island. We settled here, built cottages, and planted gardens. Three times each year, on *Pesach* (Passover), on *Shavuos* (Pentecost), and on *Sukkos* (Tabernacles), one-third of our group would go down to the shore, repeat the secret of *kefitzas haderech*, and take off for the pilgrimage to the Holy Temple in Jerusalem. Each time they returned filled with joy for having visited the Holy Temple.

"One time the group returned with anguish written all over their faces. They were dressed in sackcloth, and ashes covered their foreheads. We knew they were mourning for the Holy Temple that had been destroyed. We cried so much that our souls ascended to Heaven.

"The Heavenly Court was perplexed. After much deliberation over our fate, the Court decided that we should be granted the rewards of this world and the world to come. Their verdict permitted us to reside in the spiritual world during the week and to return to the material world for the celebration of *Shabbos*, which is a physical taste of the world to come. Now that you know our secret, you must decide if you will come with us or return to Medziboz. You cannot remain here."

Yossele thought about his wife and children. He had a hard time deciding whether to choose the physical world or the spiritual world. After a long while, he opted for the physical world. He told the rabbi that he would like to return to Medziboz. The rabbi told Yossele that he would give him the secret of *kefitzas haderech*, but warned him, "As soon as you return home, throw it heavenward so it will be destroyed."

The rabbi took Yossele down to the shore of the deserted island and gave him the secret. Quick as lightning, Yossele was standing in the center of Medziboz. He was about to throw the secret of *kefitzas haderech* heavenward when he felt a hand grabbing his. Startled, Yossele turned around to find himself staring into the face of the Baal Shem Tov.

The Baal Shem Tov said, "I sent you to bring me the secret of *kefitzas haderech*. Thank you for succeeding in this mission."

What became of Yossele?

Yossele became a *yoshev* of the Baal Shem Tov.

Give Him Life

He never deviated from his customary preparations for *Shabbos*. Exactly at noon, each Friday afternoon, he immersed himself in the *mikveh*, returned to his room, changed his everyday clothing for his *Shabbos* clothing, stood before *shtender* (the raised reading desk where he studied), and recited Psalms. He began his recitation every week with chapter one, verse one: "Happy is the man who does not follow the advice of evil people."[1]

Painstakingly, with great intent and concentration, and enunciating every word of the 150 chapters, he concluded with the last words of the last chapter: "With every breath of life in me, I will praise You."[2]

Shmuel Kaminka had just finished Psalm 147 when he was interrupted by an urgent knock at his door. At first he tried to disregard the knock, hoping that the intruder would think he was not home, but the knock turned into impatient pounding. Reluc-

[1] Psalms 1:1.
[2] Psalms 150:6.

tantly, he opened the door. A friend of his stood in the doorway.

"I have rushed over here from the study hall of Rebbe Tzvee Hirsh Nadverna," he blurted out breathlessly. "He wants to see you immediately!"

"Please tell our rebbe," Shmuel answered impatiently, "that I am almost finished reciting the Psalms. I am already on the 147th chapter. I will come in about ten minutes."

Shmuel's friend returned to the house of study and delivered the message. Rebbe Tzvee Hirsh snapped, "Go back to Shmuel. Tell him I need him immediately, and tell him that if he does not come now, he doesn't have to come at all."

When Shmuel heard the words of his rebbe, he closed his book of Psalms and ran to the house of study. As he ran, angry thoughts crossed his mind. "Why couldn't he wait until I finished? I only had three more chapters left. What could possibly have happened that was so urgent that the rebbe demanded to see me this minute? What could be more important than my concluding the recitation of Psalms?"

By the time Shmuel crossed the threshold of the study hall, he was enraged. He honestly believed that he was no longer ready to greet *Shabbos.*

As he approached his rebbe, he tripped over the sprawled body of Avraham, the town drunk. Rebbe Tzvee Hirsh paid no attention to the irate mood of his indignant student. He simply turned to Shmuel and said, "Take Avraham to the wash basin and clean him up. Then go with him to collect money so he can buy food for *Shabbos.* His wife and children are hungry. If he goes out to collect money alone, no one will give him anything because people are afraid he will spend it on liquor."

Shmuel could not believe his ears. He did not understand why he couldn't finish reciting Psalms, why Avraham the town drunk could not wait. Angrily, he dragged Avraham to the wash basin. The drunk stood up slowly, tottering uncertainly. After Shmuel washed his hands and face, he linked his arm with Avraham's and the two of them set out to collect money to buy food for *Shabbos* for Avraham's family.

Shmuel finished his task and left Avraham on the doorsteps

of his cottage. Slowly, he trudged back to his room, trying to re-capture the mood of *Shabbos*, trying to finish the recitation of the Psalms, so he could welcome *Shabbos* with joy.

He did not succeed.

Shmuel was troubled all of that *Shabbos*. He did not under-stand why the rebbe sent him when other students were avail-able, why he had to help the town drunk rather than recite Psalms. He did not comprehend the intention of his rebbe, so he decided that he would seek out a different one.

However, before he acted, he concluded that it would only be fair if he went to Rebbe Tzvee Hirsh and asked him for an explanation.

Determined in his resolve, after *havdalah* (the ceremony separating *Shabbos* from the weekday), he timidly knocked on the door of his rebbe's room.

Rebbe Tzvee Hirsh was very gracious. "Please come in, Shmuel," he beckoned. "I hoped you would come. I knew you were deeply disturbed by what I asked you to do yesterday. I would like to teach you something, something that I think is the essence of Jewish life. There is a verse in *Pirkei Avos* (*Ethics of Our Fathers*) that states, 'This is the way of *Torah*; eat bread with salt, drink water in small measure, sleep on the ground, live a life of pain, but toil in the *Torah*.'[3]

"Here in Nadverna, we translate the passage 'live a life of pain' differently than in most places. In Nadverna we translate the passage to mean, 'When you see someone in pain, give him life.'

"You see," Rebbe Tzvee Hirsh continued gently, "Avraham the town drunk was in terrible pain. He was in desperate straits. His wife and children depended upon him. They would not have had a morsel of food to eat for *Shabbos*. I called you to come im-mediately because I trusted you to help him. I knew you would

---

[3]*Avos* 6:4. Asceticism is not being advocated here. One who is wealthy is not expected to cast away his wealth for the pursuit of *Torah*. Rather, this is a general principle to develop moderation in all areas of life. It is particularly ad-dressed to the poverty-stricken person. Even if you are poor, do not neglect the study of *Torah*.

be upset that you could not finish the recitation of the Psalms, yet Avraham and his family could not wait. The Psalms could wait. Even the Almighty could wait."

Shmuel gulped. He sighed deeply. In his heart, he really had not wanted to leave Nadverna. He had only wanted to understand his rebbe's intent.

Sheepishly, Shmuel left his rebbe's room. The following Friday afternoon, exactly at noontime, he immersed himself in the *mikveh*, returned to his room, changed his everyday clothes for the *Shabbos* clothes, stood before his *shtender*, and began, "Happy is the man."

Reverence for My
Alef Beis Teacher

Yaacov Yitzchak was not always the famous Chozeh (Seer) about whom people said, "Lublin, his *shtetl,* could be compared to *Eretz Yisrael*; his chasidic court to the Holy Temple; his study room to the Holy of Holies—and the *Schechinah* (the Divine Presence) spoke from his mouth."[1]

He was born to Avraham Eliezer Horowitz, the rabbi of Josefof, about 250 years ago.

Yaacov Yitzchak was blessed with a sharp, inquisitive mind, in addition to manifesting qualities of leadership. His *alef beis* teacher (primary school teacher) was Rabbi Avraham Abley, who delighted in his pupil's ability to grasp concepts far beyond his young years. Rabbi Avraham Abley was not destined to teach the young Yaacov Yitzchak for too many years, for the Horowitz family moved to a different *shtetl.* Even so, he always wondered what happened to Yaacov Yitzchak.

Years passed. Rabbi Avraham Abley heard about the famous Yaacov Yitzchak, the Chozeh of Lublin. He tried to connect

[1]H. Rabinowicz, *A Guide to Chasidism.* London: Thomas Yoseloff, 1960.

this renowned chasidic rebbe with Yaacov Yitzchak, the young child who had given him so much pleasure, but he was never sure if they were one and the same. Often, Rabbi Avraham Abley permitted his thoughts to ramble as he imagined what had become of his former pupil. As he grew older, he became obsessed with the desire to know; he pleaded with the Heavenly Court to reveal the whereabouts of his former student.

The Heavenly Court agreed to grant his prayer under one condition: the whereabouts of Yaacov Yitzchak would be revealed just prior to the old man's death.

One night, the Chozeh dreamed that he must return to Josefof to reveal himself to his *alef beis* teacher. He also dreamed that his revelation would precede his teacher's death.

In the morning, the Chozeh recalled his dream. He struggled with its meaning. Not wanting to cause the death of Rabbi Avraham Abley, he procrastinated for days and days. Finally he decided that he would return to Josefof incognito, hoping that he could identify himself as the former pupil without revealing that he was the Chozeh.

He dressed as a simple peasant and traveled alone. He planned to arrive in the *shtetl* on the eve of *Shabbos*, pretending that he needed home hospitality, insisting that he would stay only in Rabbi Avraham Abley's house.

Rabbi Avraham Abley's wife responded when the Chozeh knocked on her door.

"How can I help you?" she queried.

"I need a place to spend *Shabbos*," the Chozeh, disguised as a peasant, explained.

"My husband is not home right now, but I expect him any moment. Please wait for him to return," she said.

When Rabbi Avraham Abley returned home, he cordially welcomed the peasant to his home. He made him comfortable, and the two men went off to the synagogue for the prayer service welcoming *Shabbat Hamalkah*.

Rabbi Avraham Abley did not persist in questioning his peasant guest about his identity, so neither he nor the townspeople knew the truth.

When the prayers were finished, Rabbi Avraham Abley and his guest returned home, recited the *kiddush* (the sanctification over the wine), and prepared to partake of the special *Shabbos* meal. After they finished eating, Rabbi Avraham Abley closed his eyes and began reminiscing about his younger years and the pupils he had taught. He called out the names of some of his former pupils. Then he called the name of Yaacov Yitzchak. Sadly, he said, "I would give anything to know what happened to him. He had such promise. I must know where he is." His voice faltered and trailed off. He clenched his fists. Tears streamed down the old man's cheeks.

"Don't be so sad," the peasant spoke softly. "I am your former pupil. I am Yaacov Yitzchak." Rabbi Avraham Abley was stunned. "Are you the Chozeh of Lublin?" he pressed on.

He could not deny who he was. "Yes," he whispered softly. "I am Yaacov Yitzchak, the Chozeh of Lublin."

Tears of joy filled the eyes of the old teacher. "I am so happy," he said. "I want to go outside and shout to the whole world that the Chozeh of Lublin is my guest for *Shabbos*."

The Chozeh of Lublin said, "Please, promise me that you won't reveal this secret to anyone just yet." The old teacher did not understand the secrecy, but he agreed. The Seer trembled, knowing the responsibility he had undertaken.

The next morning, Rabbi Avraham Abley and Rebbe Yaacov Yitzchak went to the synagogue to pray. Rabbi Avraham Abley's face sparkled with joy, although no one in the synagogue knew the reason for his joy.

The remainder of the *Shabbos* day passed uneventfully, and after dark, the Seer departed for Lublin.

Rabbi Avraham Abley thought that since his most honored guest had departed, he could reveal his presence to his friends.

The people of the *shtetl* felt badly that they had not recognized the Chozeh and had neglected to extend him the honor and respect due a sage, so they decided to jump in a wagon, ride after him, catch him on his way, and ask him to return to their village so they could recognize that he had been their guest for *Shabbos*.

When they caught up to him, the Chozeh asked how they

found out who he was. When they told him that Rabbi Avraham Abley had revealed the information to them, he began to tremble again. He turned around his wagon and returned to the *shtetl*, accompanied by the villagers. As soon as they arrived, they were told that Rabbi Avraham Abley had passed away. The Chozeh of Lublin personally arranged for the funeral of his revered teacher.

During the eulogy, he explained that he had not revealed himself to his teacher prior to this time in order that his life be prolonged. He revealed the holiness and righteousness of Rabbi Avraham Abley, so that the people of the *shtetl* would understand the merit of the hidden *tzadik* who had lived among them.

A *Shabbosdik* World

Rebbe Moshe Kobriner wanted desperately to find out how his friend Rebbe Yisrael Friedman, the princely rebbe of Rizhin, welcomed *Shabbos*.

So one week, he traveled to Rizhin, arriving early Friday afternoon. He made arrangements in the town inn and proceeded with his usual detailed preparations. First, he reviewed the entire *Torah* reading for that particular *Shabbos* morning, then he studied the corresponding chapters in the *Zohar* (the mystical secrets of *Torah*), then he recited *Shir Hashirim* (the song of songs, the love song between the Almighty and His people), then he went to the *mikveh* to purify body and soul, and then he donned white garments. When he finished all his preparations, he noticed that the sun was beginning its descent, so he turned toward the direction of his friend's mansion and hurried along the road.

When he arrived, he was ushered into Rebbe Yisrael's study. The rebbe was sitting peacefully on a soft chair, smoking his pipe. It was apparent that he had been smoking for a long time, for the room hung heavy with smoke.

The Rizhiner was not surprised to see his friend and welcomed him warmly. Rebbe Moshe Kobriner, however, was astonished to see that his friend had not readied himself for *Shabbos,* so he made his bewilderment known.

The Rizhiner pulled himself up from his chair and beckoned to his friend to join him at the window. As he ambled slowly across the room, he extinguished his pipe. Then he put his arm around his friend and held him closely. For a few minutes, they both peered into the distance silently. Finally, the Rizhiner whispered, "Moshe, do you see what I see? Do you see how the clouds of the weekday are making place for the clouds of *Shabbos*? Do you see how the sky of the weekday is parting to make way for the sky of *Shabbos*? Do you see the arrival of a *shabbosdik* world?"

Suddenly, it was apparent to Rebbe Moshe Kobriner that his own detailed, meticulous preparations for *Shabbos* were inadequate compared to the profound manner in which his friend had readied himself for *Shabbos.*

Shabbos Candles

So many of our *Shabbos* candles were extinguished during the Holocaust that for a while it seemed that Jewish life was on the verge of collapse. Yet, if we heed the words spoken by the rebbe of Riminov and consider them a sacred trust, we will be strengthened in our conviction that nothing will ever blow out our *Shabbos* candles.

One beautiful, spring afternoon, Rebbe Yechezkel Shraga Halberstam, the rebbe of Shinova, was riding in his wagon with some of his students. He wanted to share with them the rebirth of nature. They rode for a long while, reflecting upon the trees that were in bloom after a long winter, savoring the caress of rustling wind carrying the warm breezes of springtime, basking in the warmth of the bright sunlight overhead.

Unexpectedly, the glorious day reverted to winter; gray mist hid the sun, thunder echoed through the trees, lightning blazed in the distance, the trees arched from the force of the wind, cloudbursts filled the skies.

The students huddled together in the wagon, seeking warmth and shelter.

The Shinova rebbe sat in the center of the wagon, unaffected by the storm. He put his hand in his pocket, withdrew his pipe and tobacco pouch, and loaded the pipe. His students straightened up, watching, wondering how their rebbe would be able to strike a match to light his pipe in such threatening weather.

Then one student, sitting closest to the rebbe, took the matchbox from the rebbe's hand and struck a match against it in an attempt to light his pipe. Another student quickly cupped his hand over the flame; nevertheless, the match was extinguished. The students made many fruitless attempts.

Finally, the rebbe said, "Please, let me light my own pipe." With the first match he struck, the rebbe lit his pipe. The students sat silently, staring at the wondrous sight.

"If you think that was a miracle," said the Shinova rebbe, "let me tell you the story of a real miracle."

Once, when I was a very young child, my father took me to Riminov, for he wanted me to experience *Shabbos* with Rebbe Mendel Riminover. We set out early one Friday morning, on a beautiful spring day. Throughout our journey I noticed how nature was awakening from its winter slumber. Wildflowers bloomed on the roadside, the sun sparkled overhead, and billowy white clouds moved gracefully across the sky.

We arrived in Riminov in the early afternoon and went straight to the *shul* and the study hall. On our way, we saw people hurrying about, carrying *challos* and flowers, setting up their candlesticks, preparing for *Shabbos*. Many people who had finished their preparations milled around the *shul*, wishing each other "good *Shabbos*."

In the synagogue, the *shamish* was placing candlesticks and candles on all the windowsills of the open windows, for this was a special custom in Riminov.

Shortly before *Shabbos*, the glorious spring weather changed unexpectedly: gray clouds clashed, the sky echoed with thunder, lightning flashed, the winds blew fiercely. The *shamish* motioned for some of the people to help him remove the

Shabbos candlesticks from the windowsills and close the windows.

The people ran, trying to help, trying to remove the candlesticks before the downpour. But the Riminover rebbe, who was studying near the front of the *shul*, had other ideas. He stood up, raised his hands, and walked over to me, a guest in Riminov for *Shabbos.* The chattering stopped.

He put his arm around my shoulders and led me from window to window. He opened the windows and replaced the candlesticks. Now there was hushed silence in the *shul* as people wondered about what the rebbe had done.

The Riminover rebbe began to speak softly, and gradually the wind stopped blowing.

The people crowded around us. They wanted to hear what the rebbe was saying. The rebbe turned to face me. As I stood looking at him, he said, "Yechezkel Shraga, I want you to know that you have to learn how to talk to the wind. Nothing will ever extinguish the *Shabbos* candles of the Riminover rebbe."

It Depends On What You Say

The Jewish people were confined to the ghettos[1] of the Franco-Germanic lands for almost a thousand years. When emancipation was proclaimed, during the Age of Enlightenment, many Jews jumped at the promise of equal citizenship and equal opportunity. Within a few generations, they assimilated into German society and some converted, hoping that by embracing the religion of the majority of the population, they would be accepted completely.

One of the people who matured in this emancipated environment was Herr Johann Bressler. He remembered his pious grandfather but was surrounded by peers struggling with secular achievement. Because opportunities were open to Jews that had never existed before, Herr Bressler felt his actions had to prove that he was worthy of German citizenship. He became a

---

[1]The term *ghetto*, loosely used, means a place where Jews lived. The first formal ghetto, with gates and walls, was erected in Venice, Italy, around 1516. It was located near the *geto*, the iron foundry. It was compulsory for Jews to live there. However, for the past thousand years, the term *ghetto* symbolized the acts of violence perpetrated against our people in the Franco-Germanic lands.

successful businessman, mixed with the local political leaders, and frequented the salons.

He married a Jewish woman with the same background and the same life preferences, and they raised two children, a beautiful daughter and a mute son. Herr Bressler consulted the most prominent physicians regarding his son; the physicians concluded that the boy's malady was not physical, but they were unable to cure him. Herr Bressler was advised to hire a voice teacher, but the boy did not respond. He refused to imitate the sounds the teacher articulated. He refused to sing the German national anthem. He simply refused to speak.

Amidst the preparations for Herr Bressler's daughter's wedding to a non-Jew, he heard that Rebbe Shlomo ben Rebbe Dov Tzvee Hakohen Radomsker performed miracles. He decided to take time out to visit the rebbe, who, he hoped, would be able to cure his son. He was willing to try anything.

He purchased train tickets from Berlin to Radomsk and set out with the young boy. As the train sped eastward, leaving the big city behind, Herr Bressler felt that he was traveling backward in time, for the *shtetlach* of the Pale of Settlement seemed to be on a different planet than Berlin.

He was greeted pleasantly by Rebbe Shlomo. They chatted awhile. Then Herr Bressler explained why he had come to Radomsk. Meanwhile, the boy sat silently at his father's side, never uttering a sound.

The rebbe said, "I may be able to help your son, but you will have to remain in Radomsk until after *Shabbos.*"

Herr Johann Bressler was perturbed. *Shabbos* was five days away. "I can't stay here that long, rebbe," he said. "I am in the midst of arranging my daughter's wedding. It will be the social event of the season. Maybe we could compromise. I could return with my son after the wedding."

Now anger crossed Rebbe Shlomo's face. "You came here," he said in a firm voice, "of your own volition, begging me to cure your son. I told you I might be able to help him. If you leave now, I know I will never be able to help him. The choice is yours."

Herr Bressler weighed his options and decided to stay in

Radomsk for *Shabbos.* During those five days, the young boy silently explored Jewish life in the *shtetl*; his eyes saw, his mind absorbed, his ears heard.

As *Shabbos* approached, hectic preparations heralded the arrival of the Sabbath Queen: the fragrance of freshly baked *challos,* the smell and imagined taste of the cooking delicacies. The flavor of *Shabbos* pervaded the *shtetl.*

As the sun descended, people streamed from their modest cottages toward the *shul.* Herr Bressler and his son joined the worshippers. They waited for the rebbe to arrive.

When Rebbe Shlomo Radomsker arrived, he immediately walked over to the young boy and hugged him. He clasped him around the shoulders and escorted him to the pulpit at the center of the *shul.* There, the rebbe and the young boy stood together— the rebbe chanting the prayer service, and the boy, at his side, covered with the edges of the rebbe's *tallis.*

After the prayer service, the rebbe and the boy walked home hand in hand. Herr Bressler trailed behind. As they entered, the women greeted them with a warm "Good *Shabbos.*" Candlelight sparkled throughout the house.

Rebbe Shlomo began chanting the traditional *Shabbos* melody, "*Shalom Aleichem.* We wish you peace, attending angels, angels of the most sublime, the King of Kings, the Holy One, praised be He."

The family joined the singing. Herr Bressler stood silently at his place near the table, but the eyes of his young son sparkled.

Then Rebbe Shlomo lifted the wine bottle, poured the wine into his goblet, raised it, closed his eyes, and chanted the *kiddush*: "Thus the heavens and earth were finished. . . . On the seventh day, God completed His work which He had done. . . . God blessed the seventh day and hallowed it. . . ."

The young boy watched him intently. When he finished, he drank the wine, then passed the goblet around the table so that everyone present might taste the sweetness of the *Shabbos.*

"Before you drink," the rebbe said as he turned to face the young boy standing next to him, "I want you to recite the blessing for wine. I will teach you how to say it. I will say the words, and you will repeat them exactly as I say them." The rebbe began, *"Baruch."* The young boy responded, *"Baruch."* The rebbe proceeded, *"Atah."* The boy imitated, *"Atah."* The rebbe continued. When the boy finished reciting the blessing, he drank the wine, and a hushed silence filled the room.

The astounded Herr Bressler was dumbfounded. He couldn't believe his ears. His son had spoken—it was a miracle!

After he had gained control of himself, he turned to the rebbe and asked, "How can I thank you for miraculously curing my son?"

The rebbe stared at Herr Bressler for a long while. Finally he responded. "I want you to know that there was nothing wrong with your son. It's just that he could not utter the words you wanted him to say!"

The moment the boy recited the blessing for the *kiddush*, Herr Johann Bressler realized what had been missing from his own vocabulary. He returned to Berlin and completely changed his life.

Moshele Good Shabbos

The ominous sound of the goose step reverberated through the streets of Vienna, one of the most beautiful cities in the world. It was a *Shabbos* in 1938, just before the *Anschluss* (the forced annexation of Austria to Germany).

The Jews who lived in Baden, a suburb of Vienna, wanted to *daven* with a *minyan*. They understood the risk, but they calculated that if they davened quickly, they would be finished before the Nazi stormtroopers emerged from their barracks to patrol the streets.

They arranged to meet in the rabbi's house just after daybreak. They emerged from their homes, one by one, and surreptitiously headed for their destination. Furtively looking over his shoulder, ascertaining that he was not being followed, each one silently slipped into the room that the rabbi had set aside as a makeshift *shul*. When they were all together, they huddled in prayer. The room was overcast with the glimmer of a shadow of breaking dawn, for the drapes and the windows were closed tight.

They davened quickly, whispering, impatient to finish so that they could return to their own homes.

Suddenly, an unexpected knock at the door interrupted the barely audible prayers. A hushed silence spread over the men.

One of them motioned to the youngest to peep through the crack in the drapes to see who had knocked. Wending his way through the crowded room, he lifted the drapes and saw Moshele Good Shabbos standing on the doorstep. Relieved to find Moshele, rather than a Nazi stormtrooper, he began chanting Moshele's melody.

"Good *Shabbos,* Good *Shabbos!*"

Moshele was known all over Vienna as Moshele Good Shabbos, because he never stopped chanting his special *Shabbos* melody. He chanted it on Sunday. He chanted it on Wednesday. On *Shabbos* he shouted it. Moshele was on the Nazi Gestapo's most-wanted criminal traitor list. They knew he forged passports to help Jews escape from Vienna.

The boy moved aside, so Moshele could enter. He picked up the child's chant and responded lightly, "Good *Shabbos,* good *Shabbos!* What is your name?"

The child answered, "My name is Shlomo, my name is Shlomo. What is your name?"[1]

Moshele turned to the boy, looked at him intently, and then chanted, "My name is Moshele, my name is Moshele. Good *Shabbos,* Good *Shabbos!*"

Moshele and the boy entered the room, and Moshele continued singing, "Good *Shabbos,* Good *Shabbos!*"

He wrapped himself completely in his *tallis* and proceeded to join the other worshippers. They hadn't stopped for one moment, for they were anxious to finish.

The garble of their words disturbed Moshele. Suddenly, he lowered his *tallis* from his head and let it fall around his shoulders. He raised his hands and cried out in pain, "Brothers! Today is *Shabbos!* Our prayers are supposed to ascend to Heaven. Maybe this is the last opportunity we will have to *daven* together,

---

[1] The boy is Rabbi Shlomo Carlebach, the noted scholar, storyteller, and creator of chasidic melody. His father was the rabbi of Baden.

so our prayers have to ascend! Your prayers are not going any-where. We have to teach the whole world that today is *Shabbos.* Today is the day of joy!'' Tears streamed down Moshele's cheeks.

The man who was leading the prayer service turned ab-ruptly to Moshele and said softly, "Look, I can't do any better. I am so frightened. Please, if you can show us how our prayers can ascend to Heaven under these awesome conditions, then you take over for me. You lead the service."

He moved over.

Moshele pushed his way through the crowd. He walked around the room and sang out, "Good *Shabbos,* Good *Shab-bos!*'' to all the worshippers. Then he walked over to the win-dows, drew the drapes apart, and opened the windows. He walked back to the center of the room and began humming in his *Shabbos* melody, "Every living soul blesses Your Name."

Slowly, with great intensity and concentration, Moshele continued to lead the prayer service.

No one stirred. No one noticed the minutes ticking by. They were oblivious to the danger from the Nazi stormtroopers. For them, there was only One God Who had commanded the celebra-tion of *Shabbos.*

The next day was the last day that Jews could legally leave Vienna, assuming they had the proper forged documents. Moshele and his family were among those who were seated in a compartment on the last train to freedom. Nazi stormtroopers stalked the train platform, searching for illegal escapees.

Moshele was overcome with emotion. He could not leave Vienna without saying goodbye. His wife and two children pleaded with him to hide in a corner of the compartment, to re-main silent, but he could not contain himself. He opened the window of the compartment, stuck his head out, and began to sing with his same sing-song *Shabbos* melody, "Goodbye, Vienna, city of my birth. Goodbye, Vienna, city that I love!"

Immediately, two stormtroopers recognized him. They rushed into the train compartment and pulled him from the train. They beat him mercilessly, there on the platform, not be-cause he did not have the proper forged documents, but because they knew he had helped others escape. All the while he was being beaten to death, Moshele kept singing, "Good *Shabbos*, Good *Shabbos*!"

Authors' note: A few years ago, during one of his concert appearances in Antwerp, Rabbi Shlomo Carlebach discovered the son of Moshele Good Shabbos. Since he was so young during the Holocaust, he did not remember his father's melody. Rabbi Carlebach taught it to him, and he promised to teach that special melody to his grandchildren.

At a wedding in Borough Park, New York, in November 1985, I was privileged to meet the niece of Moshele Good Shabbos. Rebbetzen Mira Gartenhaus vividly described to me Jewish life in Vienna in 1938. She is the daughter of Rabbi Avraham Yehoshua Heschel, the Kapishnitezer rebbe. Her father and Moshele Good Shabbos were brothers. She told me that her uncle was known as a "man you could count on for favors." She has kept in contact with her uncle's family through the years.

She told me that Moshele's wife was named Chana. They had two children, Eliezer and Rochel. Both were incarcerated in Cyprus on their way to *Eretz Yisrael* during World War II. Eliezer returned to Europe many years after the war and made his home in Antwerp. He passed away last year. He was 56 years old and is survived by a son and a daughter. Rochel settled in Jerusalem, where she married and lives with her family [A.L.].

Today Is *Shabbos*

As I winged my way eastward across the Atlantic Ocean, I mentally reviewed what I expected to find in a country that had once been the homeland of half the world's Jewish population.

I was very involved with the struggle to free Soviet Jewry, although my visa application stated "business" as my profession. This was my opportunity to meet refuseniks, to make contacts, to encourage, to support, to teach, to tell them that there are Jews all over the world who extend their hands in friendship.

I arrived in Leningrad, located in the northwest corner of Russia. A former capital of the Tzars, it was built as a modern city in the early 1700s to be a "window looking on Europe." As soon as I settled into my hotel room and unpacked my luggage, I walked along the city's main thoroughfare, Nevsky Prospekt. I marveled at the beauty of this city, the high-spired admiralty building, the Winter Palace, the Hermitage Museum, the equestrian statue of Peter the Great. I wanted to explore, to get my bearings, before I made contact with the refusenik community. I had been instructed about how to find them and where to meet them.

The refusenik community has its own underground method of communication. It did not take long for a gathering to be arranged. That night, I was the center of attention in a refusenik's apartment. I talked and taught till the wee hours of the morning. When I stood up to leave that apartment to return to my hotel room, I felt a young woman's eyes on me. I noticed that she wore a Star of David around her neck. I said my goodbyes, promised to return, and walked away.

I waited at the entrance of the apartment. My hunch was correct. It did not take long for her to emerge into the street. I followed her. I wanted to know her story. She must have realized that she could trust me, because she whispered that she would meet me near the Arch of the Winter Palace the next evening.

Leningrad is the city of "white nights" in June and July; prolonged twilight hovers between heaven and earth for endless time before darkness finally descends.

I arrived early for our appointment and waited patiently, hoping she would not disappoint me. As she approached our meeting place, I noticed her continually peering around and behind her, making certain she was not being followed.

She nodded *shalom* and continued walking. I walked beside her. As we walked, she whispered her story.

"A few years ago," she began, "I found out I was Jewish. I began hanging around the refusenik community, surreptitiously, as I did not want to endanger my father's position in the Communist party. I wanted to find out what being Jewish meant in this country that denies religion. I wanted to find out why the refuseniks want to make *aliyah* (immigrate to Israel) so desperately. I found a Hebrew teacher. On a one-to-one basis, over a period of years, she taught me two things: the Hebrew alphabet and the laws of the observance of *Shabbos*. She taught me that these are two of the ways a Jew can maintain identity. I work as a typist six days a week, alternating Friday and Saturday. There is no way I can stop working on *Shabbos* if I want to keep my job. I have to work to support myself. I don't want the authorities to become suspicious; it would endanger my father's position.

"So when I am forced to work on Friday nights, I type in a

different way than I type on the other days of the week, in order that I remember that it is *Shabbos.* As I type on Friday night, I utter the Hebrew letters, *"alef, beis, gimmel, dalet."* When I finish a sentence, I whisper, "Today is *Shabbos."* When I finish a paragraph, I recite softly, *"Sh'ma Yisrael Adonai Eloheiynu Adonai Echad* (Hear, O Israel, the Lord our God, the Lord is One). Soon I hope to apply for an exit visa to Israel. I don't know how long it will take, but I am prepared to wait. Please," she hesitated, her voice breaking, "tell my story over and over to our friends in the West." She quickened her gait. I detected her uneasiness.

"Wait, before you disappear," I said, "I want to tell you one thing. I swear that I will be waiting for you in Lod, in Ben Gurion Airport, when you descend from the plane onto the soil of the land of Israel."

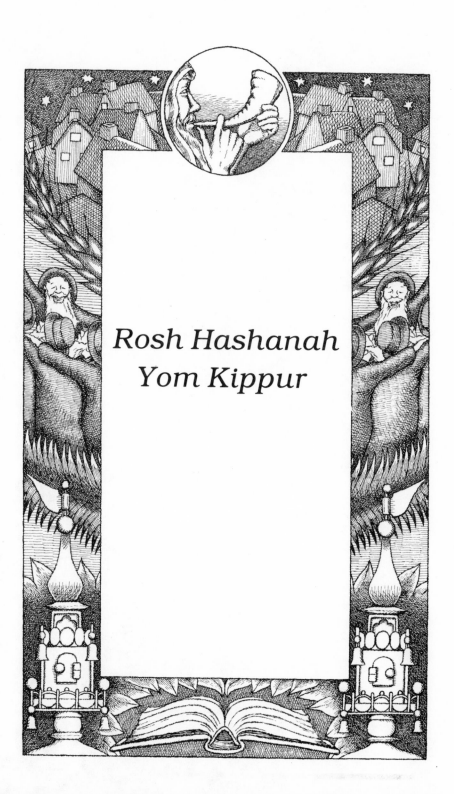

Rosh Hashanah
Yom Kippur

Rosh Hashanah, the first and second of *Tishri*, celebrates the new year, the anniversary of the creation of the world, and the birthday of man, the crown of God's creation.

Rosh Hashanah is the first day of the ten days of repentance. We were given these ten days for introspection: to evaluate our progress, to measure our achievement, to see how well we have fulfilled our purpose in His Divine Plan.

Rosh Hashanah is known by three other names: the Day of Remembrance, the Day of Judgment, and the Day of the Sounding of the *shofar* (ram's horn).

The major theme of the *Rosh Hashanah* liturgy is divided into three categories: Kingship, Remembrance, *Shofar.*

The theme of Kingship acknowledges that all mankind is the crown of His Creation. By accepting God as King, we elevate ourselves to His service and to His bidding as loyal servants.

The theme of Remembrance describes the Almighty's total recall of man's activities, past, present, and future; his yearnings, his goals, his experiences. Judgment is based upon these.

The piercing call of the *shofar* inspires repentance.

Since the time between *Rosh Hashanah* and *Yom Kippur* is a time of judgment, it is customary to bless our family and friends that they be inscribed in the book of life.

To sweeten the judgment, we dip apples into honey.

The concept of repentance was conceived before mankind was created, for the Almighty knew that repentance was necessary for the orderly functioning of the universe.

Therefore, the Almighty gave us one day a year, *Yom Kippur*—the Day of Atonement—to repent our wrongdoings and return to Him.

Wrongdoing spiritually diminishes the holiness of our soul; following God's way strengthens it.

After we stumble, we can lift ourselves up because God's Hand is outstretched to receive our repentance.

Repentance is accomplished by regretting the wrongdoing and resolving never to repeat the same offense.

Yom Kippur is the holiest day of the Jewish calendar year. It falls on the tenth day of *Tishri,* the last day of the ten days of repentance.

On *Yom Kippur,* we attempt to spiritually elevate our souls to the level of angels. We imitate their actions by refraining from all physical pleasures: food, drink, wearing leather, washing or anointing our body with cosmetics, cohabitation.

The major theme of the *Yom Kippur* liturgy is the confessional, "Our God and God of our fathers, pardon our iniquities and grant us atonement, for the sins we have committed before You," emphasizing the possibility that man can always return to God.

Torah Thoughts

Long Live the King

The holiday of *Pesach* is referred to as the holiday of remembering the exodus from Egypt, based on the historical event associated with the holiday. It is also called "the spring festival," which describes its season of the year. In general, the names associated with the Jewish holidays are descriptive of an historical occurrence or the season in which it is celebrated. Significantly, the name describing *Rosh Hashanah* falls into neither a historical nor a seasonal category, for *Rosh Hashanah* is called *Yom Hazekaron,* the coronation day of our Creator.

One of the major themes of the *Rosh Hashanah* prayer service is the coronation of the Kingship of God. We proclaim God to be King every day with the recitation of the *Sh'ma* ("Hear, O Israel, the Lord our God, the Lord is One"), and we recall the exodus and creation each *Shabbos* in the *kiddush,* which is also a proclamation of majesty. On *Rosh Hashanah* we celebrate the coronation of our King, proclaiming that our Creator, the Guide of the exodus, is our Lord, our God, and He is One.

"Reign over the whole universe in Your glory. . . . Be exalted over all the earth in grandeur. . . . May every living being recognize You as the Creator . . . and acknowledge that the Lord, God of Israel, is King, and His Kingdom rules over all.''[1]

Yom Hazekaron is the day of the coronation of our Creator, the day of the reacceptance of the Kingdom of Heaven. A parable illustrates this concept of *Rosh Hashanah.*

A king had an exceptionally able advisor who was also one of his closest friends. The two of them discussed and debated issues relevant to the welfare of their subjects. Often, the outcome was a compromise of two opinions, for their friendship remained steadfast.

Once, the advisor vehemently disagreed with the king. He decided to join forces with the king's enemies and led a violent revolution against his former friend. When the king subdued the rebellion, his former advisor was brought to trial for treason. The king played the role of the prosecutor in the courtroom and said, ''The rebellion you led against me was unforgiveable. Formerly, we were such close friends. We discussed and debated issues and always arrived at amicable solutions. We were as close as father and son. Now, it pains me greatly to sentence you to death.''

The king left the courtroom. He instructed his servants not to disturb him with pleas for pardon from the condemned or letters beseeching him for clemency.

On the appointed day, the soldiers escorted the prisoner from the jail to the place of execution at the outskirts of the city. The contingent met the king, who passed by on his horse. The king reiterated his decree to the condemned man. ''I will not pardon you. I have nothing to say to you.''

The prisoner replied in a tearful voice, ''Please, your majesty, grant me one last request. Permit me to have the privilege of running before you and proclaiming, 'Long live the king, long live the king,' until I reach the place of execution.''

The moral of the parable: no matter how much we stray from accepting the will of the Kingdom of Heaven—often deserving His disfavor for our disobedience to His will—on *Rosh Hashanah* we still proclaim our loyalty to His kingship.

---

[1]From the *Musaf* prayer service of *Rosh Hashanah*, beginning, ''Our God . . . King of all the world.''

Shofar

The *Torah* describes the rituals of *Rosh Hashanah*, the New Year, with the verses, "And in the seventh month, on the first day of the month . . . it shall be a day of introspection."[1] "And in the seventh month, on the first day of the month . . . it shall be a day of sounding (the *shofar*)."[2]

The Hebrew verb most commonly used for the sounding of the *shofar* is *tekah* (to blow, to sound). Before sounding the *shofar*, a special blessing is recited. The emphasis in the language of the blessing is on the word *lishmo'ah* (to listen), not on the word *tekah* (to blow).

If the *mitzvah* is to sound the *shofar*, why does the blessing emphasize hearing the *shofar*? Our Rabbis explained the significance of sounding the *shofar* on *Rosh Hashanah*: each and every person should hear its message, for *lishmo'ah* means not only to listen, but to make a conscious effort to hear, to take advice, to give heed.

[1]Leviticus 23:24.
[2]Numbers 29:1.

95

If the word *tekah* were used, then the sounding of the *shofar* would be external to the congregation. The *shofar* blower sounds the *shofar,* but the congregation may or may not hear. The message of the *shofar* may or may not penetrate the hearts of the worshippers.

However, when the word *lishmo'ah* is used in the blessing, the *shofar* ritual changes to an internal act: every member of the congregation must internalize listening to the call of the *shofar.*

To listen means to understand the significance, to act on the message, to internalize the action: to heed the cry of the suffering, to raise up the downtrodden, to retrospect for the purpose of self-improvement, to recognize the Almighty as the Creator and Master of the Universe, to work in harmony for the redemption of the Jewish people from exile.

Simply sounding the *shofar* (external) adds to the beauty of the prayer service, but listening (internal) demands that we change our actions in conformity with its message.

A Good and Sweet Year

One of the most meaningful customs at the *Rosh Hashanah* festival table is dipping an apple into honey. Before we eat, we bless family and friends with the words, "May it be Your Will to renew for us a good and sweet year."

Apples and honey are both sweet. Why must we sweeten that which is already sweet? The Jewish people praise God by comparing Him to an apple tree because "the apple symbolizes all the characteristics of the Almighty."[1]

From this we deduce that apples symbolize the "spiritual," the search for the Omnipresent, for Infinity, for Eternity, for *Torah.*

On the other hand, honey symbolizes the search for the "material," for comfort, home, livelihood, health. "They will be

---

[1] "The apple tree combines all excellences: as it is healing for all, so is God healing for all; as it combines two colors, so God combines two attributes—mercy and justice; as the apple has a more delicate scent than other trees, so too, God, as it is written, 'His scent is like the (trees) of Lebanon'; and as the apple has a sweet taste, so, too, God, as it is written, 'His mouth is most sweet'" (*Zohar,* Leviticus 74a).

fed the best of the wheat, and with honey from the rock, I will satisfy them."[2]

On *Rosh Hashanah,* when we dip the apple into the honey, we add the material sweetness to the spiritual, for life is a combination of both.

The apple, which is intrinsically sweet, is symbolic of the spiritual. We dip into honey, symbolic of the material, sweetening that which is already sweet. It is our way of expressing our hope that we can combine our quest for comfort, for home, for livelihood, and for health with our quest for the Omnipresent, for Infinity, for Eternity, for *Torah.*

The combination of the apple and the honey is the fulfillment of "a good and sweet year."

[2]*Psalms* 81:17.

To Eat or Not to Eat

There are many logical reasons for eating a festive meal preceding the fast of *Yom Kippur.* We feel joy knowing that the time for atonement is near, that the burden of guilt for wrongdoing we carry with us will be lifted. We are hopeful that our repentance will be accepted before the Throne of Mercy.

In addition, eating before the fast provides the necessary physical strength to sustain us through twenty-five hours of prayer and repentance. Feasting is a preparation for fasting, so that we might not suffer excessively.

The ritual of eating a festive meal prior to fasting is based upon the *Torah* verse, "And you shall fast from the ninth of the month (of *Tishri*) from evening to evening."[1] The Rabbis of the Talmud explained this verse to mean, "It comes to indicate that if one eats and drinks on the ninth (of *Tishri*), the *Torah* accounts it to him as if he had fasted on the ninth and the tenth."[2]

However, mystical thinkers have ascribed certain aspects of Jewish life to the miraculous, the wondrous, the awe-inspir-

[1]Leviticus 23:32.
[2]Talmud, *Yoma* 81b.

ing, the reverential. They classify eating on the eve of *Yom Kippur* and fasting on the day of *Yom Kippur* in this category, by equating the feasting with the fasting. On the ninth day of *Tishri*, which is the feast day, the more you eat and drink, the greater the *mitzvah*. On the tenth day of *Tishri*, which is *Yom Kippur*, the fast day, the more you deprive yourself of physical pleasures, the greater the *mitzvah*. Actually, the rituals of these two days are opposite activities, but the outcome is the same, namely, fasting and feasting eradicate evil because both activities follow the will of God. This is the miraculous, the wondrous, the awe-inspiring, the reverential. It is beyond human understanding. But isn't the concept of *Yom Kippur*, a day of atonement, in itself wondrous?

Logically, we don't know how to fix the wrongs we have committed; we must rely on the compassion of the Almighty for atonement. We don't need to understand the commandment to feast and fast; we need to have faith to follow the will of God.

Yom Kippur and *Purim*

We celebrate two holidays each year whose names are very similar in sound: *Yom Kippur* (the Day of Atonement) and *Purim*. Because of the similarity in sound, our Rabbis interpreted *Yom Kippur* to be like *Purim*, namely, that *Yom Kippur* is *ke* (Hebrew for "like") *Purim*. What possible connection can the two holidays have with each other?

Unlike other holidays, *Yom Kippur* is unique since we are commanded to abstain from all physical pleasures on this day. On *Purim*, we partake of all physical pleasures. These are seemingly opposite rituals. How are these festivals alike?

On *Yom Kippur*, the Almighty gave the Jewish people the second set of tablets upon which were written the ten commandments, replacing the first set that Moses broke when he witnessed them worshipping the golden calf. Giving the Jewish people the second set of tablets signaled the Almighty had forgiven them. They did not have to do anything. They were entirely passive, surrounded with holiness, secure in the knowledge that forgiveness meant a second chance. On *Purim*, however, the Jewish people actively reaffirmed their commitment to *Torah*,[1] for many had strayed during their sojourn in Persia.

Yom Kippur marks the Almighty's forgiving His people, a passive process. Therefore, we do nothing on this day. We abstain completely to heighten our spiritual level. However, on *Purim* the Jews were actively involved in the process of reaffirming their loyalty to *Torah*. Therefore, we celebrate by physically indulging in food, drink, and merriment.

This is the synthesis of Judaism, the combination of the physical and the spiritual.

[1] *Megillas Esther* 9:27.

Stories

Stories

If Only I Could Pray

Imagine the *shul* in Sanz on *Rosh Hashanah*! Worshippers, wrapped in oversized *tallisos* (plural of *tallis*), standing shoulder to shoulder, led in prayer by Rebbe Chayim Halberstam, the Sanzer rebbe. No sound is audible, except for the chanting of prayers ascending to the Throne of Glory.

Afterwards, a few of the rebbe's disciples ask him to teach them the secret of prayer. "Why do you think I am the expert on prayer?" he responds. "Let me tell you a short story about Maxele from St. Petersburg, who was an expert on prayer."

You know that St. Petersburg was off limits to Jews, unless they had business considered necessary for the economic welfare of the Russian government. Very few Jews qualified. Maxele's father was one of the exceptions. The life that he lived in St. Petersburg was totally compatible with the non-Jewish world, for he assimilated rapidly into Russian society.

Many years passed, and Maxele's father aged. When he realized that his time was approaching to leave this world, he called his son and said to him, "Maxele, it is almost time for me to leave this world. Before I die, I want you to swear to me that you will always remember that you are a Jew."

Maxele turned to his father and said, "I will swear to you that I will always remember that I am a Jew . . . but please, tell me, what is a Jew supposed to do?"

Maxele's father answered, "If I could relive my life, I would give anything to find out what a Jew is, what a Jew is supposed to do. The truth is: I don't know. When I was twelve years old, I was kidnapped to serve in the Tzar's army. I spent twenty-five years in the army and was never permitted a furlough to see my family. By the time I was released, I had forgotten my Jewish heritage almost entirely. Since I had excelled in the army, I was permitted to settle in St. Petersburg. I only know that I was born a Jew, and I remember that on *Rosh Hashanah* a Jew goes to *shul*."

Maxele's father passed away soon after. The following *Rosh Hashanah* Maxele searched for a *shul* in order to fulfill the oath he had made to his dying father. He did not know what to do, but he entered a *shul* and sat down in the rear. No one paid any attention to him. He sat for a while, unable to participate, not understanding anything that was happening. He just sat and watched.

After a while, Maxele stood up. He lifted his eyes heavenward and prayed. "God in Heaven! Until this moment, I have forgotten that I am a Jew. I am illiterate because I was never given the opportunity to study your *Torah* or to find out what is expected of me. I make a vow to You that from this moment on, I will try to find out what a Jew is supposed to know and do. In spite of my lack of knowledge, I have always recognized that You are One and Your Glory fills the whole world. I love You with all my heart, so please don't forget me, Maxele from St. Petersburg."

The Sanzer rebbe's voice trailed off. His disciples noticed that he was crying. He said to them, "You wanted me to teach you the secret of prayer. I want you to know that I would like to be able to pray once in my life like Maxele from St. Petersburg."

What the Rebbe Knew

Yaakov was one of ten young men whom Rebbe Pinchas of Koretz supported with a weekly stipend in order that they might study *Torah* day and night. The study of *Torah* was their vocation and their avocation; they had no interest in worldly matters.

Yaakov was the leader of the group, and it was his responsibility to go to Rebbe Pinchas' house each Friday afternoon to pick up ten rubles and distribute them to his friends, one ruble for each friend, in order that they might have money for *Shabbos* and for the remainder of the week.

One Friday afternoon, Yaakov picked up only nine rubles. He was very surprised that he was shortchanged; he believed it was an honest mistake, but when he returned to the rebbe's house to tell him the problem, he was told that the rebbe could not see him.

Yaakov knew that his friends were just as dependent upon their weekly stipend as he was, and he did not want to shortchange them. So he gave each one their due, leaving himself without money for *Shabbos* and the week. In order to sustain himself and his family, he pawned his fur hat, believing that when the mistake was rectified he would be able to redeem it.

That Friday night in the *shul*, all the disciples of Rebbe Pinchas wore their fur hats, all except Yaakov. He was wearing a weekday hat. He hoped the rebbe would notice, but alas, Rebbe Pinchas did not even glance at him.

The following Friday afternoon, Yaakov went again to pick up the weekly stipend. He hoped he would have an opportunity to talk to the rebbe, to clarify what he believed to be an error. But when he arrived, the rebbe silently handed him nine rubles and escorted him outside, closing the door gently in his face. Yaakov knew then that the previous week's episode was not a mistake. He distributed the money to his friends, went home, picked up his *Shabbos* clothes, and pawned them in order to have money for *Shabbos* and the week. He had hoped that when the rebbe saw him dressed in weekday clothes on *Shabbos*, he would realize his mistake and rectify it. But, alas, Rebbe Pinchas paid no heed to Yaakov the whole of that *Shabbos* either.

People from the surrounding area had been invited to spend that *Shabbos* with Rebbe Pinchas, and they came to Koretz from all over. They streamed to the *shul* as the sun was setting, and by the time the prayer service was over, brightly lit candles sparkled throughout Koretz. In the rebbe's house, long, banquet-sized tables were set with white tablecloths, crowned with the fragrance of freshly baked *challos,* ready to accommodate the visitors. All of them sat joyfully around the tables, chatting, smiling, imbibing the warmth and glow of *Shabbos*, singing, listening to the rebbe's *kiddush,* his words of *Torah.* Only Yaakov sat in a corner by himself, dressed in his weekday clothes, scowling.

The third Friday, Yaakov was determined to speak to the rebbe, but when he went to pick up the weekly stipend, Rebbe Pinchas opened the door only a crack, handed him an envelope with nine rubles, and closed the door.

Yaakov was distraught. He didn't have money for *Shabbos.* He didn't have anything else to pawn. He didn't understand what he had done to deserve this treatment. He walked toward his house, unhappy and downtrodden. On the way home, he met an old friend who had become a wheat merchant. The wheat merchant stopped Yaakov and asked him why he looked so miserable. Yaakov couldn't control himself any longer. Tears streamed down his face. He began to stammer. Slowly he revealed the cause of his misery.

His friend listened attentively and then said, "On the next market day, I will provide you with flour. You will go to the market and sell it. With the profit, you will buy more flour, and you will continue to buy and sell flour. Eventually you will become capable of supporting your family comfortably."

Yaakov weighed his friend's proposition. He really did not want to give up his place in the study hall, but he also knew he had no choice. He knew he had the responsibility of taking care of his family. So he thanked his friend for the offer, shook his hand, wished him "Good *Shabbos*," and told him he would be waiting for the next market day.

The *Shabbos* meals in Yaakov's house that week were meager. He did not have his *Shabbos* hat or his *Shabbos* clothes. There was no singing, no joy, only the hope that the following week would be better.

On the appointed day, the wheat merchant delivered a load of flour to Yaakov. He took it to the marketplace, sold it for a profit, invested in more wheat, and returned home in much better condition than when he had left. In a very short time, Yaakov moved from a booth in the marketplace to a neighborhood store. He invested his profit in other merchandise. Soon he moved his business from the neighborhood store to a warehouse to accommodate his flourishing business. He was selling a lot more than wheat: fabric, spices, household goods, tools, leather. People heard that the quality of Yaakov's merchandise was better than that of the other merchants in the area, so they gradually switched their business accounts and dealt with him exclusively. His reputation as an honest businessman spread.

Meanwhile, the administrator of the duke's estate heard about the new businessman, and he went to investigate. He was delighted with the quality of Yaakov's merchandise and the manner in which he did business, so he reported his findings to the duke. The duke inspected the merchandise and agreed with his administrator's opinion. He became one of Yaakov's steady customers.

The administrator continuously praised Yaakov's business ability. One day, the duke decided to meet him personally. By observing him for a while, the duke saw that Yaakov was gentle and honest. Moreover, the merchandise was displayed attractively, the customers seemed satisfied, and the warehouse was managed efficiently.

The duke introduced himself and promised Yaakov he would return again. He kept his word and visited him in his warehouse many times. One day the duke invited Yaakov to visit him in his mansion. Intrigued by the invitation, Yaakov accepted.

When he first arrived, the duke made him feel comfortable. Then he began to speak in a serious tone. "I have grown to trust you these past few months. I admire your ability to achieve. Look around this mansion," he continued. "I have everything I want: a vast estate, wealth enough to purchase anything my heart desires, servants, but, alas, I haven't any children. I know I will die soon, and my name will not be remembered. Therefore, I have hired a sculptor to sculpt a statue of my likeness for my gravestone. I want the eyes of the statue embedded with two precious stones that can only be purchased in Amsterdam. Because I have grown to trust you, I want to commission you to travel to Amsterdam to purchase those precious stones for me. I will pay you handsomely and take care of your family while you are away. I will arrange your travel to a port on the Baltic Sea, and from there, passage by boat to Amsterdam."

Yaakov was surprised by the duke's proposition. Mentally, he weighed the conditions. In his mind, it seemed to be a quest after folly; moreover, Yaakov knew that sea travel could be very dangerous. On the other hand, he wanted to return to his place in the study hall. By accepting the duke's proposition, he would have to travel for a short time, but would then be able to return to the study hall independent of the rebbe's weekly stipend. He reflected, deliberated, and mused how pleasant the future could be with the money the duke offered him, but he could not decide. He asked the duke for three days to think about it; he wanted an opportunity to discuss the duke's proposition with Rebbe Pinchas.

Instead of going to his warehouse early the next morning, Yaakov went to seek the advice of Rebbe Pinchas. When he arrived at the study hall, he was told that Rebbe Pinchas had requested that no one be admitted to his private room. Yaakov was not too disappointed, because he had two more days to decide, but the next morning and the next, the rebbe refused to receive disciples. Yaakov knew that it was his own responsibility to decide. He returned to the mansion and told the duke that he would accept the proposition. The duke rejoiced and immediately proceeded to make arrangements for Yaakov's trip. The date for departure was planned for the first Sunday of the following month.

Yaakov traveled with a lot of baggage: clothing, suitcases filled with food, his *tallis* and *tefillin*, holy books to study along the way, and the money to pay for the precious stones.

The trip was uneventful. When he arrived at the port city, he transferred his baggage to the boat and settled down in his assigned room, waiting for the boat to set out to sea. Yaakov did not know that the captain had paid special attention to the amount of baggage he was carrying.

While the boat was at sea, a sailor asked Yaakov for a favor, and he left his room in order to help. Unbeknown to him, the captain had set up the sailor as an accomplice to remove Yaakov from his room so he might have ample time to search the baggage. When the captain searched each piece, he saw the amount of money Yaakov was carrying. He devised a plot whereby he could steal Yaakov's money.

The next morning, the captain announced that the passengers would be able to stop to rest on an island. After a few hours, he would signal the time to return to the boat by blowing three whistles. He made certain that Yaakov did not hear the number of whistle signals. Then, he took Yaakov aside, put his arm around him, and told him that four whistles would be the signal to return to the boat.

The passengers descended the gangplank of the boat when it dropped anchor, and they spread out around the island, enjoying the freedom, the foliage, the sunshine, the warmth. Since the captain had announced that the rest period would be a few hours, Yaakov carried with him his suitcase of books. He left the rest of his baggage locked in his room on the boat.

He found a tree, sat down comfortably, opened his suitcase, took out a book, and began to read. Some time later, he heard the first whistle. Some of the passengers began walking back to the docked boat, but Yaakov knew he had plenty of time. He continued reading. He ignored the second and third whistle signals also, since he believed he had time to return to the boat on the fourth signal.

Alas, the captain ordered the sailor to raise anchor after the third whistle signal, the passengers filed quickly up the gangplank, and the boat cruised away from the island. Yaakov lifted his eyes from his book and saw the boat in the distance. He ran toward the edge of the island, screaming and waving frantically, but to no avail. Yaakov was stranded. He realized that he might be stranded for a long time. Rather than succumb to depression, he walked around, surveyed the island, discovered fruit trees, a brook, and a cave for shelter.

He decided to gather some rocks and build a lookout tower, so he would be able to signal the next passing boat. As the pile of stones grew higher, he climbed up to see the area of the entire island. In the distance, he noticed a fire burning. He scrambled down from the lookout tower and ran toward the fire. Much to Yaakov's surprise, a man sat tending the fire.

Breathlessly, Yaakov blurted out his story; the man listened listlessly. Yaakov tried to find out how long he had been stranded on the island, how he had survived the weather, how he had sustained himself, but the man did not blink an eyelash. It was apparent to Yaakov that the man considered him to be an intruder. Yaakov decided to try one more time to engage the man in conversation before he retreated to his side of the island. This time, the man said, "I'll only tell you one thing. My name is Hershel."

That night the two men slept on their respective sides of the island, but the next morning Yaakov returned to Hershel's side of the island and tried to draw him into a conversation. Yaakov did all the talking. He expressed his concern, over and over, for the welfare of his wife and children. He openly discussed his lonesomeness for his family. He yearned to be back in Koretz. Hershel listened but did not speak. Yet, as the days grew into weeks, Hershel began to trust Yaakov. He showed him how to pick the best fruit at the peak of ripeness and how to catch the most delicious fish from the brook.

During his free time, Yaakov studied from the books he had brought with him to the island. Sometimes he asked Hershel to join him. When they were together, all Yaakov spoke about was his longing for his wife and children. The two men became companions.

One day Hershel calmly confided to Yaakov that he had deserted his family. Yaakov was shaken, but he did not react. He continued his routine, as if it had no effect on him. About a week later, he asked Hershel to accompany him on his walk to the edge of the island where he had built the lookout tower. He climbed to the top to scan the horizon for approaching boats. Hershel seemed to pay no interest in this activity.

The next week, Yaakov noticed a boat approaching the coast in the distance. He scrambled up his lookout tower, removed his shirt, and waved it frantically, screaming at the top of his lungs. His display caught the attention of the boat's captain, and he sent a sailor in a rowboat to the island to pick up Yaakov and bring him to the boat.

Yaakov's imminent departure aroused much pain in Hershel's heart, for Yaakov would return to his family. Hershel had been reminded almost daily how precious family was, and he began to regret that he had abandoned his.

As Yaakov prepared to step into the rowboat, Hershel called out, "Wait for me! I'd like to return to Koretz with you. I'd like to go back to my family!" Both men stepped off the deserted island onto the rowboat, the first step toward home.

The captain wondered why two men were living on a deserted island, and he listened sympathetically to Yaakov's plight. He offered them passage as far as the next port. Yaakov and Hershel joined the vagrants and wandered from *shtetl* to

shtetl towards Koretz. Since most *shtetlach* with a Jewish population took care of the poor, they found places to sleep and eat
along the way. As they approached Koretz, they heard the town's
beggars discussing the recent death of the duke and the tragic
fire which destroyed all his property.

They arrived in Koretz on a Friday afternoon, and from the
excitement in the *shtetl,* it seemed as if preparations were
underway for a special *Shabbos.*

Yaakov was worn out and dirty, and his clothes were rag-
ged. He did not have the strength to face his family, so he slipped
into the *shul* for the prayer service and then followed the crowd
to Rebbe Pinchas' house. Hershel shadowed Yaakov's every
step.

When all the visitors were seated around the long banquet-
sized tables with white tablecloths, crowned with the fragrance
of freshly baked *challos,* Rebbe Pinchas, standing at the head of
the table, raised his hands for attention. Instead of beginning
with *kiddush,* he cleared his throat, looked toward the back of
the room where Yaakov and Hershel sat, and motioned to them
to come forward. Yaakov moved through the crowd toward
Rebbe Pinchas, followed by Hershel. Rebbe Pinchas embraced
Yaakov and then, still holding him around the shoulders, said in
a gentle voice, "Tonight, we have a special guest. Tonight we
welcome Yaakov back after a long absence. It is time I explained
to you why he was away for so long. I had to devise a plan
whereby he would willingly go to the place where Hershel was
hiding in order to bring him back to Koretz and his family.
Yaakov was successful in his mission, for Hershel is standing
here beside him."

Rebbe Pinchas stopped speaking for a moment and smiled
at Hershel. Then he continued, "Now it is time for Yaakov to return to his family and his place in the study hall." When he finished speaking, Rebbe Pinchas of Koretz filled his wine cup and
began chanting the *kiddush.*

That *Shabbos* was the most joyful *Shabbos* of Yaakov's life.

Repentance

Rebbe Yosef Mayer of S'finka, a *shtetl* near Marmoresh in the Carpathian mountains, rejoiced in the happiness of his followers and cried with them in their pain. He warmly received rich and poor, the influential and the humble beggar. He was interested in the welfare of every Jew. Rebbe Yosef Mayer could not rest until he had helped ease the suffering of every unfortunate person who knocked at his door.

Once, a very troubled Jew arrived in S'finka to seek the advice of the rebbe. The date was the sixth day of the Hebrew month of *Elul* in the year 5659 (1899). Pain was written all over his face.

It was customary that the *gabbai* (the rebbe's secretary) wrote people's problems on a piece of paper and gave them to the rebbe. When the *gabbai* approached the troubled Jew and asked him how he could help, he said brokenheartedly, "I have come to ask the rebbe to teach me how to repent for a sin that I have committed."

The *gabbai* asked, "What is the nature of this sin?"

The troubled Jew answered, "I am embarrassed to tell you.

No sin of this kind has ever been committed by any Jew since the beginning of time. I will only tell it to the rebbe."

Sympathetic to the troubled Jew's pain, the *gabbai* showed him to the rebbe's room.

The rebbe stretched out his hand to make the troubled Jew feel at ease and queried, "How can I help you?"

"Rebbe," the troubled Jew said, "I have committed a sin that has never been committed before by any other Jew since the beginning of time."

"What did you do?" asked the rebbe.

The troubled Jew stammered, "I did not fast last *Yom Kippur!*"

"Why didn't you fast last *Yom Kippur*?" asked the rebbe.

"It's a long story, rebbe. Let me tell you what happened. I live in a tiny Carpathian mountain village with my wife. We are the only Jews in the area. Last year *Yom Kippur* was observed on Monday, but according to my calculations, the Holy Day was Tuesday. Therefore, on Monday my wife and I feasted, for, as you know, it is as great a *mitzvah* to feast the day before *Yom Kippur* as it is to fast on *Yom Kippur*. That afternoon, I harnessed my horses to the wagon, and we set off for the *shtetl*, to pray with other Jews in *shul.*

"When we reached the *shul*, the sun was descending in the heavens. We hurried inside, expecting everyone to be ready to begin *Kol Nidre* (the opening prayer of *Yom Kippur*). Instead, the worshippers were reciting *Ne'ilah*, the closing prayer. I looked at my wife. We were aghast at our mistake and overcome with remorse. We decided that we would observe *Yom Kippur* according to our calculations. We remained in *shul* that night and the next day. We fasted and prayed by ourselves. Now, I have come to ask you how to repent for this sin which no Jew has ever committed since the beginning of time."

The troubled Jew's voice trembled. The rebbe paced back and forth across his room. Suddenly he began to shiver. A piercing scream came from his mouth, and he began, "Master of the Universe! Have compassion on Your people. Redeem them from this bitter exile. Look how they are spread out among the na-

tions. In order to earn a livelihood, they have to live by themselves, away from a Jewish community. They don't even know
when *Yom Kippur* occurs!"

Silence. The rebbe stopped praying. The troubled Jew did
not say a word. The rebbe held him, and they cried together.

Then the rebbe said, "You prayed the *Kol Nidre* service
when everyone else recited *Ne'ilah.* I can't tell you to give charity
money to atone for the sin you committed, for if you had extra
money, you would surely have purchased a Jewish calendar.
This is your repentance. Promise me," continued the rebbe,
"that from now on, you will try to have more contact with the
Jewish community, especially from the beginning of the month
of *Elul.* That way you will be able to calculate the correct date of
Yom Kippur. Don't ever hesitate to ask help from another Jew. I
bless you with a better source of income than you are earning so
that soon you will be able to live among your own people."

Don't You Know It's *Yom Kippur?*

Rebbe Yehuda Layb (Laybele) Ayger was born into a misnagdic[1] family about 150 years ago.

His grandfather, Rabbi Akiva Ayger, was a brilliant *Torah* scholar who stood firmly against the rising assimilationist tendencies of his generation. His writings included glosses on the Talmud and responsa and commentaries on the *Torah*. Yet he was remarkably humble.

His father, Rabbi Shlomo Ayger, was as illustrious as his own father had been.

Why is it so important to start this story with the family background of Rebbe Laybele Ayger? At this particular period in Jewish history, there existed a tremendous conflict between *chasidim* and *misnagdim*,[2] and young Laybele Ayger, at the age

---

[1]Opposed to the chasidic movement.

[2]The *chasidim* believed that the unlearned could approach the Heavenly Throne of the Creator through prayer and good deeds. Serving God with joy, song, and dance in addition to the study of *Torah* created an emotional environment of love and caring. The *misnagdim* insisted on intensive *Torah* study and the strict interpretation of *halachah* (Jewish law). They believed that the performance of the commandments was the ladder to reach the Heavenly Throne of the Creator. Although their styles were different, both *chasidim* and *misnagdim* had the same goal: namely, to raise the Jewish people to the highest possible level of holiness.

of seventeen, wanted to leave the misnagdic environment in which he was raised to study in a chasidic *yeshivah*.

He begged his father for permission to leave Posen, his native city, in order to study with the rebbe of Kotzk. The chasidic *yeshivah* of the Kotzker rebbe was famous for the high level of achievement of its students. However, *misnagdim* believed that Kotzker *chasidim* behaved peculiarly. In addition, the leaders of the two sects literally prohibited their followers from having anything to do with each other.

It was natural, therefore, that Rabbi Shlomo Ayger refused his son's request. But Laybele was persistent. Finally, his father relented, and Laybele joyfully made preparations to travel to Kotzk. As he was about to leave Posen, his father exhorted him, "You may go to study in Kotzk, but don't become like them."

Laybele arrived at the Kotzker *yeshivah* and immediately immersed himself in study and in the Kotzker way of life.

That *Yom Kippur* night, at the conclusion of *Kol Nidre*, the evening prayer service, Laybele decided to remain awake all night to study. He found a place for himself at a long bench and table in the large, empty study hall, for everyone else had gone home to sleep. It was very quiet. He opened a volume of the Talmud and immersed himself in the printed word.

Suddenly, three students entered the study hall, walked over to the table where Laybele was studying, pushed him off his bench, and sat down in his place. Laybele had learned that there is always enough room for everyone, so he decided to move away rather than protest on *Yom Kippur* night.

The students did not study. Rather, the eldest asked his companions if they had already made *kiddush* (sanctification of Sabbath and festival wine).

Laybele gasped, horrified!

One of the younger students shook his head in the negative. Thereupon, the eldest instructed the third companion to go over to the closet, get a *kiddush* cup and a bottle of wine, and bring them to the table. When the eldest returned to the table, he poured wine into the *kiddush* cup, lifted it up, and prepared to recite the blessing.

Laybele was panic-stricken and bewildered! He thought, "The *Torah* commands that every Jew fast on *Yom Kippur*." He could not understand why three students of the Kotzker rebbe were in the study hall preparing to make *kiddush* on *Yom Kippur* night!

Laybele could not restrain himself and he began shouting, "What are you doing?"

The eldest replied, "Why? What's wrong? Tonight is a festival. We are going to make *kiddush*." Laybele responded, "But don't you know that *Yom Kippur* is a fast day?" The eldest retorted, "So what!"

Laybele demanded, "Don't you know that all Jews are supposed to fast on *Yom Kippur*?"

The eldest inquired, "Who said so?"

Laybele answered, "God said so in His *Torah*." The three companions asked in unison, "Who is God?" They stared at Laybele.

Laybele could not answer. He was stunned. Then there was utter silence. After ten frightful minutes, the three companions walked over to Laybele. The eldest put his hands gently on Laybele's shoulder and said quietly, "Laybele, you have been in Kotzk almost a whole year. You still don't know who God is! You haven't learned anything yet."

They retreated, slowly returning to the table. The eldest poured the wine back into the bottle, walked over to the wash basin, rinsed the *kiddush* cup, and put everything back in the closet.

Laybele was shaken by the entire experience. He closed the volume of the Talmud that he had been studying and mulled over what had happened. Toward dawn, Laybele Ayger decided to become a Kotzker *chasid*. Subsequently, he became a great chasidic rebbe.

The Wine Bottle That
Never Stopped Flowing

Before one becomes a rebbe, one usually travels around the various *shtetlach* (villages) to see how the Jewish people are faring.

Once, a young rebbe-to-be arrived in a *shtetl* and noticed a tremendous amount of commotion in the town square. He saw that a poster was being nailed to a center tree in the town square. He edged his way over to the tree and read the poster. The poster announced the forthcoming marriage of the youngest daughter of the richest man in town and invited all the townspeople to join in the wedding celebration.

A poor man standing nearby turned to rebbe-to-be and said, "You look like a stranger in town. Why don't you wait around for the celebration? In this town, the rich always honor the poor and the strangers when they celebrate a joyous occasion. You will be seated at a table where important people sit, and you will be served the best food."

The rebbe-to-be decided to wait around to see if the poor man spoke the truth. On the day of the celebration his words were fulfilled. The father of the bride seated the strangers and the poor people at the same table as his most important guests.

After the sumptuous meal was over, just before the recitation of the grace after meals, the father of the bride walked around from table to table and poured wine in each guest's goblet. The rebbe-to-be noticed that all the wine was poured from the same bottle. The wine in the bottle literally never stopped flowing. The rebbe-to-be marveled at this. Waiting for the conclusion of the grace after meals, he approached his host and asked how it was possible to fill so many wine goblets from the same bottle of wine.

The father of the bride answered, "If you have time, I will tell you the story of the wine bottle that never stops flowing."

True to his word, after the last guest left, the wealthy man sat down next to the rebbe-to-be. He pointed to the lavish table decorations, linens, and remainder of a sumptuous banquet and somberly began to tell his tale.

It was not always like this. Once, I was very poor. I lived in a small *shtetl*, far removed from any large area of Jewish settlement. I tried to eke out a living as a *mohel* (a ritual circumciser) but I knew very few people, and very few people knew me. Sometimes I would travel to larger towns, hoping to find a newborn to circumcise, but no one wanted to avail themselves of my services.

One time, a few days before *Yom Kippur*, a father of a newborn son breathlessly ran through my *shtetl*, demanding to know where the *mohel* lived.

"I need a *mohel*, I need a *mohel*," he shouted as he ran. "My newborn son needs to be circumcised on the morning of the day before *Yom Kippur*, the eighth day after birth."

I heard his shouts, so I ran out of my house and told him that I was a *mohel*, that I would be only too happy to circumcise his son, that I would do the circumcision gratis. I only requested that he make the circumcision early in the morning, so I could return to my family before the holy day began. The father of the baby agreed. On the morning of the eighth day, I arose early, packed my *tefillin* and my instruments, and started off. I wanted to reach my destination in order to have time to pray before the circumcision.

When I arrived, the father was not in his house. The mother told me he had gone to the town square to gather a *minyan* (quorum of ten males) for the circumcision ritual. I ran out to look for him. I knew that a *minyan* was not needed, and I was anxious to circumcise the baby and return to my *shtetl*. As I was searching for the father, I saw a man in the distance. He looked like a charity collector and carried a big satchel. I ran over to the man and asked, "Do you want to be the *sandek* (the person holding the baby during the circumcision) and share the joy of bringing a baby boy into the covenant of our father Abraham?"

He kept walking and answered in a singing melody, "Time is money, time is money."

I stepped in front of him so he could not proceed. I demanded to know what he wanted in order to remain for the circumcision. He asked me, "What do you have to offer?"

I told him, "I have nothing to offer except my *tefillin*."

"I'll take them," he said.

We returned to the house. I took my *tefillin* and put them into his satchel. Then I circumcised the baby. Afterward, I asked him in which direction he was going. I thought he might be walking in my direction, and I could accompany him. But he sang out again, "Time is money, time is money," and disappeared as suddenly as he had appeared.

I began the long trek back to my *shtetl* alone, happy that I had been instrumental in helping the father and mother bring their newborn son into the covenant of Abraham. I never expected to see the tax collector or my *tefillin* again.

I arrived home, weary from my journey. To my surprise, I noticed my *tefillin* lying on the table when I entered my house. I asked my wife, "How did you find my *tefillin*?"

She told me, "A stranger knocked at our door. He looked tired and thirsty. I invited him in. First, he took your *tefillin* out of his satchel and laid them on the table. Then, he asked me for some wine. I told him that we have not been able to afford to buy wine for many months."

My wife continued telling me what happened. She said, "He turned around and looked up at an old wine bottle on a top shelf, lifted it, and tilted it over a cup that was standing on the table. I knew that the wine bottle had been empty for many months, but wine began flowing from the bottle. My eyes opened wide in amazement at the awesome sight. Wine flowed into the cup and filled it. The stranger lifted the cup and drank. When he finished, he said to me, 'I bless you that the wine in this bottle will not stop flowing until you marry off your youngest daughter.' Then he walked out of our house and disappeared."

From then on, I prospered. I circumcised many children and earned a decent living for my family. For the first time in my life, I even had some money. I invested it in business. Soon I became the richest man in town. Many years passed. During all these years, I was privileged to use my wealth to help many people less fortunate than myself. I was hospitable to strangers, I supported widows and orphans, I helped establish a few people in business, and I supported scholars who devoted themselves to the study of the *Torah.*

My children matured and I married them off, one by one. At each wedding dinner, I poured wine only from this bottle. Tonight, I have celebrated the marriage of my youngest daughter. I know that the blessing of the tax collector was fulfilled.

I Am a Jew

Rebbe Layb Sarah's wandered from *shtetl* to *shtetl*, performing acts of kindness, distributing or collecting charity, advising, helping, serving those in need.

He planned to be in a certain *shtetl* for *Yom Kippur*, but because of a sudden fierce rainstorm accompanied by gusty, howling winds, he realized he would not have enough time to reach his destination in time for the holy day. He decided to remain in a tiny nearby village located off the path of the main mud-clogged road.

In the village, he found a tiny *shul* and entered. Inside, eight people stood around, half of them contemplating the idea of repentance, the other half idly chattering, commiserating with their neighbors about the difficulty of living a Jewish life in such a tiny village. As soon as Rebbe Layb Sarah's walked in, they came to attention, for they recognized him. They extended him every possible hospitality: they helped him change his rain-soaked garments and bade him sit quietly until he had warmed himself. The people noticed that Rebbe Layb Sarah's glanced continuously around the small room, wondering if there would be a tenth man for the *minyan*. They assured him that two men lived nearby at the edge of the forest, and they had promised to be present for the *Yom Kippur* prayer services.

On the strength of that promise, Rebbe Layb Sarah's began preparations for *Yom Kippur*. From his backpack, he removed and donned a white *kittel* (prayer robe) and a large white hat, wrapped himself in an oversized *tallis*, and recited the preliminary prayers beseeching the Almighty for mercy in His Judgment.

The eight men watched the door and waited. Including Rebbe Laybe Sarah's, the count was nine, one short of a *minyan*. Anxiously, they watched and waited.

Although the rain had stopped, a gray cloudy mist remained. The moment to begin *Kol Nidre* was rapidly approaching, but there was no *minyan* in the tiny *shul*. It was apparent that the two men from the edge of the forest who had promised to join the *minyan* would not appear.

Consternation covered Rebbe Layb Sarah's face for it was too late to travel elsewhere, and it was apparent that there would be no *minyan* in this place. He turned to the elder and queried, "Isn't there another Jew living nearby?" The elder threw his hands up and shook his head negatively. Then Rebbe Layb Sarah's rephrased his question. "Isn't there even an apostate Jew living nearby, perhaps?" The elder was surprised at the question, but it triggered a response. "Yes," he answered, "there is an apostate Jew nearby. He is the local *poretz* (landowner). He married the daughter of the previous *poretz* forty years ago. Her father promised him that if he converted, he would be his beneficiary. They had no children. She died a few years ago. He has had nothing to do with us in all these years."

Rebbe Layb Sarah's responded, "I want you to know that the gates of repentance are never closed, not even to an apostate, not even to a person who has groveled in dirt all his life. Even in such a person you may find a spark of holiness. Show me where the *poretz* lives." The elder pointed toward the direction of the *poretz*'s mansion. Rebbe Layb Sarah's quickly removed his *tallis* and ran towards the mansion. When he arrived, he knocked on the door but entered without waiting to be invited inside.

In the meantime, the *poretz* came to the entry and stood frozen at the sight of the breathless Rebbe Layb Sarah's, dressed in a white *kittel* with a large white hat. The two men stood silently and stared at each other. The *poretz* thought about calling his bodyguard to grab the intruder and lock him in the dungeon for trespassing, but he was unable to move. The minutes ticked by. The sun had set. An hour passed.

Finally, Rebbe Layb Sarah's broke the frozen silence.

My name is Layb Sarah's. I want to tell you my story. The *poretz* of my mother's village had a son who noticed her every time she came to the village marketplace. He tried repeatedly to gain her attention, but she ignored him continuously. The more she ignored him, the more he persisted, to the point that he imagined he was madly in love with her and decided that he would marry her.

She was so alarmed by the young man's persistent nagging that she told her father. He realized that the situation could get out of hand. He knew that the only way to save his daughter from the *poretz*'s son was to marry her off to a Jew as quickly as possible. He did not think the *poretz*'s son would continue paying attention to her if he knew she were married. The only unmarried Jewish man in the village was the tutor, who earned his livelihood by teaching the children in the village. He was a kind, scholarly man, much older than my mother, and he lived in my grandfather's house. My grandfather asked him if he would consent to marry his daughter. The tutor agreed on the condition that if the marriage did not work out after a year, he would willingly grant her a divorce. She agreed to the match in order to be freed from the unwelcome attentions of the *poretz*'s son. After a year, the old tutor wanted to fulfill the conditions of the marriage, so he volunteered to divorce her. She refused to accept the divorce. Instead, she said to her husband, "I pray that God will bless us with a son who will follow in the righteous footsteps of his father."

God answered her prayer, and I was born. My mother

named me Layb, but I am known as Layb Sarah's, in honor of my mother, who married the old tutor to escape from the *poretz*'s son.

My mother withstood the test, but you did not. You sold your soul for gold and silver. But I want you to know that the gates to repentance are never closed. This is the moment for you to repent. Tonight is *Yom Kippur*. The Jews of this tiny village need you for a *minyan*. Come with me, join us—the tenth man is the holiest to God.

The face of the *poretz* paled. His body quivered. Mentally, he reviewed his life. He lowered his eyes, ashamed of the tears streaming down his cheeks, and whispered, "I will come with you."

Rebbe Layb Sarah's and the *poretz* ran back to the *shul*. Surprised whispers murmured across the lips of the eight men who had been waiting. Rebbe Layb Sarah's motioned to the elder to give the *poretz* a *tallis*. The *poretz* spread the *tallis*, raised it, and let it fall over his head and shoulders, completely wrapping himself in it.

Rebbe Layb Sarah's removed both *Torah* scrolls from the ark. He gave one to the elder and one to the *poretz*. He stood between them and began chanting the haunting melodic introduction to *Kol Nidre*.

> By the authority of the Heavenly Court,
> And by the authority of the earthly court,
> With the consent of the Omnipresent One
> And with the consent of this congregation,
> We declare it lawful to pray with sinners.

The *poretz* stood like a bent reed. From time to time he sighed, he cried, he beat his breast the twenty-five hours of *Yom Kippur*, the twenty-five hours of the great fast day. Each time the confessional prayer was recited, the trembling voice of the *poretz* pierced the air and penetrated the souls of the other worshippers.

When the worshippers were nearing the end of *Ne'ilah* (the closing prayer of *Yom Kippur*), the *poretz* walked over to the open ark and lay his head inside. He kissed the *Torah* scrolls and began screaming, "Hear O Israel, the Lord our God the Lord is One" one time; "Blessed Be His Holy Name For Ever and Ever" three times, and "God is the Righteous Judge" seven times.

After the seventh repetition, he died.

For the *ma'ariv* prayer service, there was no *minyan* in the tiny *shul* in the tiny village.

Rebbe Layb Sarah's personally directed the arrangements for the *poretz*'s funeral. At the eulogy, he told the story of the *poretz*'s life. He concluded by repeating a verse from the liturgy of the *Ne'ilah* service on *Yom Kippur*: "You wait for him until his dying day; if he repents, You readily accept him."

Rebbe Layb Sarah's recited *kaddish* for the *poretz* each *Yom Kippur*, the anniversary of his death.

A *Yom Kippur* Melody

A very wealthy and prominent man, Yaakov ben Mayer, had an only daughter named Rivka. She was the apple of his eye, and he did everything to insure her happiness. He looked forward to the time when she would find her soul mate, marry, and raise a family. Tragically, Rivka was born with a physical defect, so none of the eligible young men in the town would even consider marrying her.

The distraught father thought about arranging a match for his beloved daughter with one of the young men from distant towns. The more he thought about his plan, the more he believed his idea had potential. Finally, he decided to test his plan. He finished up some of his business affairs, made travel arrangements, and set out in search of a husband for his daughter.

Each time Yaakov ben Mayer arrived in a town, he would settle in the local inn, go to the *yeshivah,* and observe the students at their lessons. He knew that any young man he would consider eligible for his daughter would be studying in a *yeshivah.* He even joined the students during their free time, trying to find out about their personalities. In one town, he became acquainted with a young man, a poor but brilliant, God-fearing student named Moshe. After thoroughly investigating his background, he decided that Moshe was an appropriate choice of a husband for his beloved daughter.

Convinced that his choice was right, he approached the head of the *yeshivah* and beseeched him to arrange the match. The head of the *yeshivah* asked Moshe, the perspective groom, if he would marry Rivka, and he readily consented.

Moshe and his future father-in-law returned home.

Yaakov ben Mayer made elaborate preparations for the marriage. He bought clothing and linen for the young couple and built them a beautiful home. He furnished it with both necessities and luxuries. When the house was finished, he invited friends, relatives, all the town dignitaries, and the scholars to share in the joyous occasion of his daughter's wedding.

At the wedding dinner, the groom addressed the guests, as was the custom. His presentation impressed even the scholars. The guests rejoiced with the young couple, and Moshe and Rivka settled down to married life. Moshe continued his studies in the *yeshivah*, in his new hometown, and Rivka tended to her household chores. He was never upset by her physical defect.

Moshe spent his days learning *Torah*. In the evenings, he rejoiced with Rivka. He gradually became accustomed to a comfortable lifestyle. The memory of his impoverished years faded from his mind.

However, the *yetzer hara* (the evil inclination) was not satisfied that Moshe and Rivka were content.

It stirred up temptation and jealousy in Moshe's mind until he was so unsettled that he began to sneak away from the *yeshivah* in order to explore the world. He wandered around the marketplace for hours, watching the women shop, searching for trinkets, neglecting his studies.

It was not difficult to compare the lovely women he saw in the marketplace with his physically defective wife. Temptation, nurtured daily, exploded. One day he decided that he would divorce Rivka. He only had to deal with one problem: money. He had become accustomed to comfort. He knew that if he divorced

Rivka, he would find disfavor in the eyes of his father-in-law, immediately causing him to return to a life of poverty. For a while he tried to cope, balancing temptation with immersion in *Torah* studies, but he did not succeed. Temptation overcame Moshe.

Thinking over his situation, he decided on a practical solution. He would set up a situation whereby he would be the direct cause of his father-in-law's and wife's public embarrassment. Then they would be only too happy to grant him a large financial settlement in exchange for a divorce. He would then be free to leave town.

Moshe put his plan into action. He stopped attending the *yeshivah* and prayer services. He wandered aimlessly about all day and returned home in the middle of the night. His wife and father-in-law saw through his plan. Although they were pained and very angry, they refused to pay the extortion money he demanded for a divorce. Finally, realizing that they would not accede to his demand, Moshe picked himself up one day and disappeared from the town.

Moshe wandered from village to village. He had no money, and his clothes became worn. Hunger overpowered him.

Once he passed through a village and noticed that a widowed, non-Jewish storekeeper was searching for a helper. He applied for the job and was hired on the spot. Moshe wanted to succeed. He put all his effort into the job. The business flourished, and the widow became very wealthy. Working together daily brought the widow and the ex-*yeshivah* student into close contact. They grew to love each other and decided to marry.

Moshe and his new wife became prominent merchants. They sought ways to expand their business further. Moshe took upon himself the responsibility of traveling to the big cities to buy merchandise.

He traveled in style: a coach drawn by four horses, stocked with food, blankets and pillows, carried him from city to city. As he traveled, he accumulated merchandise.

Large fields separated towns along his route. The fields were filled with farmers busily harvesting the summer wheat. Once, he came across a group of farmers who were singing a

haunting melody as they harvested. The melody was vaguely fa-
miliar, so Moshe stopped his coach and joined the farmers. The
melody reverberated through the fields. Moshe's voice rang out
loud and clear, and the farmers lowered their voices and listened.
Only Moshe's voice was audible. The farmers wondered how this
non-Jewish-looking merchant knew the melody to *Kol Nidre*,
one of the most sacred prayers recited on *Yom Kippur*. Eventually Moshe realized he was the only person singing. He began to
tremble, as if he were awakening from a nightmare. He recognized the melody the farmers had been singing. He stopped singing, embarrassed, determined to be silent, but the haunting melody kept echoing in his head.

Moshe calculated months and days.

"It must be near *Yom Kippur*," he thought.

"Jews all over the world will be gathering for atonement, to
repent their evil ways. I am a Jew." Moshe was overcome with
shame. Suddenly, he yelled, "What am I doing in this masquer-
ade? I need to return to my people!"

Not knowing what took hold of him, Moshe jumped from the
coach, leaving the food, blankets, pillows, and merchandise he
had thus far accumulated. He ran for days, ignoring hunger,
thirst, and sleep.

After days of running, he finally stumbled near a small
house, owned by a Jew named Yosef, who happened to be a disciple of the Baal Shem Tov.

Yosef saw the bedraggled stranger and went out to meet
him.

"Who are you?" he asked. "Please come inside. Let me help
you."

Moshe shook his head. He didn't need help. He would not go
inside the house.

Yosef persisted. Reluctantly, Moshe entered and sat down
on a low stool near the door.

Yosef hurried to bring food and drink for the stranger.
Moshe sipped one drop of water and ate one small morsel of
bread. He refused to utter a word.

Finally, after days of trying to coerce his guest to eat, to drink, to speak, Yosef gave up. He left the beggar to his self-imposed world of suffering.

Moshe remained in Yosef's house for two years. He fasted during the weekday daylight hours and ate only a small slice of bread and a cup of hot water each night. Once a week, Moshe ate a complete meal in honor of *Shabbos*. He continued to flagellate himself, hoping that physical deprivation and contrition were the keys to forgiveness.

One cold, blustery winter day, while Moshe was sitting on his stool outside of Yosef's house, an old man appeared from nowhere and whispered to him, "It has been announced by the Heavenly Court that your repentance has been accepted. The Heavenly Court wants you to stop inflicting further physical pain upon yourself."

Moshe was startled. With great trepidation, he asked the old man, "Who are you? How do I know that you are revealing the truth?"

The old man answered, "The Heavenly Court knows that you are waiting for a sign that your repentance has been accepted at the foot of the Throne of Mercy. In a few days, you will have your sign. It will be brought to you by a passerby who will confirm my words."

When he finished speaking, the old man disappeared.

Moshe would not change his self-imposed suffering until he was certain that the old man had spoken the truth. He waited for the passerby.

A few days later, a hunter knocked on Yosef's door. Yosef, ever hospitable, invited him inside and made him comfortable. They chatted for a while. Then the two men shared a glass of wine and a piece of honeycake. The hunter said he would like to tell a strange story. Moshe, who was sitting on a stool near the doorway, perked up his ears to listen to the details.

The hunter began to speak. "Do you know the story of the wealthy merchant who was traveling through the forest, his wagon loaded with merchandise? He jumped off, as if possessed, ran for days, and then disappeared without a trace."

The words tumbled out of the hunter's mouth. He paused to catch his breath, then continued at a slower pace.

"His wife sent a search party for him. It returned without a trace of her husband. She was very distraught. If this were not enough, another tragedy struck. Shortly thereafter, just a few weeks ago, a fire broke out in his house. His wife was killed, and all his possessions were devoured by the flames."

Moshe listened with mixed emotions to the hunter's story. He was pained by the details of the fire but felt relief that the hunter's story corroborated the old man's.

When the hunter departed, Moshe told Yosef why he had spent the past two years sitting silently on the stool in his house. When he finished, he thanked Yosef for his hospitality and his care. Then he set out for the town he had left and the wife he had deserted.

Trembling and embarrassed, he arrived at his former home, knocked on the door, and entered cautiously. The minute he saw his wife, he began to plead for forgiveness, for the pain and suffering he had caused her. Rivka, righteous woman that she was, forgave him. Her father also forgave Moshe and concluded that his strange behavior had been caused by the wanderlust of youth.

Moshe resumed his former lifestyle, the same lifestyle which had singled him out as the worthy choice for the daughter of the town's wealthiest and most prominent man.

He immersed himself in the study of *Torah* once again and dedicated his efforts toward helping those less fortunate than himself. Moshe and Rivka were privileged to raise children who followed in their footsteps: children who were scholars and communal leaders.

L'Chayim! L'Chayim!

There are two types of stories that have been transmitted from generation to generation about Rebbe Yisrael ben Eliezer, the Baal Shem Tov, the founder of the chasidic movement. The stories that were told by his disciples about his deeds fall into one category; the stories that he told himself fall into an entirely different category.

This story was told by the Baal Shem Tov himself as he sat with a group of disciples near the grave of the "holy drunkard," unmarked by a tombstone, covered with weeds and reeds in a clearing in the midst of a thick forest.

Before he began to tell the story, the Baal Shem Tov poured a bottle of wine over the grave and shouted, *"L'chayim, l'chayim!* Holy drunkard! *L'chayim!"*

His students waited patiently for him to speak because they were astounded by his actions. The Baal Shem Tov began this story in a gentle voice.

Once, about 150 years ago, when Ivan the Terrible was Tzar of all Russia, there lived two Jewish families who were financially better off than most of the Jews who struggled to eke out a meager living. One family was blessed with a son, the other, with a daughter, and both sets of parents decided it would be advantageous for their children to marry. After the wedding, the parents set them up in a business as part of the dowry.

The groom, Shimon, was very happy with the arrangement. He wanted to dedicate his days and nights to the study of *Torah* and Talmud, so he agreed that his young wife Masha would run the business, and he would remain a student in the study hall.

The young bride had other ideas. She wanted the business to prosper immediately. Each night, when he arrived home, she told him about the wonderful world of business, concluding her monologue with, "If you would only take time to help me in the store, we could earn much more money. We could afford furs and jewels and travel." Shimon was very happy with the amount of money the profit of the store provided for them, so he always answered, "We are rich enough." But the conversation between Shimon and Masha was always on the subject of money and the things that money could buy.

One day a salesman came into the store and showed Masha 20,000 rubles' worth of merchandise. She began to calculate the profit she could earn if she bought the merchandise from him, but before she had a chance to discuss financial arrangements, he informed her that he never discussed business matters with women. "If you want this merchandise," he said with a sneer, "you had better call your husband."

Masha told the salesman to wait, and she ran to the study hall to fetch her husband. When Shimon came outside, he demanded to know why it was so important for her to disturb his learning. She explained the situation to him as she dragged him back to the store.

Shimon half-heartedly signed the papers and accepted the merchandise, then returned to the study hall. The next morning Masha asked, "Why don't you stop at the store on your way to the study hall to see how beautifully I have displayed the new merchandise?"

Shimon stopped for a few minutes. He watched the customers come into the store. They examined the merchandise and ran to call their friends to see it. No one in the town had ever seen such quality merchandise. It sold rapidly. The profit was enormous. Shimon became fascinated with the world of business.

He arrived at the study hall very late that morning. The next morning he spent more time in the store. Then he helped order more new merchandise. Soon, he spent the entire morning in the store, then the entire morning and part of the afternoon. In two weeks' time, Shimon spent entire days at the store. He stopped studying. Shimon was a successful businessman!

Now all he thought about was earning more and more money.

One day, Masha said to him, "We stock merchandise in this store through a salesman who buys his supplies in St. Petersburg. If we could eliminate the salesman, the middleman, and buy our own merchandise, we would be able to double our profit."

Shimon listened to his wife and then said, "You know that Jews are not permitted in St. Petersburg.[1] How can I possibly go to the big city? If I am caught, I will be jailed or executed."

Masha looked Shimon squarely in the eye and proclaimed, "So you'll act like a non-Jew for a few days! I have a Russian nobleman's outfit. You can tuck your *tzitzis* (ritual fringes) inside your shirt and wear a fur hat. You will appear to the city people as if you were a rich businessman."

Shimon didn't see anything wrong with the plan, so he donned the Russian nobleman's outfit and set out in his carriage for St. Petersburg. He made arrangements to stay in a fine inn, and then he presented himself at the factory where the merchandise he wanted to buy was made. The owner, realizing that Shimon was placing a very large order, greeted him cordially. He wanted Shimon to feel comfortable during his visit to St. Peters-

---

[1]The policy of the Russian government toward strangers, particularly Jews, was hostile from the middle of the sixteenth century when Ivan IV, "the Terrible," consolidated the empire.

burg, so he arranged a dinner party in his honor. Because he was so impressed with the size of Shimon's order, he invited other wealthy businessmen to the party also. He wanted Shimon to meet the right people.

Shimon was in a quandary when he arrived at the dinner party. He had never before eaten non-kosher food, but he knew that if he refused the delicacies that were served, his host would become suspicious that he was Jewish. He wanted to make sure no one found out his secret, so he ate along with the other guests. While they ate, dinner music was played by a quartet specially hired for the occasion.

After dinner, Shimon's host said to him, "I have a very beautiful daughter. I don't know if you noticed her at dinner, but I would be very happy if you would ask her to dance." Shimon wondered how he, a married man, could dance with a strange young lady, but he didn't think about it too much. He walked over to her, asked her to dance, and they glided across the dance floor.

Suddenly, the young lady ran from the dance floor. Her father pursued her and demanded to know how she could insult his honored guest, his best customer, by running off in the middle of a dance.

"Father," she said, "as we were dancing, his fringes fell out of his shirt. He is a Jew."

The host ran over to Shimon and angrily demanded, "Why didn't you tell me that you are a Jew? You could be my best customer, but a Jew is a Jew. Unless you convert, I will kill you." The gun he carried in his belt was pointed at Shimon's head.

The music and the dancing stopped. The horrified guests stood in a circle around Shimon. Silence reigned in the room. Shimon knew he could no longer pretend. His feet, which had been dancing five minutes before, quaked in their boots. Not knowing what to do, Shimon stammered, "Give me three days to think about conversion."

His host answered, "Since you are such a good customer, I will grant your wish."

The party was over. Shimon returned to the inn. He struggled with his conscience for three days. He thought he might be able to sneak out of the inn and return to his wife. But he was fascinated with the noble lifestyle of St. Petersburg. He admitted that it was his wife who had insisted on this pretense anyway, that it was her fault that he was in this predicament. Then he reflected on the most vital question of all: What good will I be to God if I die? What will God gain? He decided to convert, knowing full well that he would not return to his wife, the small town, or the stifling lifestyle he would be leaving behind.

After three days, Shimon agreed to convert. Afterward, his host asked him if he liked his beautiful daughter. When Shimon answered yes, the host suggested that they marry.

Shimon married his host's daughter and moved into the mansion. He became a partner in the factory. The newlyweds, Shimon and Catherine, lived together for ten years. They had five children.

One day, Shimon checked a calendar to arrange a business deal. He noticed that his particular calendar had one Jewish holy day marked off, and that day was *Yom Kippur*, the holiest day of the Jewish calendar year. As he stared at the words *Yom Kippur*, the Jewish Day of Atonement, he realized *Yom Kippur* was that very day.

The pretense of the wealthy Russian businessman vanished, and Shimon lay his head down on the desk and sobbed. After a while, he regained his composure and went for a walk in the well-tended gardens of the mansion.

He decided to stop by to talk to the gardener, who was known as the "happy drunkard"—despite his drunkenness, the gardener took great pride in tending the gardens on Shimon and Catherine's estate. "Maybe," thought Shimon, "he will cheer me up. He is always so happy."

Shimon searched for the drunkard and found him sitting on a rock on the side of the road. He was crying.

"Why are you crying?" Shimon asked the drunkard. "You are always so happy. I wanted you to cheer me up! What is the matter with you?"

"If you swear not to tell anyone my secret, I will tell you," he sobbed. Shimon swore never to reveal the drunkard's secret.

The happy drunkard whispered, "I am a Jew, and today is *Yom Kippur.* On *Yom Kippur,* every Jew appears before God as holy as an angel. How do I appear before God today?"

Shimon listened in awe to the story. Now, they were both crying. The happy drunkard asked Shimon why he was crying. Shimon said, "If you swear to me never to reveal my secret, I will tell you." The happy drunkard swore.

Shimon told his story to the happy drunkard. He didn't omit one detail. He told him how he had been determined to be a learned Jew ten years before, how his former wife had convinced him to become a businessman, how he had arrived in St. Petersburg, converted, remarried, and prospered in his new life.

The happy drunkard listened to Shimon's tale and then responded, "You know that today is *Yom Kippur.* I want you to swear to me that you will do whatever I tell you to do."

Again, Shimon swore.

The happy drunkard continued. "Tell your wife and father-in-law that you have an opportunity to transact a tremendous business deal in Amsterdam. Take your money with you and leave this place. Return to your town and your former wife. When you arrive home, tell her that you were kidnapped and were just released. Tell her you will never set foot into the store again. Spend your days and nights in the study hall and go home only for the Sabbath. The people here will wonder about your disappearance for a while, but they will think that you were captured. Now, go in peace."

Shimon followed the happy drunkard's directive and returned to his town.

Catherine mourned his loss for a long time, for she loved him dearly. Gradually, she accepted the fact that he must have been captured, for she believed he would never desert her or their children.

Some days brought consolation, other days, anguish. On the anniversary of his disappearance, Catherine could not stop crying. She wandered aimlessly in the gardens, trying to chart a future course for her life, when she saw, from a distance, the happy drunkard sitting by the side of the road on a rock.

She thought, "Maybe the happy drunkard will cheer me up," but as she drew nearer, she noticed he was crying.

She approached him and began to speak softly. "I thought you might be able to cheer me up, but I see that you are crying. Please tell me what is troubling you."

The happy drunkard answered, "I can only tell you what is troubling me on one condition. Swear to me that you will not tell anyone what I will reveal to you."

Catherine thought she might be able to help, so she swore. The drunkard then proceeded with his story. "I want you to know that I am a Jew. Today is *Yom Kippur,* and on this day every Jew appears before God as holy as an angel. How do I appear before God today?"

Catherine listened silently. When he finished his story, she said, "I understand how you feel. Now let me tell you my story. My husband, Shimon, disappeared exactly one year ago today, and no one has heard from him since. My family and I assume that he was captured, but we miss him very much." Tears streamed down Catherine's cheeks.

The happy drunkard asked gently, "Do you want to know what happened to Shimon?"

Catherine's eyes opened wide in disbelief. "I will do anything if you tell me what happened to Shimon and where I can find him," she pleaded.

"Then swear to me that you will do exactly as I tell you."

Catherine swore.

The happy drunkard proceeded. "First, swear to me again that you and your children will convert to Judaism. Then, go back to the mansion and tell your father that you can no longer live without Shimon. Tell him that somebody gave you a clue where he might be. Then take your children and travel to that town. The Almighty will show you the way."

Catherine returned to the mansion and told her father that she was taking her children with her to search for Shimon. She told him about the clue and concluded that since she could no longer live without her husband, she was setting off immediately to find him.

Catherine traveled to the town where Shimon lived. She knew she would need a place to stay, so she went to the local inn to make arrangements for herself and her children for a few days. Then she asked the innkeeper if he were acquainted with a Jew named Shimon.

"Shimon!" he responded with surprise. "Shimon is the wealthiest Jew in town!"

"I must meet him," said Catherine. "Can you please arrange for me to meet him?"

"That is quite impossible," answered the innkeeper. "You see, he doesn't talk to anyone. Everybody in this town knows that he studies in the study hall all week and only returns home for the Sabbath. He has been doing this only since he returned from a lengthy business trip. He was away for ten years."

Catherine opened her purse, took out a few rubles, and put them in the innkeeper's hand. "I beg you," she pleaded, "you must help me. You must arrange a meeting between us."

The innkeeper furled his brow and then said, "I have a plan. There is one way that I am sure you can meet Shimon. Each Friday afternoon, his carriage—drawn by eight horses and a uniformed footman—comes to the study hall to pick him up. On the way home, he stops at the ritual bath. If you like, I can take you to the bath house, and you can wait outside in the courtyard."

Catherine rejoiced at the thought of seeing her husband. She led the children into the carriage, and the innkeeper drove them to the courtyard of the bath house.

Shimon emerged from the bath house, complacent, happy, ready for the Sabbath, but when he saw Catherine and his children standing in the courtyard, he trembled.

After he regained his composure, he said, "Catherine, it is almost time for the Sabbath. You will come to my home and be my guest. Do not tell my wife Masha who you are or who the children are. I will merely say that you are a business acquaintance. After the Sabbath, I will take care of everything."

Immediately after the Sabbath, Shimon took Masha and

Catherine to his rabbi. He told him the story of his life, not omitting one detail. He emphasized that Masha only discussed money and business matters. He blamed her as the cause of his dropping out of the study hall and traveling to St. Petersburg. He told the rabbi that he felt that there was more to life than the pursuit of material possessions.

Then Shimon told the rabbi about Catherine's love and devotion. "She," he whispered, looking at Catherine, "gave me the strength to return to my people and my heritage."

Shimon gulped after he finished his story, then sighed an anguished sigh. "Tell me the truth, rabbi," he continued. "Which of these two women was ordained by heaven to be my soul mate?"

The rabbi didn't speak for a long time. Shimon's question weighed heavily on his soul. Shimon, Masha, and Catherine waited, waited, and waited. After what seemed to be an eternity, the rabbi spoke. "I want you to know, Shimon, that your true soul mate is Catherine from St. Petersburg."

Shimon divorced Masha. The rabbi taught Catherine the fundamentals of Judaism, and she and the five children converted. Then the rabbi married Shimon and Catherine in a religious ceremony.

Catherine's father missed her very much. He longed to see his grandchildren. A year after Catherine set out to search for Shimon, her father was wandering aimlessly in the garden, trying to find solace. He happened to find the happy drunkard sitting by the side of the road on a rock. He was crying.

Catherine's father approached him and said, "I thought you might be able to cheer me up. I am so lonesome for my daughter and grandchildren. I see, however, that you are crying. Something must be troubling you terribly. Please tell me what it is."

The happy drunkard answered, "I can only tell you what is troubling me on one condition. Swear to me that you will not tell anyone what I will reveal to you."

Catherine's father swore. The drunkard then proceeded with his story. "I want you to know that I am a Jew. Today is

Yom Kippur, and on this day every Jew appears before God as holy as an angel. How do I appear before God today?"

Catherine's father said, "I understand why you are crying. Now, let me tell you my story. I have an only daughter and five grandchildren, and I don't know where they are. I miss them so much."

The happy drunkard said, "If you swear to me that you will follow my instructions exactly, I will tell you where they are."

Catherine's father swore.

The happy drunkard proceeded with his instructions. "Sell all your belongings here, and convert to Judaism. Then, travel to that town. When you arrive, you will find that your daughter has been reunited with her husband. She will welcome you with open arms." Then the happy drunkard's voice trailed off and he began to mumble. Only Catherine's father understood when he said, "If you leave this place, what will happen to me? Please, let me go with you."

After following the instructions, Catherine's father and the happy drunkard set off for the town. As they approached the town, the happy drunkard passed away. Catherine's father buried him in a grave covered with weeds and reeds in a clearing in the midst of a thick forest.

The Baal Shem Tov peered intently at each one of his students and said, "This grave site is the burial place of the holy drunkard. I know you were astounded when I poured the bottle of wine over the grave and shouted, '*L'chayim*, holy drunkard, *l'chayim!*' Now you understand that he was called the 'holy drunkard' because he helped so many people. I'm sure you agree that he deserved to be remembered with, '*L'chayim*, holy drunkard, *l'chayim!*' "

Berel's *Din Torah* with God

An air of hushed expectancy hovered over the *shul*. Rebbe Layve Yitzchak of Berditchev stood before the pulpit, ready to chant *Kol Nidre*. He waited, silently. People thought that he was waiting for their attention, so they tried to focus their thoughts on the holiness of the moment. But he waited and waited. The sun's rays passed below the tree tops, but the Berditchever still stood silently.

After an interminable time, the Berditchever turned to the *shamish* and asked, "Has Berel the tailor arrived in *shul* yet?"

The *shamish* looked around at the hopeful faces of the worshippers. Unable to find Berel among them, he answered, "No, rebbe, he has not yet arrived."

"Then please go quickly to his house, and bring him here," the rebbe said.

When Berel arrived with the *shamish*, Rebbe Layve Yitzchak turned to greet him. Staring him directly in the face, he demanded, "Berel, why were you delaying the prayers of Israel?"

Berel answered breathlessly, "I couldn't help it, rebbe. I have no one to act as a judge between me and Him. Do you want to know why I have to summon Him to a *din torah* (judgment)? I was not going to make the issue public, but since you asked me to come here, I will tell you what happened. I will let you arbitrate between us."

Berel took a deep breath and pulled himself up to his full height, preparing to play the role of the defense against the Antagonist. He began:

This is what happened. Summer was rapidly giving way to autumn. As the weather changed, chill penetrated the crisp air. The *poretz* (landowner) asked me to sew a new winter coat for him. He wanted it styled full-cut and ample enough for his big body. Happy with the opportunity for a little extra business, I took my sewing bag, scissors, and yardstick and set out for his mansion. He gave me a roll of beautiful woolen textured fabric, and I set to work. As I cut and measured the pattern, I realized that I would have fabric left over. I decided that since I was a very poor man, the father of ten children—one a daughter of marriageable age—I would use the leftover fabric to sew vests. I planned to sell them and use the money for my daughter's dowry.

I sewed the *poretz* a magnificent garment. Believe me, I did not skimp on the fabric. After I finished the coat, I sewed the vests from the leftover scraps. When I finished, I realized that I needed a way to take the vests with me. I devised a plan. When I brought the *poretz* his new coat, I told him how desperate my family was for food. He was not a cruel man, so he ordered a servant to bring me a giant-sized loaf of bread with which to feed my hungry family. I thanked him and took the bread to the sewing room. There, I cut the loaf in half, dug out the soft part of the dough, and ate most of it. I then placed the vests in the hollow, fitted the two halves of the crust together, placed the bread in my sewing bag, and set out for home.

I had walked about a mile or a mile and a half down the road when I heard the sound of horses' hooves chasing after me. I froze in my tracks. A servant of the *poretz* was shouting, "Wait, Berel, wait, Berel! The *poretz* wants to see you."

I looked around and found a bush. Pretending innocence, I

sat down to wait for the servant to catch up to me. In the meantime, I unloaded my sewing bag, mentally marking the bush where I left it. I don't have to tell you how frightened I was. The servant motioned to me to jump on the horse, and in no time I was standing in front of the *poretz*. I was quivering in my shoes. I could not imagine how the *poretz* found out what I had done with the bits and pieces of leftover fabric. Much to my surprise, the *poretz* was not angry. He simply said, "Berel, I like the coat you sewed for me very much. I called you back because you forgot to sew a hook across the back so I could hang it up."

I took the coat, returned to the sewing room, sewed on the hook the *poretz* wanted, and gave it back to him. Then I started out for home again. I walked the same way I had walked originally, but when I approached the bush where I left my sewing bag, I saw that it had disappeared. This time I was not frightened; I was filled with anguish. I sat down and cried.

"Master of the Universe! You are not poor. You don't have ten children. You don't have a daughter of marriageable age. The *poretz* will never miss the little bits and pieces of fabric I took. Why did You permit someone to come along and steal my sewing bag? Would it have been so bad for me to have a few extra bits and pieces of fabric that the *poretz* didn't need anyway? It would have given me a little extra income. If this is the way You treat Your chosen people, then I don't want to be counted among them."

I returned home, downcast, filled with pain, determined to stop being Jewish.

When I sat down to eat, I omitted the ritual hand washing and the grace after meals; I stopped praying three times a day; I went to sleep without reciting the *Sh'ma*; I did not attend the *selichos* prayers (prayers asking for forgiveness); I refused to listen to the sounding of the *shofar*. I did not want to be included among "the chosen people."

Today is *Yom Kippur*, the day of atonement, the holiest day of the Jewish year. I am ashamed of what I did. I have to ask Him to forgive me for what I did, for neglecting His *mitzvos*. Since He is a Compassionate God, I know He will forgive me, but only on one condition—that He forgives everything. If He forgives me, then I will forgive Him. Now that I have told you everything that happened, rebbe, you arbitrate between me and Him!

Rebbe Layve Yitzchak sat down. He put his head in his hands and thought for a few minutes. Then he rose and said, "Berel, you are right. Don't waiver from your conditions. I have decided that you have won this *din torah*. When He forgives you, He will forgive every Jew."

Then Rebbe Layve Yitzchak turned to the pulpit and started to chant *Kol Nidre.*

Kol Nidre in
a Russian Prison Camp

American Jews take religious freedom for granted. On the other side of the world, in Soviet Russia, religious freedom is denied to two-and-a-half million of our brethren. Let me tell you a story that took place in Moscow, just twelve short years ago, to illustrate how some Jews struggle for religious freedom.

Simchas Torah, celebrating the conclusion of the *Torah* reading cycle and the resumption of a new *Torah* reading cycle, is a time of great joy in Moscow. Joy permeates the air as young Jews, unafraid of the Communist regime, emerge from every corner of the city to identify with their people, to sing, to dance, to rejoice.

Twelve years ago, torrential rains poured down upon the heads of the dancers who gathered in front of Moscow's Choral Synagogue on Arkhipova Street to celebrate *Simchas Torah*. It seemed that the more intense the rain, the more intense the dancing. Yet, one middle-aged man was dancing with even more gusto than the other dancers. His face sparkled with ecstasy.

Rabbi Shlomo Carlebach, the chasidic folksinger, scholar,

and storyteller, was visiting the Soviet Union at the time.[1] He approached the middle-aged man and asked, "My friend, do you dance with this enthusiastic fervor every year on *Simchas Torah?*"

The man was not afraid to talk to Shlomo, even though Shlomo was dressed in typical religious garb—skullcap, ritual fringes, and Star of David.

He answered, "My name is Josef. Many years ago I was incarcerated in a Siberian labor camp, serving a life sentence at hard labor. I never believed I would be released. I have so much to celebrate. Let me tell you my story."

Rabbi Shlomo Carlebach, always the good listener, gently led Josef away from the dancers so he could concentrate, because the fervor of the *Simchas Torah* dancers had made it impossible to hear.

"This is what happened," Josef began.

I was incarcerated because I was a Jew. I knew the charges were false, but I had no defense. I spent almost ten years in a Siberian labor camp. For most of those long, cold, bitter years, I had no contact with any other Jews. Then, one day, I heard that another Jew had been incarcerated in a cell on the other side of the same prison camp. I decided to seek him out, despite personal danger. I desperately wanted to see another Jew, to talk to another Jew, to say *"shalom aleichem"* to another Jew before I died in that forsaken wasteland.

I made plans to sneak to the other side of the prison camp. I knew that what I planned to do was against prison camp rules, but I did not care. I had to see another Jew. When I found him, I tiptoed over to him. He was walking in the courtyard where the prisoners exercised, and I fell into step beside him. I whispered, *"Shalom aleichem, landsman"* (greetings, my friend and neighbor).

[1]Rabbi Shlomo Carlebach told this story to us when he returned from Moscow in the autumn of 1967.

He turned his head slightly and whispered, "Not now! We are not permitted to talk. The soldiers on the ramparts can shoot us at any minute. They know we are Jews. They will not hesitate to shoot if we break the rules!"

I ignored my fellow Jew's plea and continued to whisper to him, "Do you know what tonight is?"

"How am I supposed to know what tonight is?" he demanded.

"Tonight is *Yom Kippur,* the Day of Atonement, the holiest day in the Jewish calendar year," I continued.

"So what!" he exclaimed, his whisper growing louder and more agitated. "What good does being Jewish do for us? Where has it gotten us? So what if tonight is *Yom Kippur!* I've been in one prison camp after another. I just don't care anymore."

I persisted. "Listen, I've been in this prison camp for almost ten years. All this time, I've searched for another Jew. Knowing that tonight is the holiest night in the Jewish calendar year, we must share this night together in some way. Let's sing *Kol Nidre* together. Do you remember how the melody is chanted?"

Tears filled my friend's eyes. He whispered, "I used to sing *Kol Nidre* with my father in the synagogue as a young boy. I haven't heard it chanted since then."

I begged him to join me in singing. He began to hum the melody softly. He hesitated with the words. Finally he recalled them.

As he sang, his voice grew louder and more distinct.

We did not notice the commotion in the watchtower, for we were so absorbed in what we were doing. It seemed that the guards were aiming to shoot us for disturbing the peace. Then we heard shouting. The captain was ordering the guards to halt.

"Let them be," he ordered.

He descended from the watchtower and walked over to us. We trembled when we saw him standing beside us. He aimed his gun but held it steady. Then he demanded gruffly, "What are you two Jews doing?"

I answered as politely as I could. "We are singing a song."

"Then sing more," the captain commanded.

"Please don't disgrace us by making us sing more. We know you will shoot us. Do it now. Get it over with!" I pleaded.

The captain's voice suddenly became more amicable.

"I am not going to shoot you," he said. "Please continue to sing that melody. I want to hear it."

We resumed singing. As we sang, we saw tears fill the captain's eyes and roll down his cheeks.

When we finished, the captain spoke.

"As you began to sing," he said, "I had a vague recollection of hearing that melody before. Suddenly, memories of going to the synagogue with my father swept over me. I pictured myself as a little boy, huddled underneath my father's *tallis.* When I was twelve years old, I was forcibly conscripted into the Tzar's army. I had no connection with my family for years. I was promoted in the army until I reached the rank of captain and have made a career of serving my country. Now I realize that I am still a Jew, although it has been at least forty-five years since I had anything to do with my people. Tonight I understand that I am still part of the Jewish people."

Spontaneously, the three of us began chanting *Kol Nidre* again. Our eyes overflowed with tears. I do not know if I will ever experience such a holy moment again.

After we finished, the captain promised that he would do everything in his power to hasten our release from the Siberian labor camp. It took time; the waiting was interminable. I even doubted the captain's sincerity. We waited the better part of a year. Then, a few weeks ago, orders for our release were received. I came here to Moscow to celebrate *Simchas Torah* with my people. Bless me that next year I will be free like you. Bless me that next year I will be able to dance in the streets of Jerusalem on *Simchas Torah.*

Rabbi Shlomo Carlebach blessed Josef and promised to tell his story to Jews the world over.

The *Baal Teshuvah*

Hershel Nussbaum remembered his early teenage years. He only needed to look at the blue, tattooed number on his arm to remind himself of his struggle to survive in Auschwitz. After the Allied liberation, he tried to piece together his life, searching unsuccessfully for family, wandering from one displaced-persons camp to another all over battle-scarred Europe, finally obtaining passage to America.

He settled in Brooklyn, finding hospitality in the home of a distant relative. Hershel Nussbaum was determined to continue with life. Even after the Holocaust, he sincerely believed in the eternity of the Jewish people. He was certain that the study of *Torah* would revitalize the Jewish people, whose numbers and spirit had been decimated by the worst catastrophe in their long history, so he enrolled in a *yeshivah*. He wanted to continue his studies on the exact page he had finished when he was incarcerated.

It was obvious to his teachers that Hershel Nussbaum was a special student. He was blessed with an inquiring mind and keen understanding. He was also patient, diligent, and respected by his fellow students. He sported a dusty blond beard and curly hair. The emaciated survivor became sturdy and muscular after a few years in America.

Hershel progressed rapidly toward rabbinical ordination. Soon, the *rosh yeshivah* (dean of the school) called him into his office for a private meeting.

"I hear," said the *rosh yeshivah*, "that you plan on a pulpit in the Midwest after you are ordained. Hershel, why do you want to leave the New York area?"

Diffidently, Hershel lowered his eyes and answered, "I am so determined to spread *Yiddishkeit* (Jewish life) in America that I feel I must begin my rabbinate in another part of the country. There are so many Jews who are searching for guidance and inspiration."

"In that case," replied the *rosh yeshivah*, "I give you my blessing. I know you will succeed in your determination to teach and reach out to Jews."

Shortly before he was ordained, Hershel married Rachel, who came from an observant family and was as committed as he was to the eternity of the Jewish people. Rachel liked the idea of becoming a *rebbetzen* (rabbi's wife). Together, they dreamed about establishing an open house where young people would feel comfortable in discovering the mysteries and joys of Jewish life.

After Hershel was ordained, he was invited to the pulpit of a synagogue in a large midwestern city. Hershel and Rachel investigated the city and found that there were Jewish schools there— a *yeshivah* and the first few grades of a Jewish day school. It seemed like a good place to settle. They agreed that this was a chance to begin concretizing their dreams.

Hershel and Rachel settled into the role of rabbi and *rebbetzen*. The community leaders did everything in their power to welcome them. In return, the couple extended themselves to the community. A warm relationship developed between the congregation and them.

They raised a large family.

The children emulated their parents' warmth, value system, commitment to Jewish life—all except the youngest. From the time that Baruch was a fifth grader, he daydreamed his classtime away. Sometimes he tucked a comic book inside his Bible. Sometimes he had a large, illustrated book describing the first space-age discoveries at Cape Canaveral. He read these over and over, never tiring of the repetition.

It was not difficult for Baruch's fifth grade teacher to see the comics and the space-age storybooks tucked inside his texts. He phoned Baruch's parents one night. "Rabbi Nussbaum," he said, "this is Baruch's teacher. I'm calling to tell you that your son is substituting comics and space-age storybooks for the Bible. I'm not sure exactly how to handle the situation. I just wanted you to know the problem."

"I will talk to Baruch tonight," promised Rabbi Nussbaum. When Baruch returned home from school, he was greeted by a scowl on his father's face.

"Baruch," Rabbi Nussbaum said, "your teacher is concerned that you are reading comics and space-age storybooks instead of studying the Bible."

"Dad, listen," Baruch stammered. "It takes so long for him to explain a lesson. I understand it the first time. I don't want to talk or play around, so I read other things quietly until everyone in the class understands. What else can I do?"

Rabbi Nussbaum had no answer. The next day, Baruch tried to give his teacher undivided attention, but he was bored. The world outside his classroom fascinated him.

He was so bright, so curious, so creative. As he matured, he imagined himself wearing a space suit rather than being immersed in the pages of the Talmud. Surreptitiously, he spent more time in the public library than inside the house of study at his *yeshivah* high school. He allowed his creative energies to flow together with his imagination in the exploration of the world around him. He excitedly followed the research advances in space and space medicine. During his college years, his parents saw him exchange their religious world for the secular. They nodded to each other, their eyes sharing the pain of disappointment. Their dreams of their children's commitment to another strong Jewish generation were gradually shattered.

They hardly spoke to Baruch, for when they addressed him, he answered only to the name of Barry. A silent struggle ensued between the parents and their son. Hershel and Rachel hoped that their son's straying from their religious value system was but a passing fancy, and they prayed for this stage in his life to be over soon. However, Baruch/Barry remained determined to pursue secular learning among secular friends. More and more Barry adapted himself to and pursued the customs of his secular friends and the general culture at the expense of Judaism. More and more his parents restrained themselves; they were opposed to his ways, but they loved their son.

One night, Barry found his parents waiting for him when he entered the house. "Sit down," they said. "We would like to talk to you." Barry did not know what to expect. He sat down, facing his parents.

"We heard," they began, "that you are keeping company with a young woman."

Barry was totally unprepared for this turn of events. He had actually delayed the news of his forthcoming marriage for many weeks, fearing his parents' disapproval.

"Yes," he answered. "I was planning to introduce you to Marcy very soon. Her father is a doctor, almost ready to retire. Their family has lived in this city for the past three generations. We have a lot in common. We met in graduate school. She is studying medicine. She hopes to take over her father's practice. Don't worry. Marcy is Jewish!"

Hershel and Rachel tried to remain calm. Rachel was the first to speak. "Yes, she might have been born Jewish, but what does she know? What *mitzvos* does she observe? Is she committed to our way of life?"

This sudden confrontation put Barry on the defensive. He retorted defiantly, "I love Marcy, and I am going to marry her." He rose to leave. "And by the way, her father invited me to live in their house until we get married!" He stalked out of his home.

People in Rabbi Nussbaum's close-knit congregation were sympathetic to his plight. Many, patients of Marcy's father for years and years, decided to change doctors as an act of protest, as a way of expressing to their beloved rabbi their concern. They knew that the doctor had been Barry's mentor and that he had influenced the rabbi's son to pursue the scientific in exchange for the religious world.

Barry and Marcy were very uncomfortable in this close-knit community. One night, they discussed their feelings openly with Marcy's father. They explained to him how determined they were to continue their education. Marcy spoke first. "We did not intend that our relationship should become a cause célèbre in this town. We care deeply for each other. We want to graduate in our chosen professions, and then we plan to get married. What do you think we should do?"

Marcy's father did not hesitate in his reply.

"I know how uncomfortable you both must feel. I'm a little uncomfortable, too. My practice has suffered somewhat. However, I suggest that you both apply for admission to Indiana University to complete your education. You, Marcy, might gain admission to the university hospital at Purdue, and you, Barry, can choose your doctoral program from among the courses of study offered at Bloomington. I know there is a vast choice of course offerings at Indiana University, including biochemistry, medical biophysics, medical genetics, molecular and cellular biology. The campuses are within commuting distance. You will be able to visit on weekends. I am prepared to supplement the financial aid and scholarship money you will hopefully receive."

Marcy and Barry listened carefully. They followed her father's advice. That fall, they moved to Indiana University.

At first, one or the other commuted each weekend. Then their schedules became more demanding, and they decided to visit on alternate weekends.

One *Shabbos* morning, Barry decided to take a walk on campus. He passed the room where the head of the Judaic studies department had gathered with some students for a *Shabbos* service. The windows were open, and the melodies of the prayers floated down to Barry's ears. Pangs of loneliness welled up within him as he recalled the melodies sung at his father's *Shabbos* table. Without thinking, he ran up the stairs, bursting excitedly into the room. He sat down as a spectator, not a participant; it had been so long since he had set foot into a synagogue.

After the service, the head of the Judaic studies department introduced himself.

"My name," he said, "is Yisrael Mendelowitz. "I've been teaching on this campus for a few years. We have a growing Judaic studies department. Students from all over the Midwest gather here, on a secular university campus, to pursue a major in Judaic studies. I welcome you."

Barry felt very warm and comfortable talking to Yisrael Mendelowitz. They talked most of that Sabbath afternoon. When they parted, Barry promised he would return often.

During the week, Barry mentally replayed the tape of his conversation with Yisrael Mendelowitz. Something intrigued him about this warm, friendly human being.

The following weekend, he shared his experience with Marcy. He insisted that she come to his campus the following weekend to meet Yisrael Mendelowitz.

Together, they attended Sabbath services; afterwards, they lingered and talked. They told Yisrael their plans for their respective careers. Out of the clear blue sky, Yisrael queried, "Do you know Judaism's attitude on the questions you are researching in your doctoral programs? Do you know that modern Jewish theological thinkers are concerned with organ transplants, genetic engineering, space travel, nuclear warfare, the effect of alcohol and drugs on the unborn fetus?"

Neither Marcy nor Barry knew that Jewish theologians were dealing with issues in the world of science and research. Yisrael's questions were intellectually stimulating, and they enjoyed his company.

Gradually, they spent more and more time in the company of Yisrael Mendelowitz. They were intrigued by his knowledge, by the way he readily answered and encouraged their questions. The subjects they discussed together ranged from belief in God to being Jewish in a secular world, accounting for unethical religious Jews, the necessity of observing the *mitzvos* (commandments), the necessity of living a Jewish way of life, and the role of the Jewish people in the world.

The autumn turned to winter, winter to spring, spring to summer. Barry and Marcy juggled their schedules, setting aside time to study with Yisrael Mendelowitz each week. They also spent many Sabbaths with him. He had challenged their entire value system, and now they sought answers. He stressed over and over that they did not have to exchange their careers for Jewish life.

Toward the end of the second year, Barry was awarded his doctorate, and Marcy finished her internship. When they told Yisrael Mendelowitz that they were leaving Indiana to settle on the East coast, Yisrael said, "We've really grown attached to each other during these past two years. I could not make this suggestion to you if I didn't care about you as human beings. I would like to propose that you both take a year off—a sabbatical—time to reflect upon who you are, where you are going, what the Almighty expects of you! There are so many men's and women's *yeshivos* in Jerusalem that cater to the *baal teshuvah* (one who returns to Judaism). Why don't you spend next year in Jerusalem?"

Silence pervaded the room. Both Marcy and Barry looked intently at each other. Yisrael Mendelowitz had lovingly planted a seed for two years; he had nurtured it, watered it, fertilized it. Now the seed was ready to bloom.

Exhilirated, Marcy and Barry shouted, "What a wonderful idea!"

Barry, the Ph.D., and Marcy, the M.D., boarded an El Al flight for Jerusalem, the holy city. They each registered in the *yeshivah* recommended by Yisrael Mendelowitz. The year of intense devotion to Jewish studies flew by. They immersed themselves in the study of *Torah*.

That June, Barry/Baruch and Marcy/Miriam were married in Jerusalem on Mount Zion. Hershel and Rachel flew to Jerusalem to share in the joy of their son's marriage.

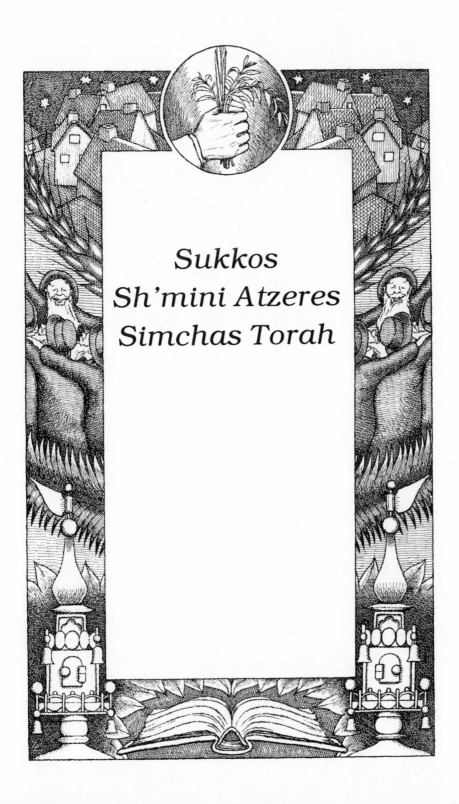

Sukkos
Sh'mini Atzeres
Simchas Torah

Sukkos is one of the three pilgrim festivals, one of the three times during the year when the Jewish people ascended to Jerusalem to worship in the Holy Temple.

These holy days derive their name from the *Torah*: "You shall dwell in *sukkos* (temporary huts) for seven days . . . that your generations will know that I made the children of Israel to dwell in temporary huts when I brought them out of the land of Egypt."

In the *Torah* and the liturgy, *Sukkos* is described as the festival of joy, for the symbols of these holy days lend themselves to celebration.

We reside (eat, sleep, study) in the *sukkah*, a temporary, flimsy hut roofed with *s'chach* (cut tree branches) for seven days, from the fifteenth through the twenty-first days of the month of *Tishri*.

During these days, we take an *esrog* (citron) and *lulav* (palm branch) together with *hadasim* (myrtles) and *aravos* (willows) and recite a blessing over them. A single procession around the synagogue with the *esrog* and *lulav* is an integral part of the morning prayer service.

In ancient times, two additional causes for rejoicing during *Sukkos* were the completion of the harvest season and the ceremony of the drawing of the water.[1]

The last three days of *Sukkos* have additional significance.

Hoshanah Rabah, the twenty-first day of *Tishri*, has special solemnity, for it is considered to be the end of the grace period when the final verdict of *Yom Kippur* is sealed. On *Hoshanah Rabah*, the procession with the *esrog* and *lulav* during the morning prayer service is increased from one time to

---

[1]Water was poured on the altar of the Holy Temple in a ceremony of song, music, dance, torchlight, and *shofar* blasts.

seven, followed by beating a bundle of five willow branches on the ground five times.

Sh'mini Atzeres, the twenty-second day of *Tishri* and the eighth day of the *Sukkos* week, is the time of the year when we pray for rain. The fertility of *Eretz Yisrael* is dependent on winter rains.

The last day of this joyous week, *Simchas Torah*, the twenty-third day of *Tishri*, marks the conclusion of the *Torah*-reading cycle and its immediate resumption. The joyous celebration of seven processions with the *Torah* scrolls around the synagogue is heightened by song and dance, for *Torah* is the essence of Judaism.

Torah Thoughts

The *Sukkah* of Faith

Logically, it would be proper to celebrate our *Pesach seder* (commemorating the exodus from Egypt) outdoors in the *sukkah,* for the *Torah* instructs us, "So that your future generations may know that their ancestors dwelled in a *sukkah* when I brought them out from the land of Egypt."[1] Yet, we celebrate our *seder* indoors, in the dawn of springtime, and we dwell in a *sukkah* in the fall, when the summer sunsets wane and rain inundates the earth.

We leave the security of the permanent house that protects us from the elements for a vulnerable, temporary dwelling that emphasizes the risk of being exposed to the elements.

Dwelling in the *sukkah,* in the shadow of "His Faith,"[2] is an act of faith that removes the vulnerability, the insecurity, the risk. It helps us understand that the *sukkah* is symbolic of the clouds of glory which hovered over and protected the Jewish

[1]Leviticus 23:43.
[2]*Zohar,* Leviticus 63b.

people in the desert. It helps us understand our frailty and dependence upon the creator of all.

Most important, dwelling in the shadow of "His Faith" contrasts the difference between the Egyptian and the Jewish mentalities. The Egyptian Pharoah boasted, "The Nile is mine, and I created it."[3] He was convinced that he was in control of his world, that the overflow of the Nile was his doing.

Of the Jewish people, however, it is said, "Israel has faith in God; He is their help and their protection."[4]

[3]Ezekiel 29:3.
[4]Psalms 115:9.

Sukkah: The Eternity of the Jewish People

In connection with the concept of the *sukkah* of faith,[1] the nations of the world demanded the Almighty to reveal to them the secret of Jewish eternity. They suspected that our patriarch Abraham, the progenitor of the Jewish nation, had something to do with Jewish eternity, for they often heard the quote, "And he placed his faith in God, and God considered him to be righteous."[2]

Abraham's righteousness and loving-kindness were intertwined with faith, the foundation of holiness. Abraham's great-grandchildren followed in his footsteps. They exhibited their readiness to live by faith when they accepted the *Torah* and swore to uphold its commandments.

The nations were puzzled about how the observance of the commandments manifested this faith, so they pleaded, "Offer us also the *Torah* anew and we shall obey it. . . . The Holy One,

[1]*Zohar*, Leviticus 63b.
[2]Genesis 15:6.

Blessed Be He answered. . . . I have an easy commandment which is called *sukkah*. . . . Go and carry it out."[3]

Why did the Almighty choose this particular commandment, the commandment of *sukkah*—symbolizing faith—with which to reveal the secret of the eternity of the Jewish people? He chose this commandment because the Jewish people are connected to the Creator, not through logic, not through knowledge, not through understanding, but through faith, the faith of Abraham. The commandment of *sukkah* symbolizes this faith. Just as faith remains a mysterious phenomenon, so does the secret of the eternity of the Jewish people.

[3]Talmud, *Avodah Zarah* 3a.

The *Mitzvos, Sukkah,*
and *Shabbos*

Rabbi Chananya ben Akashya said, "The Holy One, Blessed be He, desired to confer merit upon the Jewish people, so He gave them *Torah* and *mitzvos* in abundance."[1]

There are many different kinds of *mitzvos* that provide for our physical and spiritual welfare, each more precious than the other. The *mitzvos* have been divided and classified by our scholars from time immemorial. Some of these categories are: *mitzvos* between man and man and between man and God; *mitzvos* that are time-bound and those that are eternal; *mitzvos* that are required only of a Jew living in *Eretz Yisrael* or of Jews living in *Eretz Yisrael* and the Diaspora; *mitzvos* that have reasons and *mitzvos* that are accepted without reason, because the King decreed them; positive, active *mitzvos* and *mitzvos* that are negative, prohibited; *mitzvos* for different parts of the body—*tefillin* for the head and arm, the prohibition of slander for the tongue, hearing and understanding the Oneness of God for the ear, covering the eyes at *Shabbos* candlelighting time to distinguish between *Shabbos* and the weekday.

[1]Talmud, *Makkos* 23b.

Among the many *mitzvos* that embrace the entire body of the Jew, two *mitzvos* are special—the *mitzvah* of *sukkah* embraces the physical body completely; the *mitzvah* of *Shabbos* embraces the spiritual nature of the Jew.

The *mitzvah* of dwelling in the *sukkah* embraces and elevates the person completely when in the *sukkah*. One enters the *sukkah*, and the *mitzvah* surrounds one's entire being. But when one leaves the *sukkah*, one leaves the *mitzvah*, because the *sukkah* has limitations. The *mitzvah* of sanctifying the *Shabbos*, however, embraces and elevates the spiritual longing of the Jew. It is the Almighty's gift of eternal peace to His people. It surrounds us without limitations. We cannot walk out of *Shabbos* the way we walk "out of" the *sukkah*, because *Shabbos* surrounds us spiritually twenty-five hours each week. We take the light of *Shabbos* with us wherever we are, wherever we go.

Through the performance of the *mitzvos*, of *sukkah* and *Shabbos*, we realize how graciously the Almighty provides for our physical and spiritual welfare.

The *Esrog* and *Lulav*

A curious *midrash*[1] explains the *Torah* verse, "And you shall take for yourself on the first day the fruit of a beautiful tree, leaves of palm branches, twigs of myrtle, and willows of the brook, and rejoice before the Lord your God for seven days,"[2] to mean that the first day of *Sukkos* is the first day for an accounting of our transgressions.

Since *Sukkos* is a joyous festival, why does the *midrash* interpret "the first day" as an accounting of our transgressions?

It is no coincidence that *Sukkos* follows *Yom Kippur*, the Day of Atonement, a day of general reckoning for all transgressions. In our brokenheartedness on *Yom Kippur*, we are cognizant of the fact that we have no redeeming features whatsoever. Yet, we turn to the Almighty to plead for forgiveness for "if a man has pain, he visits the Healer."[3]

When we repent out of brokenheartedness, we do not know

[1]*Tanchumah*, Leviticus 22.
[2]Leviticus 23:40.
[3]Talmud, *Baba Kama* 46b.

how to pinpoint each detail of our overall transgressions, so we pray for general forgiveness.

Five days later, on *Sukkos*, the brokenheartedness lifts to make way for the festival of joy. In the midst of joyous celebration, we have the opportunity to reflect and pinpoint our specific failings. With each failing that we correct, our joy increases.

The *esrog*[4] and *lulav*[5] represent specific parts of the body that pinpoint the areas marked out for improvement.

> The *esrog* symbolizes the heart (for the sin we have committed with a stubborn heart).
>
> The myrtles symbolize the eyes (for the sin we have committed with haughty eyes).
>
> The willows symbolize the lips (for the sin we have committed with slanderous talk).
>
> The palm branch symbolizes the spine (for the sin we have committed by running to act with evil intent).

On the first day of *Sukkos* we take these four species—the heart, the eyes, the lips, and the spine—and bind them together. By waving the four species, we reflect on improving the areas of the body that they represent. Symbolically, we are binding those parts of the body closer to the service of the Almighty. Then we are truly ready to rejoice before the Lord our God.

---

[4] A yellow, thick-skinned fruit resembling a lemon, with a knobbed end at its base.

[5] Palm branches surrounded by myrtle and willow leaves and bound together.

Sh'mini Atzeres

"Seven days you shall eat *matzah*. . . . And you shall observe the feast of the *matzos,* for on that day I brought you forth from Egyptian bondage"[1] (*Pesach*).

"And you shall dwell in a *sukkah* for seven days . . . in order that future generations will know that I made the children of Israel dwell in a *sukkah* when I brought them forth from Egyptian bondage"[2] (*Sukkos*).

When comparing the two festivals which celebrate the exodus from Egyptian bondage, we perceive a profusion of symbolism, particular to either *Pesach* or *Sukkos.*

Both festivals are celebrated for seven days. Among the *Pesach* symbols are the *matzah,* the *marror* (horseradish or bitter herbs), the *zeroa* (roasted bone), the *charoses* (mixture of nuts, apples, wine, and spices), the *beitzah* (roasted egg), the *karpas* (celery, parsley, or boiled potato), and the *chazeres* (romaine lettuce) adorning the *seder* plate; the cup of Elyahu; the four cups of wine; and the salt water—each reinforcing the underlying reason

[1]Exodus 12:15, 17.
[2]Leviticus 23:42, 43.

for the festival: to remember the bitterness of slavery, to rejoice in freedom.

Among the *sukkos* symbols are the *sukkah* and the *ooshpeyzin* (the spirit of a different patriarchal guest invited each night, one of the seven faithful shepherds of the Jewish people, Abraham, Isaac, Jacob, Joseph, Moses, Aaron, and David), the *esrog* and *lulav*, the *hoshanas* (willows), the libations of water ceremony,[3] and the seventy sacrifices offered when the Holy Temple stood in Jerusalem for the welfare of seventy peoples who were the forerunners of the nations of the world.

These seven days of *Pesach* and *Sukkos* seem to be complete and rich festival celebrations. If so, why does the *Torah* add an eighth day, *Sh'mini Atzeres*, at the conclusion of the festival of *Sukkos*, particularly when the month of *Tishri* marks the observance of *Rosh Hashanah* and *Yom Kippur* as well? Why don't we add an additional day to the festival of *Pesach*?

The accepted explanation is, "The separation of the Jewish people from the Divine Presence is too difficult to bear, so the Almighty added one more day, that His people might linger in His presence a little longer."[4]

However, expanding "your separation is too difficult for Me" into its deepest meaning, we learn that

the separation between one Jew and another, the disunity, the lack of love of fellow Jew, is very difficult, very painful for Me to bear. Therefore, I give you, My people, *Sh'mini Atzeres*, an eighth day for joining yourselves together in peace (*atzor*—to bind), to heal your wounds, to tighten the grip between one Jew and another, to reunite those who are separated from each other and from Me.

I give you this extra day following *Rosh Hashanah*,

[3]*Hoshanahs*—a bundle of five willow branches beaten on the ground five times on *Hoshanah Rabah*, signaling the official close of the season of repentance—and the joyous ceremony of the libations of water—celebrated in ancient days when the Holy Temple still stood—are symbolic of the trust we have in the goodness of the Almighty that the earth will be blessed with rain.
[4]Rashi, Leviticus 23:36.

Yom Kippur, and *Sukkos,* My people, because you, yourselves, prayed on *Rosh Hashanah* and *Yom Kippur:* "Let all of us be bound together to do Your will with a perfect heart."[5]

You also pray continuously that I "spread over you My *sukkah* of peace."[6]

I beg you, My children. . . look how closely you have been drawn together by the celebration of these festivals. . . . Please don't destroy the unity that you have attained.[7]

[5]*Rosh Hashanah* and *Yom Kippur amidah.*
[6]Evening service, Sabbath and Festivals.
[7]Rebbe Avraham Slonim.

Simchas Torah

Did you ever wonder why *Simchas Torah*—the festival celebrated with joy and dance marking the completion of the *Torah*
reading cycle and its immediate resumption—follows *Rosh
Hashanah* and *Yom Kippur* rather than *Shavuos*, the festival of
revelation?

The answer to this mystery can be traced to a talmudic
dictum.

Rabbi Simai said, "When Israel stood at Sinai, 600,000
ministering angels came and set two sparkling crowns upon the
heads of each Jew, one crown for *na'aseh* (we will do) and one
crown for *v'nishma* (and we will listen)."[1] During revelation, the
sparkling crowns of *na'aseh v'nishma* connected themselves to
the souls of every Jew standing at Sinai and to the souls of every
Jew yet to be born. It was as if the sparkling crowns formed the
attachment between the letters of the *Torah* and the Jewish
people. These letters of the *Torah* sustain and spiritually elevate
our souls, enabling us to reach the Divine Presence as we strug-

---

[1]Talmud, *Shabbos* 88a.

gle with the complexities of life. Every time we make the conscious choice to do a *mitzvah*, the *Torah* letter within our soul glistens; however, when we err, the glistening *Torah* letter within our soul dims.

If we constantly err, the dim letter fades, flickers, and can eventually be obscured. Just in time to stop the creeping haze, *Yom Kippur* arrives, pointing the way toward repentance, toward rekindling the radiance of our letter. Suddenly, we have another chance to illuminate our letter once again. When the gates of prayer close as the sun descends on *Yom Kippur*, the letters representing the souls of every Jew sparkle, just as the letters sparkled at revelation. Knowing that our letters are again glistening, we have reason for great rejoicing. The festival celebrating this great rejoicing is *Simchas Torah*, following soon after *Yom Kippur*.

Stories

The Price of a *Mitzvah*

Rabbi Elyahu ben Shlomo, the Vilna Gaon, was the undisputed halachic authority of the eighteenth century. As a youngster, he was considered a child prodigy. After his *bar mitzvah,* he was recognized as an outstanding *Torah* scholar. He was master over complex talmudic texts, elucidating tractates with elaborate commentaries.

The title "Gaon" was given to him by the people of the Vilna (Lithuania) Jewish community as a sign of the awe that they felt for this man, who personified religious leadership. When people asked him how he merited this title, he answered in Yiddish, "If you wish, you can also become a Gaon." The Vilna Gaon led an exemplary life of *Torah* leadership until his dying days.

On the eve of his last *Yom Kippur,* it was evident to his family and disciples that his strength had ebbed. He called his family and friends to his bedside to bestow his blessings before he passed from this world to the next.

His physical condition deteriorated rapidly. On the third day of *Sukkos,* his disciples carried him into the *sukkah.* They brought with them a most magnificent *lulav* and *esrog,* so that he might fulfill the commandments of the festival. As he raised the *lulav* and *esrog* in his frail hands, he began to weep. His disciples were astounded that he cried over his impending death. He noticed their puzzled looks and whispered in a halting voice, "It is so difficult for me to depart from this world. This beautiful *mitzvah* of blessing the *lulav* and *esrog*, that can be purchased for a few *zlotys*, brought me joy all the years I lived in this world and elevated me to reach the Divine Presence. I will never be able to fulfill this commandment again."

The Vilna Gaon's *yahrzeit* (anniversary of his death) is observed each year on the third day of *Sukkos*.

Don't Burn Down This *Sukkah*

Before they were rebbes, the brothers Zusia of Anipol and Elimelech of Lizensk were *maggidim* (itinerant preachers).

They traveled from *shtetl* to *shtetl*, visiting Jews who lived in widely scattered communities throughout the Pale of Settlement[1] (Poland and White Russia). Among the *shtetls* they visited were Koretz, Zhitomir, Polnoye, Rizhin, Kamenitz, Lemberg, and Ropshitz. They traveled in order to bring the Jews who lived in these isolated communities closer to the Almighty. To do this,

[1]In the year 1792, in an official act of the Russian government, Tzarina Catherine the Great decreed that the former Polish kingdom, which Russia annexed, be called the Pale of Settlement. She prohibited Jews from venturing forth from this territory. The word "pale" is derived from the Latin *palus*, meaning a stake or pole, and it was an area surrounded by poles that restricted or confined people who were under the jurisdiction of another country. The Pale of Settlement was located between the Baltic and Black Sea from north to south, and by the surrounding partitioning countries of Russia, Prussia, and Austria on the east and west sides. The Jews were confined to small villages in the Pale of Settlement, the western provinces of the empire, to prevent their spreading to other parts of Russia. They were treated as a hostile population, different from other Russian citizens, unworthy of equal citizenship.

they told stories, they inspired, they tried to influence, they taught, they showed their love for the downtrodden.

The two brothers usually traveled during the day while the people struggled to eke out a living. They arrived at their destination as the people returned from work. When the people heard that Rebbe Zusia and Rebbe Elimelech were in town, they would rush to listen to their words of wisdom before they returned home. After the brothers finished teaching, they usually spent the night in the *shtetl* inn, continuing their travels the following day.

Once Rebbe Zusia and Rebbe Elimelech passed through a small *shtetl* near Cracow. Looking intently at each other, they decided that there was something strange about that place.

"This place smells bad," said Rebbe Zusia to Rebbe Elimelech. "I don't think we should remain here overnight, as we usually do."

It must have been Rebbe Zusia's "holy inspiration" that gave him the ability to forsee that one hundred years from that time, the name of that place would be Auschwitz.

During one of their trips, Rebbe Zusia and Rebbe Elimelech arrived in a certain *shtetl* between *Yom Kippur* and *Sukkos*. News of their visit spread quickly through the *shtetl*. The wealthiest Jew ran out to meet them. He insisted that they stay with him for the *Sukkos* holiday. He said, "I am so happy to welcome you to our town. Please, stay here with me for *Sukkos*. I will do everything to make both of you comfortable. I have a beautiful *sukkah* and a magnificent *esrog*. Your presence will truly honor my family and me." The brothers agreed to spend *Sukkos* as guests of the wealthy man.

The first night of *Sukkos*, the wealthy man, his family, and his invited guests finished eating their meal in the *sukkah* and retired to the comfort of the house to sleep. Only Rebbe Zusia and Rebbe Elimelech remained outdoors. They insisted on sleeping in the *sukkah*.

At first, the wealthy man was a bit perplexed, since the first chill of autumn had pierced the air. Then he recalled his promise to make them comfortable, so he dragged two mattresses, two pillows, and some blankets into the *sukkah*.

Rebbe Zusia insisted on sleeping on the ground, so Rebbe Elimelech piled his brother's mattress and pillow on top of his own. He wrapped himself in all the blankets, snuggled up like a bear hibernating during winter snow, and, quick as a wink, Rebbe Elimelech fell asleep.

He was awakened to the sound of his brother's whisper, "Master of the Universe! Zusia is a little bit cold. Could you please do something to warm up this *sukkah* . . . just a little something?" Rebbe Zusia was accustomed to conversing with the Almighty personally.

Rebbe Elimelech was used to his brother's personal prayers. But he was very surprised when a warm breeze rustled the trees outside and wafted gently through the *sukkah*. Zusia said, "Thank you, Master of the Universe. Zusia is a little bit warmer."

Rebbe Elimelech removed one of the blankets, turned over, and fell asleep again.

A while later, Rebbe Elimelech was again awakened to the sound of his brother's whisper. "Master of the Universe! Zusia is still a little bit cold. Could you please make it a little warmer in this *sukkah* . . . just a little bit?" Once more the wind blew; this time it was gustier, more sultry than the time before. Zusia said, "Thank you, Master of the Universe. Zusia feels better. Zusia is a little bit warmer."

Rebbe Elimelech removed the second blanket, turned over, and thought he would then be able to sleep peacefully.

But about an hour later, he was awakened again by the sound of his brother's whisper. "Master of the Universe! Zusia is still a little bit cold. Could you please make it a little warmer in this *sukkah* . . . just a little bit?"

Now, sweltering, gale-force winds howled all around. The temperature rose; the inside of the *sukkah* felt like a tropical island.

Rebbe Elimelech removed the third blanket and turned over. He lay staring at Rebbe Zusia, scowling. Angrily, he muttered, "Zusia, enough already, enough! Stop praying to the Master of the Universe for warmth. Next time, you will surely burn down this *sukkah*!"

We Have Only Each Other—
Let's Not Fight

Because Rebbe Nachum Tzernobler was the most outstanding disciple of Rebbe Yisrael ben Eliezer, the Baal Shem Tov, he inherited his rebbe's *tefillin*. Rebbe Nachum Tzernobler was very poor. His only valuable possession was the *tefillin*.

It happened one year that it was practically impossible to obtain an *esrog* because of drought. Rebbe Nachum was very sad. He loved *Sukkos* and the *mitzvah* of *esrog* and *lulav* so much that he would do anything to obtain an *esrog* and *lulav*!

For two days after *Yom Kippur*,[1] Rebbe Nachum walked around the marketplace, desperately searching for a way to obtain an *esrog* and *lulav*. On the third day of his futile search, he overheard two people talking.

"Do you know that Moshe Chaim, the richest man in this town, has the only *esrog* and *lulav* in the whole vicinity?" one confided. "In fact, he invited me over to his house to see it! He said it was the most beautiful *esrog* that he has had in years!"

---

[1]*Yom Kippur* is five days before *Sukkos*.

"I wonder how he obtained it! I thought it was impossible to find an *esrog* because of the drought!" the other responded.

Rebbe Nachum's eyes opened wide in amazement. His ears strained to hear the conversation. The two people described the beauty of the *esrog* they imagined that Moshe Chaim had purchased in honor of *Sukkos.*

Believing that Moshe Chaim could do the impossible when it came to a *mitzvah*, Rebbe Nachum made mental plans for how he could convince Moshe Chaim to sell his *esrog.*

The practicalities of life haunted him. Even if he could convince Moshe Chaim to sell his *esrog,* he had no money to pay for it. He sat down in a corner of the marketplace and began to weep.

"How can I, Nachum Tzernobler, a poor Jew, buy Moshe Chaim's *esrog*?" he sobbed.

Suddenly, an idea flashed through his head. He had a plan. Maybe it would work! Quick as lightning, he ran through the streets, directly to Moshe Chaim's house. He knocked on the door, still breathless. Moshe Chaim opened the door.

"Why, Rebbe Nachum, how nice of you to visit me. Won't you come in? What can I do for you?" he asked in a surprised voice.

"I heard," panted Rebbe Nachum, "that you have the only *esrog* in this entire vicinity. I want to buy it from you."

Moshe Chaim looked at his guest and said adamantly, "I don't know where you heard that I have an *esrog* for *Sukkos.* Anyway, it is not for sale! Besides," Moshe Chaim lowered his voice, "if, perhaps, I should change my mind and sell it to you, how would you pay for it?"

Moshe Chaim waited for an answer. He was interested in listening to Rebbe Nachum's offer. Without hesitating, Rebbe Nachum replied boldly, "I have something that is priceless. Give me the *esrog,* and I will give you the Baal Shem Tov's *tefillin.*"

Moshe Chaim gulped. He could not believe his ears.

"All right," he said, "it's a deal. In exchange for the Baal Shem Tov's *tefillin,* I will sell you my *esrog.*"

Rebbe Nachum Tzernobler sprinted homeward, the precious *esrog* in his hand. He had never been happier in his life. He knew that this *Sukkos* would be his best.

His wife wondered why he was so happy. The holiday was rapidly approaching, and she had no money to buy food for her family for the holiday.

"My husband," she queried, "please tell me what wonderful thing happened that made you so happy? This morning, when you left, you were so sad."

Rebbe Nachum boldly took the *esrog* and placed it on the table. His wife's eyes opened wide.

"Where did you get the money to buy this *esrog*?" she demanded. "We have no money to buy food."

"I exchanged the Baal Shem Tov's *tefillin* for this *esrog*," he said calmly.

Angrily, she picked up the *esrog* and threw it to the ground. The luscious fruit lay smashed, the *pittum* (the distinctive knobbed stem) four feet away.

Rebbe Nachum's face was livid. He stared with unbridled fury at his wife, heartbroken at what she had done.

Then, realizing that what he had done was not completely correct, he calmed himself, walked over to his wife, and put his arm around her shoulder.

"Yesterday," he lamented, "we owned a most precious possession, the Baal Shem Tov's *tefillin*. Today, we owned a beautiful *esrog*. Now we have neither. We only have each other. Let's not fight. Good *yom tov*, good *yom tov*!"

How Will They Survive?

There was a tremendous difference between the lifestyles of Jews living in Tzarist Russia and the Jews living in the emancipated countries of France, Germany, and Italy during the eighteenth and nineteenth centuries.

In the emancipated countries, the walls of the ghettos had been broken after approximately one thousand years. The Jews breathed with deep relief at their new-found freedom, gradually acculturating to the society around them. Within a few generations, they had assimilated into the economic, intellectual, and social climate that had opened to them. As a result, the level of intense Jewish scholarship dropped considerably.

In Tzarist Russia, the Jews were not permitted to participate in the secular society. Consequently, the leaders of both *chasidim* and *misnagdim*[1] emphasized learning as the key to Jewish survival in an openly hostile environment.

Pinchas, the son of Rebbe Mayer Halayve, the Apter Rebbe,

[1]See footnote 2, page 118.

was a very curious young man. He never hesitated to ask his father about any subject that disturbed him.

Knowing the differences between Jewish life in France, Germany, and Italy, on the one hand, and Tzarist Russia, on the other, he innocently asked his father one day, "How will the Jews of France, Germany, and Italy survive? Here in Russia we have so many rebbes, so many great scholars, so many committed leaders. We might even have some of the *lamed vav tzadikim*[2] in our midst. In France, Germany, and Italy, there are no great leaders. How will they survive?"

Rebbe Mayer Halayve was used to his son's questions. Mentally, he filed this question, along with many others, in the deep recesses of his mind. Then he turned to Pinchas and said, "Pinchas, my son, one day you will see."

Pinchas soon lost interest in his question, but his father didn't forget. He waited for an opportunity to show his son how "they will survive."

Pinchas was one of the brilliant students who studied day and night in the study hall of Apt. Because he had married young, his father sustained the young couple by providing them with two rubles each Friday afternoon.

One week, the Apter rebbe distributed stipends to all the students he supported, but he omitted his son. Pinchas thought his father inadvertently forgot him, but when he did not receive his stipend the following week, he was concerned. He did not know how he would be able to pay his rent or his grocery bill.

He did not want to openly ask his father why he had not received his stipend for two weeks. Noticing how perturbed Pinchas was, one of his friends asked how he could help.

"Please go to my father," Pinchas pleaded, "and ask him why he did not give me my stipend for two weeks."

At first the friend hesitated. He did not have the nerve to approach the rebbe, but when he saw the pain on his friend's face, he decided to go.

---

[2]*Lamed vav tzadikim* are the thirty-six righteous men who, because of their meritorious lives, cause the world to exist.

Timidly, the friend knocked on the door of the rebbe's study room. Not knowing what to say, the friend stuttered, "Pinchas wants to know why he hasn't received his stipend for two weeks."

The Apter rebbe became very angry. He began shouting, "Pinchas my son is eighteen years old. Let him go out to earn a living! Does he think I will support him for the rest of his life?"

The friend gasped. "But rebbe," he pleaded, "the only thing Pinchas knows how to do is be a rebbe like you. What can he possibly do to earn a living?"

The Apter rebbe thought for a minute, then calmly said, "Tell my son to go to Germany to sell *esrogim* for *Sukkos!*"

The friend went to Pinchas. He told him what his father had said. Pinchas was heartbroken and hurt. He did not understand why his father had suddenly decided to stop his stipend without discussing the matter with him. Pinchas knew he was studying with greater diligence each day. He also knew that his father's decision would force him to leave Apt right after *Tisha B'Av*.[3] He did not understand what he had done to incur his father's wrath.

Pinchas was confused, but he had no choice. He told his wife what he had to do, took the money he had saved for emergencies, and set out for Italy, where he knew he could purchase a wagon-load of *esrogim*. He calculated that he would reach Italy before the beginning of the month of *Elul* (the month preceding *Rosh Hashanah, Yom Kippur,* and *Sukkos*). He planned to purchase the *esrogim* and point his wagon homeward, selling his merchandise as he passed through the small Jewish communities in Northern Italy, Austria, and Germany. He hoped, with good fortune, that he might return to his father's side before *Rosh Hashanah.*

Pinchas traveled during part of the day and settled in inns along the way by mid-afternoon so he could spend some hours studying. He greeted the townspeople when they returned home

---

[3]*Tisha B'Av*, the national day of Jewish mourning, marking the destruction of both holy temples in Jerusalem, is observed on the ninth day of the Hebrew month of *Av*, corresponding to the summer months of July or August.

from work, tried to sell his wares, slept the night, and repeated the process each day, drawing nearer and nearer to Apt. The people of the small Jewish communities treated him kindly. Most of them hadn't given much thought to purchasing *esrogim* during the month of *Elul*, but when Pinchas told them his story, emphasizing how much he wanted to be back in Apt for *Rosh Hashanah*, they willingly bought his *esrogim*. As his wagonload of *esrogim* decreased, and his money increased, Pinchas calculated that he would have enough to sustain his wife and himself for the coming year.

Just before *Rosh Hashanah*, Pinchas had only one-fourth of a wagonload of *esrogim* left to sell. Disappointed that he hadn't sold the entire wagonload, he made arrangements to spend *Rosh Hashanah* in an inn along the way. After *Rosh Hashanah*, he continued his journey.

Most of the remaining *esrogim* sold quickly between *Rosh Hashanah* and *Yom Kippur*. He had only ten more to sell. He reckoned that he could sell the last ten with ease on the day after *Yom Kippur*, so he set off in the direction of Apt, leaving himself three days to arrive home before *Sukkos*. His joy knew no bounds. After not having spent *Rosh Hashanah* and *Yom Kippur* with his father, he savored the flavor of sitting in the *sukkah* at his father's side.

Pinchas's joy was short-lived! He sold the *esrogim*, hired a wagon driver who boasted a short cut to Apt, and instructed him that they would leave shortly after daybreak the next day. But the sun barely peeked through the gray, cloudy sky that morning. It didn't take long for the clouds to change to mist, the mist to drizzle, the drizzle to downpour. Soon the roads became muddy. Pinchas realized that he would not be able to travel that day. There was no way he could reach Apt before *Sukkos*. Wretched with disappointment, he resigned himself to the fact that he would have to spend the first days of *Sukkos* in the village inn. He sat despondently, looking out the window, watching the rain.

The rain continued the next day and the next day. Pinchas made arrangements with the innkeeper to extend his stay for a few more days.

He did not know anybody in the village except the few people who had purchased his remaining *esrogim*. He hoped that when he went to the synagogue on the first night of the festival, one of the village people would invite him to eat the festival meal in their *sukkah*, but the people ignored his presence. He sat down by himself in the rear of the synagogue.

As the prayer leader began chanting, Pinchas put his head down on his hand and sobbed. When he opened his eyes a short while later, he was all alone. He didn't know what to do because he would not eat if he were not sitting inside a *sukkah*.

Suddenly, a man stormed into the synagogue. It was apparent that he was the town baker; his tall white hat and pants were covered with flour. He had not changed his clothes for the holiday. He sat down in the center of the synagogue, opened a prayerbook, and started to chant the weekday prayers. He ran his words together, mispronouncing every other syllable.

Pinchas laughed inwardly. His inner pain dissipitated.

"Let me show you how the holiday prayers are chanted," Pinchas said gently as he moved over to the bench where the baker sat. Pinchas patiently pointed out the differences between the holiday and weekday prayer service to the baker. He waited for him to finish, then greeted him. "Good *yom tov*! Good *yom tov*! Do you have a *sukkah*?"

The baker responded warmly, "Yes, I have a small *sukkah*. It is located on top of the roof of my modest cottage. If the wind and rain haven't carried it away, I would like to invite you to eat in it with me. I don't have much food to share with you, only a *challah* (braided bread) and a small herring, but you are most welcome to share half."

Pinchas thought of Apt and his father's beautiful *sukkah*. He would be sitting at his father's right side. The disciples would be sitting around a long, festive table, singing and studying. He accepted the invitation of the poor Jew who, he thought, could not read Hebrew correctly.

As they emerged from the synagogue, Pinchas felt the cool breezes of a clear, comfortable, moonlit night. They walked slowly to the baker's modest cottage, climbed a ladder to the roof, and entered the *sukkah.* The baker invited the seven holy shepherds of Israel—Abraham, Isaac, Jacob, Joseph, Moses, Aaron, and David[4]—into his *sukkah* and chanted the *kiddush.* They shared the *challah* and the herring. As they were finishing the simple meal, they heard heavy footsteps clomping up the ladder to the roof. The intruder, dressed like the baker and carrying a volume of the Talmud, entered the *sukkah.* The baker motioned to him to sit down next to him. He opened the volume of the Talmud, and they began to study.

Pinchas was surprised that the two men could study, but his thoughts were so far away in Apt that he paid no attention to them. The men studied all night, watched the sunrise, motioned to Pinchas to join them, and went off to the synagogue for the morning prayer service for the first day of the *Sukkos* festival.

Afterward, Pinchas returned to the inn and slept a few hours. Toward evening, he returned to the synagogue. The previous night's scene repeated itself in every detail. Pinchas again ate half of the *challah* and half of a herring, a meager festival meal, in the baker's *sukkah.*

After the meal, another intruder, dressed like the baker, clomped up the ladder, entered the *sukkah,* and sat down. He opened the volume of the Talmud that he carried and began studying with the baker. The thoughts in Pinchas's mind again wandered to his father's *sukkah* in Apt. He paid no attention to the men who sat and studied through the night in the baker's *sukkah.* Pinchas continued dreaming of Apt during the second day of the festival. On the third day, the first day of *chol hamo'ed* (the four intermediate workdays of the festival week), he decided to return to Apt. He hoped that he would arrive home in time for *Sh'mini Atzeres* and *Simchas Torah,* the last days of the *Sukkos* festival. However, as soon as he prepared to depart the village, the rain, which had subsided during the first two days of the festival, resumed.

---

[4]It is a custom to invite the spirit of one of the seven holy shepherds of Israel into the *sukkah* each night of the festival. Along with this custom, it is a tradition to open our *sukkah* to the poor of the community.

Pinchas resigned himself to spending the remainder of the *Sukkos* festival in the small village. He did not think it strange that the weather permitted him to attend the evening prayer service in the synagogue and eat in the baker's *sukkah* each night, for it rained only during the daylight hours. He did not think it strange that each night of the seven-day holiday, a different intruder visited the baker.

After *Sukkos, Sh'mini Atzeres,* and *Simchas Torah,* Pinchas prepared to return home. The daytime rains had stopped completely, and the roads had dried. He reached Apt in a few days. As soon as he arrived in Apt, Pinchas ran to see his father. He was breathless when he knocked on the door of his father's study. Rebbe Mayer Halayve had to calm his son, for no sooner had he seen him then he began to wail.

"Oh, Father!" wailed Pinchas. "If only you knew how miserable I have been for the past two months. I had to spend *Rosh Hashanah, Yom Kippur,* and *Sukkos* in inns in little villages, where hardly any Jews live. All the time I dreamed of being here with you."

The Apter rebbe raised his hand to halt his son's wailing.

"Pinchas, my son," he said, "why didn't you pay more attention to the bakers when they were studying? Didn't you recognize any of them? Didn't you know that those bakers were born with the souls of Abraham, Isaac, Jacob, Joseph, Moses, Aaron, and David?"

Then the Apter rebbe softened his voice. "Pinchas, my son, do you know now who lives in Germany? Do you know why I sent you? Do you know now how they will survive?"

Authors' note: This story has been told and retold for many generations. It is being retold here to honor the memory of my great-great-great-grandfather, Rebbe Mayer Halayve Apter, may his merit bring blessings to the entire household of Israel.

I'll Bless This *Esrog* While Standing on a Horse

Rebbe Mordechai Neshchizer was very poor. He found it difficult to eke out a living for his family. Yet, as the *Yamim Nora'im* (the Days of Awe—*Rosh Hashanah* and *Yom Kippur*) approached, he began to cut down even his meager expenses so that he might have enough money to purchase a beautiful *esrog* to enhance the beauty of the *Sukkos* holiday. He did this each year.

One year, Rebbe Mordechai found it more difficult than usual to save the money he needed to purchase an *esrog.* It seemed that the price was enormous. He waited and saved until the day before the holiday. Finally, he counted his rubles and found that he had saved six, so he set out by foot for the marketplace in Brod in search of a beautiful *esrog.*

As Rebbe Mordechai walked toward Brod, he thought about the beautiful *esrog* he would purchase. He pictured himself reciting the blessing over the *esrog* and the *lulav* on the first day of the holiday. Even these thoughts filled him with great pleasure.

As he neared Brod, he saw a Jew sitting on the edge of the road. The Jew was weeping.

Rebbe Mordechai stopped to see if he could help his fellow Jew and began to ask, "My dear brother, why are you weeping? How can I possibly help you?"

The man looked up, hesitated, and slowly stopped weeping. He began to speak softly. "I am a water carrier," he gulped. "I delivered buckets of water to the people in this town every day in a horse-drawn wagon. Today my horse died, and I will not be able to deliver water anymore. I will become a pauper. I will have to go around begging."

Rebbe Mordechai listened to the water carrier's story. Gently he said, "If you could find a new horse in the marketplace this minute, how much would you have to pay for it?"

The water carrier thought for a minute and then said, "Rebbe, I think I could buy a new horse for six rubles." Rebbe Mordechai put his hand in his pocket and withdrew the six rubles that he had saved to buy the *esrog*. As he placed the six rubles in the water carrier's hand, he instructed him to go to the marketplace and purchase a new horse.

Rebbe Mordechai returned home without the *esrog*, but he was very happy. As he walked into his modest cottage, he sang out to his wife, "Praised be the Lord for His Mercy and Kindness. Praised be the Lord for providing me with such a beautiful way to fulfill the *mitzvah* of blessing the *esrog* and *lulav*. While all other Jews are performing the *mitzvah* by holding the *esrog* and *lulav* in their hands, I will perform this *mitzvah* while standing on a horse."

The Case of
the Disappearing *Sukkah*

Wars wreak havoc on the inhabitants of feuding countries who become innocent victims of the struggle. They suffer hunger, destruction of property, loss of freedom, and often, death.

The *yishuv* (Jewish settlement in *Eretz Yisrael*, particularly in Jerusalem) suffered more than usual during the years of World War I, for natural disasters, typhus, malaria, and famine added to the general misery of war. In addition, the financial support from Jews living in Allied countries was cut off by the Turks, who sided with the Axis powers. Yet the Jews of the *yishuv* attempted to maintain as normal a life as possible under those horrible conditions. Although food and water were scarce, disease was rampant, and misery abounded daily, a small ray of joy settled over the *yishuv* during the observance of *Shabbos* and the celebration of festivals. The *yishuv* particularly looked forward to being invited to sit, even for a few minutes, inside Rebbe Mendele Twersky's amazing *sukkah*.

Much to their disappointment, Rebbe Mendele Twersky erected an ordinary *sukkah* that year, in the autumn of 1915. Its simple wooden walls contrasted noticeably with the elaborately decorated walls of the amazing *sukkah* he had erected for the previous ten years, ever since he had made *aliyah* (immigrated) to *Eretz Yisrael* from Russia.

Speculation surrounded the mystery of the disappearing *sukkah* walls; it added considerably to the excitement of the holiday preparations. Every Jew in Jerusalem had an opinion as to where the elaborately decorated walls of Rebbe Mendele Twersky's former *sukkah* had gone, but no one knew for sure.

They only knew that the walls of the amazing *sukkah* were shrouded in legend: they looked like the Garden of Eden; the letters that were painted over the design on the walls revealed the mystical secrets of *Torah;* the walls once belonged to the Baal Shem Tov and were inherited by his best disciple, who passed them down to his best disciple, for five generations, until they became the property of Rebbe Mendele Twersky.

The excitement quickly turned to temporary dismay when they saw Rebbe Mendele Twersky sitting in an ordinary *sukkah* during the first two days of *Sukkos.* Some people even thought that he was playing games, that he would erect his amazing *sukkah* during *chol hamo'ed*—the intermediate days of the holiday. Others passed by his house and whispered to their friends, "The walls of the *sukkah* are not tied to the side of his house like they always are!"

The seven days of the festival passed, and Rebbe Mendele Twersky sat in an ordinary *sukkah.* The *yishuv* finally realized that the treasured landmark, the amazing *sukkah,* had disappeared for some unknown reason.

How did Rebbe Mendele Twersky's *sukkah* disappear? It would have been easy to ask him outright, but no one wanted to. It was simpler to speculate, to circulate rumors, to presume various hypotheses, to gossip, to capitalize on the excitement that burst forth again after the holiday ended.

The autumn weather turned colder and colder; the winter rains began to fall. The days in the autumn months of *Cheshvan* and *Kislev* dragged on. Only the case of the disappearing *sukkah* added a spark of excitement to their miserable existence.

Three months passed; the people of the *yishuv* did not forget the case of the disappearing *sukkah*. After almost ninety days, there still was no clue. The mystery hung over the *yishuv* like the clouds that threatened daily rain.

The sixth day of the month of *Teves* marked the *yahrzeit* (the anniversary of the death) of Rebbe Yechezkel Halberstam. The leaders of the *yishuv* gathered to dedicate communal study time to his memory. After they finished, they sat around long tables, sharing their thoughts and stories about their rebbe, and ate a meager meal. There the case of the mysterious *sukkah* was solved.

Yisrael Mayer Gottlieb rose to his feet. He cleared his throat for attention. All eyes focused upon him. He began to speak in a soft voice.

"Before we recite the grace after meals, I would like to say a few words. There has been so much speculation about the case of the disappearing *sukkah* in the past three months that now I would like to dispel the mystery. Actually, all of you think you have been studying here to honor the memory of one of our leaders. However, let me tell you that there was another purpose. This is what happened. Many months ago, my grandson Shlomo was stricken with typhus. The doctors feared that he might never recover. In desperation, I ran from one doctor to another. Finally, one suggested that he might be helped if he could bathe in hot water twice each day. I did not know what to do. There was neither oil nor wood available with which to heat water for his baths. Rebbe Mendele Twersky and I are old friends. I had to confide in someone, so I went to him with my problem. He did not hesitate for one second to find a solution. He grabbed me by the hand, dragged me to the side of his house where the walls of the amazing *sukkah* were stored from year to year, cut the rope that bound them to the house, and said, 'Quick, take the walls of the *sukkah*. Chop them in pieces the size of firewood, and use them to heat water for Shlomo's baths. I know he will recover.'

"I was speechless. I could not argue with him, for he started to cut the rope. While I stood there, glued to the spot, he ran for some young men and directed them to chop the walls of the *sukkah* into firewood. They carried the wood back to my house. I heated the water and bathed my grandson. As you all know, he recovered, thank God. So you see, we learn not only to honor the memory of the dead, but to celebrate the rebirth of Shlomo my grandson. Now the case of the disappearing *sukkah* is solved."

Rebbe Yisrael Mayer Gottlieb sat down. Stunned silence echoed in the room as the people of the *yishuv* realized what had happened to the walls of the amazing *sukkah*. They were used to save the life of Shlomo, Rebbe Yisrael Mayer Gottlieb's grandson.

Because of a Little *Sukkah*

He was innocent of any crime. He did not mingle with the refuseniks or the dissidents. He never went near the big Moscow synagogue on Arkhipova Street. He did not protest from the balcony of his apartment building. He refrained from all activist activities. He had never defamed the Soviet state. He had never stolen anything, maimed anyone, or spoken evil about the government. He had never even received a traffic ticket. He was a lawful, peace-abiding citizen of the U.S.S.R., yet he was constantly harassed, for Saul wanted to live the life of a Jew, together with his wife and two sons.

Saul was harassed day and night. He felt the shadow of KGB agents following him from his home to his job. They knew where he stopped, and for how long. They knew who his friends were.

Sometimes he stopped on the way home from work to join the *minyan* for the evening prayer service, each evening meeting in a different place. Other evenings, friends dropped by at his apartment; he taught them the Judaism he remembered from his father's house. He was part of the network of Hebrew teachers who were threatened with arrest on trumped-up charges and who dared to keep Judaism alive in a country where religion and God are aliens.

Saul's wife constantly feared for his safety. She pleaded with him to leave the big city for a while, to flee to the small rural town where her brother lived, where police surveillance might not be so stringent. She enlisted the help of their two sons, beseeching them to convince their father to leave.

At first, Saul stubbornly refused to listen to their pleas. He felt responsible to the *minyan*, to his pupils. He recognized that his presence provided moral support for them.

Finally, he compromised. "I promise I will leave right after *Rosh Hashanah*," he said. "I want to hear the sounding of the *shofar* with my friends."

When *Rosh Hashanah* passed with no increase in harassment, Saul reneged on his promise. "Please, understand," he told his wife and children, "how much I want to remain here until after *Yom Kippur*. I assure you I will be all right. After the holy day, I will certainly leave for safer ground."

Towards the end of the *Yom Kippur* prayer service, Saul detected pain in the eyes of his *minyan* friends. He knew they wanted him to leave for a safer place, as he promised, but he also realized that they would not be able to rejoice in the celebration of *Sukkos*, "the festival of our joy," without him. So once again, Saul postponed his trip.

He dared to build a little *sukkah*, attaching it to the storage room of his apartment. It was difficult to camouflage the *sukkah* completely, since the top had to be open to the sky, but it was barely noticeable from the side street that ran past his yard.

The first two nights of the *Sukkos* festival, Saul assigned specific times for his *minyan* friends to drop by his hidden *sukkah* to recite the *kiddush* and the blessing, "Who has made us holy with His commandment to dwell in the *sukkah*."

Saul's wife pleaded with him to have compassion on their sons and her, not to postpone his flight to safety any longer. As tears streamed down her face, Saul renewed his promise to flee.

"Tomorrow night," he said, "I will teach my *minyan* friends one last time. It will be my way of saying goodbye to them. I will leave the next morning. I promise."

Saying goodbye to his *minyan* friends was very painful. He didn't know if he would ever see them again, so he lingered until late into the night. When he returned to his apartment, he was very thirsty. He poured himself a cup of water. Remembering that his chasidic grandfather never ate or drank even a drop of water outside of the *sukkah*, Saul took the cup of water and went outdoors to his hidden *sukkah*. Still wearing his coat, for the autumn air was chilly, he placed the cup on the table. He sat down, recited the blessing, and drank. Then he put his head on his hand, closed his eyes, and let his thoughts wander. He was very weary.

Suddenly, he heard banging, shouting, and commotion in the hall of his apartment building a few feet away. "Open the door!" they shouted. "Where is he, where is he?" they demanded. He imagined them searching his apartment, overturning the furniture, throwing his holy books onto the ground, ripping the *mezuzos* from their places on the doorposts of his home.

Then Saul clearly overheard one of them saying, "I don't understand. I was certain we would find him here. He must have flown the coop." They trudged around the apartment and the hall, shining their lanterns into every crevice.

Finally, Saul heard the door to his apartment slam. He was safe in the *sukkah*. As he listened intently, he heard their footsteps fade.

Saul determined that the temporary danger had passed. Without returning to his apartment, he ran down the side street, through alleyways, across vacant yards, toward the train platform at the outskirts of the city.

He reached the platform as the train slowed to a stop to load and unload the few passengers who traveled at that hour of the night.

Saul did not look at the locomotive's sign indicating its destination. He hopped on the train and settled down in the third class compartment, praying that no one would recognize him.

Back in the big city, his wife was relieved that Saul was not home when they broke into and searched their apartment. She did not know where he was, but, somehow, she was confident that he was safe.

Two weeks passed. Finally a letter arrived, postmarked from the town where her brother lived. Her sister-in-law wrote that her husband was not well, that a visitor diagnosed with the same illness stopped by to see them, and both men decided to go to a health spa until they recovered fully. She concluded the letter with, "Until we all meet again."

Saul's wife understood that both her brother and husband were being hounded by KGB agents and that both were temporarily safe.

She waited and waited for another message. Finally the families were reunited in a little village, far from the big city. Tearfully embracing his wife, Saul whispered, ". . . because of a little *sukkah*. . . ."

Humble Above All Men

Chaim combined *Torah* study with business; he was successful at both. He was as comfortable in his role as advisor to young people attempting to set up new businesses as he was as an authority on Jewish law. People from all over the vicinity sought his advice.

Chaim's business prospered without much guidance from him, so he spent days and nights delving into *Torah*, Talmud, and Jewish law in his private library, which was covered with wall-to-wall shelves of scholarly volumes. Oftentimes, he passed up meals, remaining secluded for days at a time. He enjoyed none of the luxuries his wealth could afford him; traveling, fancy wardrobes, and lavishly furnished housing did not interest him. His friends thought he was eccentric, but his family understood the reasons he chose solitude.

He lived this way for twenty-two years. Toward the end of that year he came across a talmudic passage that changed his life. On that day he read, "Rabbi Mayer says: "He who studies the *Torah* but does not teach it is alluded to as one who has despised the word of the Lord."[1] He was dumbstruck.

[1] Talmud, *Sanhedrin* 99a.

"What am I doing in seclusion?" he demanded of himself.
"I have been studying all these years by myself. I have not spoken to another person in all this time. I have not influenced another human being. I have not even shared an *alef* (the first letter of the Hebrew alphabet) with a child."

He closed the volume of the Talmud he was studying and spent hours thinking how he could teach what he had learned. Resolutely, he emerged from solitary confinement, determined to spend at least part of each day teaching.

Early the next morning, instead of praying by himself, as was his usual custom, he went to the synagogue. From his home he walked slowly past the marketplace, taking the longer route, for he had not seen the sparkling sunshine for twenty-two years. He passed the stalls, looked in wonder at the merchandise, and breathed deeply, inhaling the fresh air. Off in the distance, he noticed the blue sky, the gently rolling clouds, the verdant foliage, the ocher hills.

"This is my first opportunity to teach," he thought excitedly. He stopped a passerby.

"Look at the magnificence of God's creation," he said. "Look at the beauty of the Almighty's work."

The passerby paid him no attention. He thought the intruder was odd; he busily hurried to his destination.

Chaim was disappointed. "My first opportunity to teach another human being about the glories of creation and I failed! He rebuffed me entirely. Maybe he was too busy, too poor, or too ignorant to understand what I was trying to teach him," Chaim rationalized. "Oh well, the day is young, and I am sure there will be other opportunities."

Chaim continued toward the synagogue. He arrived a few minutes before the prayer service began and sat down on one of the benches in the center. No one stopped gossiping to welcome the stranger among them. Absentmindedly, men wrapped themselves in prayer shawls and donned *tefillin*. The prayer leader led the service; the men mumbled the words, trying to follow his lead. Chaim was appalled at the lack of concentration and intent of the worshippers. They raced mechanically through the prayers, hurriedly removed their *tefillin* and prayer shawls and left immediately. No one remained to exchange a *Torah* thought. No one greeted him.

"After all," he whispered to himself, "when I prayed by myself, I really felt that I was communicating directly with the Almightly. What kinds of Jews live in this town?"

Chaim was confused. He was pained by the apathetic attitude of the few Jews he had met on his first excursion outdoors in twenty-two years, and he felt clearly superior to them.

"I still need to find someone to teach," Chaim thought. He left the synagogue and walked in the direction of the study hall. From the open windows of the study hall, he heard the sing-song melody of the talmudic passages the young men chanted as they studied. "Maybe here, in the study hall, I will be able to share my twenty-two years of learning with others," he uttered.

Chaim entered the study hall, walked over to the table where the young men studied, sat down, and listened to their discussion. He listened patiently for what seemed to him an interminable time, but the young men came no closer to understanding the intricacies of the talmudic passage.

"Excuse me," interrupted Chaim. "Maybe, I can help you understand this passage. Let's look at the previous passage together. Doesn't it contradict this passage? Obviously, had you looked at Tosafos (primary commentary printed on every page), your dilemma would have been easily resolved! Now, let's see how we can understand this passage together!"

Chaim explained clearly and carefully, penetrating the depth of the issue. The young men sat totally absorbed in his explanation. When he finished, they thanked him, and he left.

Chaim felt wonderful. He had shared his knowledge with young men who were studying.

"I really think I am such a good teacher," he thought. "I bet if I continue to teach, people will recognize me as the leading scholar of this generation!"

Chaim circulated around town for the next few days, trying to create opportunities to teach. Each time he walked away from a group of students he helped, he grew more and more arrogant, but no one recognized his ability.

Once, when he walked around the marketplace looking for prospective students, he overheard two people planning a trip to Lizensk to spend *Shabbos* with Rebbe Elimelech. He stopped to eavesdrop.

"You know," said one, "I have saved enough rubles to go to Lizensk next week. I am so looking forward to it. I hear that just spending *Shabbos* with Rebbe Elimelech is the highest religious experience!"

"I've heard that, too," responded the other. "I am waiting for *Rosh Hashanah*. I want to have time to save enough money to take my whole family with me. I want to be in Lizensk when Rebbe Elimelech sounds the *shofar!*"

Chaim was surprised at the excitement of the two men.

"Why are they so anxious to travel all the way to Lizensk to be with Rebbe Elimelech when I am just as great a scholar as he? Why don't they come to me? After all, I studied for twenty-two years. I understand the intricacies of most talmudic passages," he thought. For a few moments, Chaim was calm.

Suddenly, he began screaming, "I know what I have to do! I have to go to Lizensk. I have to find out why Rebbe Elimelech is accepted as one of the leaders of this generation while I am not even considered a close runner-up. I will go to Lizensk for the last two days of *Sukkos*. I will be in Lizensk for *Simchas Torah*, when Rebbe Elimelech dances with the *Torahs*."

He set off during *chol hamo'ed* (the intermediate workdays of the festival week). He arrived in Lizensk on the eve of *Hoshanah Rabah*.[2]

He settled in an inn and then walked around the town, try-

---

[2]*Hoshanah Rabah* is the end of the penitential period that begins with *Rosh Hashanah*. It follows *Yom Kippur*, the Day of Atonement, as an unofficial grace period. Many people prolong their good wishes to their relatives, friends, and neighbors by greeting them with a *shanah tovah*, "a good year," from *Rosh Hashanah* until *Hoshanah Rabah*.

ing to find the study hall. He saw hundreds of people streaming forward: the tailor, the butcher, the dairyman, the bookbinder, the candlestick maker, the blacksmith. Unobtrusively, he stepped into line with the crowd and walked with them. The study hall was mobbed. Only a few seats remained empty at the back. Chaim slid into one of the seats and prepared himself to listen intently to find out why people flocked to Rebbe Elimelech, why people huddled together for the privilege of listening to Rebbe Elimelech's words of wisdom.

Rebbe Elimelech began to speak in a low voice. "Tonight," he said, "I want to teach the meaning of the verse, 'And now Israel, what does the Lord your God demand of you? To respect and fear Him!' "[3]

First, he illustrated the verse with a parable, then he applied the parable to the moral meaning. As he spoke, his voice grew more intent, more excited, more agitated. His eyes focused around the room: he turned in all directions. Clearly, he was searching for someone. The room was hushed in thick silence. Suddenly, Rebbe Elimelech called out, "Respect and fear of the Lord is not found in the streets, nor in the marketplace. It is not found in the heavens. He who wishes to purchase it does not have to search. Nor does he have to immerse himself in study. Do you want to know where respect and fear of the Lord is found? It is found in the heart of every Jew. I wish that your fear of God be as your fear of man."[4]

The impact of his ringing words left everyone in that room stunned. No one moved.

Chaim believed that Rebbe Elimelech spoke directly to him, only to him. He began to tremble. His hands shook, his heart throbbed, his knees twitched, his feet staggered. He fainted. He fell to the floor, under the row of seats in front of him.

Until Rebbe Elimelech finished, Chaim lay under the bench unnoticed. As the people stood, one tripped over his body. He bent to pick him up and stretched him out on a vacant bench. A

[3]Deuteronomy 10:12.
[4]Talmud, *Berachos* 28b.

doctor in the crowd took Chaim's pulse and said, "Don't worry, he just fainted from the heat in this room. He will be fine in a little while!"

But Chaim lay unconscious on the bench in Rebbe Elimelech's study hall that night and all of the next day. Most people were so involved in their holiday preparations that they were oblivious to Chaim's plight.

Toward evening, throngs of people rushed into the study hall, for it was the eve of *Sh'mini Atzeres*, the eighth day of the festival week. The first person to sit down on the bench near Chaim realized that there was something wrong. He rushed to find Eleazar, the son of Rebbe Elimelech.

"Go and tell your father," he shrieked, "that there is a body lying on one of the benches in the back of the study hall. It seems to be breathing!"

Eleazar ran to find his father. Breathless, he told him that a body was lying on one of the benches in the study hall.

Rebbe Elimelech said, "Calm down, Eleazar. Don't ask me to explain what I want you to do. Just go and do it! Take my walking stick and place it on the man's body. When he awakens, tell him I want him to spend the last two days of the holiday with me."

Eleazar was puzzled, but he followed his father's instructions.

As soon as the walking stick lay across Chaim's body, he regained consciousness. He stirred and stretched, blinked his eyes, sat up, and lowered his feet to the ground.

"Where am I?" he asked. But he remembered where he was, why he had traveled to Lizensk, what he had hoped to find out.

Observing Rebbe Elimelech during *Sh'mini Atzeres* and *Simchas Torah* provided Chaim with the clues he needed to discover the character of a great leader, for Rebbe Elimelech was compassionate, humble, patient, and caring. His words were uttered with love, his song with great feeling.

After the festival, Rebbe Elimelech said to Chaim, "Before you return home, I want to bless you to learn to love every human being, to always show care and concern for your fellow man. I pray that the people you teach will seek you because of your humility. Remember, our teacher Moses was 'humble above all men that were upon the face of the earth.'[5] Now, go in peace."

Chaim returned home a changed person. He always tried to emulate the deeds of Rebbe Elimelech of Lizensk. He spent the remainder of his life caring for the less fortunate, teaching those who sought to study with him, and learning. He became one of the respected leaders in his town.

[5]Numbers 12:3.

Berel's *Chumash*

Of all the chasidic rebbes, only the Rizhiner lived as befitting a descendant of the royal house of King David. People described the furnishings of his chasidic court as "majestic." His followers flocked to Rizhin to spend *Shabbos* or holidays with Rebbe Yisrael Friedman, the rebbe of Rizhin, to experience the delight of serving the Almighty with joy.

Celebrating holidays with joy was the mark of *chasidism.* In Rizhin, this joy was multiplied and magnified a hundredfold during *Sukkos,* and it climaxed on *Simchas Torah,* the last day of the fall holiday season.

Simchas Torah preparations in Rizhin were elaborate. Displayed at the front of the *shul,* the *Torah* scrolls were adorned with mantles of velvet, richly embroidered with ornate designs. They were crowned with silver. Jeweled breastplates and pointers dangled around the scroll. *Simchas Torah* flags were ready for the marchers, who followed the *Torah* procession around the *shul.* The marchers themselves, dressed in their holiday best, thronged about, waiting, cherishing the moment.

Excitement mounted in Rizhin. *Simchas Torah* was about

to begin. Normally, the rebbe of Rizhin signaled the beginning of the festivities immediately after the evening prayer service. From his place on the pulpit, he would turn to face the congregation, then nod to the prayer leader, who would begin chanting, "You have made it known that You are God."

This year, the rebbe was frozen in his place. His eyes stared at the entrance of the *shul,* he breathed slowly, steadily, but not a muscle moved. The congregants glanced anxiously at their rebbe, then turned away. They were too afraid to inquire what was wrong.

The minutes dragged by slowly; they waited and waited, more impatient, more worried. A hushed silence pervaded the congregation. It seemed as if it were *Yom Kippur,* not *Simchas Torah.*

Then, a commotion broke the hushed silence as the door at the rear of the *shul* opened and banged shut. Laybish the milkman, followed by his young son Berel, entered the *shul,* and they rapidly trudged down the aisle, heading straight for the pulpit, for the outstretched hands of the Rizhiner rebbe. The Rizhiner, ignoring the milkman's grimy clothing and soot-covered face, said softly, "Good *yom tov,* Reb Laybish, Good *yom tov,* Berel. I have been waiting for you."

Laybish answered, "Good *yom tov,* rebbe. I came as soon as I could. I'm glad I'm not too late for the *Simchas Torah* celebrations." Then, conscious of the condition of his dress, Laybish whispered, "Everything, the house and all its contents, were consumed in the fire."

The rebbe turned to Berel and asked, "Where in the *Torah* is it written that you must celebrate *Simchas Torah?*"

Berel lowered his eyes and answered sheepishly, "I really don't know."

The rebbe replied, "The reason you don't know is because the *Torah* does not command us to celebrate *Simchas Torah.*" He turned to one of his students and queried, "Do you know where the Talmud describes the celebration of *Simchas Torah?*"

The student thought a minute, then answered guardedly, "Tractate *Megillah* 31a in the Talmud mentions the ninth day of *Sukkos*, the *Torah* readings, and the *Haftorah* selections, but it does not mention the joyous celebrations, the *hakafos* (joyous processions with the *Torah* scrolls), the conclusion of the *Torah* reading cycle, and its immediate resumption."

The Rizhiner walked over to his chair on the pulpit, beckoned Berel to him, and sat the child on his lap. Holding Berel's shoulders, he continued speaking. "You see, Berel, the celebration of *Simchas Torah* is not written in the *Torah* or in the Talmud. Listen to me carefully, and I will tell you the origin of our celebration. The custom of celebrating *Simchas Torah* with the joyous processions of the *Torah* scrolls, the conclusion of the *Torah* reading cycle, and its immediate resumption, was instituted by our Rabbis during the fourteenth century as a reaction to persecution. The Crusades in the Franco-Germanic lands decimated Jewish communities, and the expulsions and blood libels were perpetrated against our people because we refused to forsake *Torah*. We never let three days go by without reading or studying *Torah*. The minute we finish the book of Deuteronomy, we joyfully begin again with Genesis, the creation of the world. The joy is so overwhelming, so spontaneous, so marvelous, that we dance and sing on *Simchas Torah*. Do you understand why we will celebrate tonight, Berel?"

Berel was not sure he understood the rebbe's explanation, but he nodded his head nevertheless. Then the rebbe asked, "Berel, what are you clutching in your hand?"

Berel answered, "This is my *chumash* (Bible)." The Rizhiner turned to Laybish and asked him how Berel happened to have a *chumash*.

Laybish said, "There is no school in the *shtetl* where I live, so I taught Berel the fundamentals of our religion myself. He wanted to learn more than I was able to teach him, but I could not afford to hire a teacher, so I sent him to a neighboring *shtetl*. He had to subsist on dark bread and water, since I could give him no money. In order to pay for his lessons, he assisted the *shamish* by sweeping the study hall each night. He saved the few *zlotys* the *shamish* gave him. Instead of buying food, he bought that *chumash.*"

The rebbe looked at the scorched *chumash* in Berel's hand. He rumpled Berel's singed hair and flicked the ashes from his grimy shirt. "How did it happen?" asked the rebbe.

Berel whispered, "We had just left for Rizhin to join in the *Simchas Torah* celebrations. From behind us, we heard the animals bellowing in the barn. We turned around to see what happened. We saw that everything was blazing, the house and the barn. My father ran back to the barn to try to save the animals. I ran back to the house. I had to save my *chumash.*"

The Rizhiner listened carefully to Berel. Then he held up his hands to the congregation, his face shining, resplendent. He stood up, walked to the center of the pulpit, and said, "We are not great when we observe the commandments of the *Torah*, for that is our responsibility. We swore at Mt. Sinai to observe. Who among us would break a vow? Tonight, we heard the story of a young boy who risked his life to save *Torah*, which is not demanded of him by law. Can you imagine the joy in Heaven over such an act? The joy spills over in the form of dancing in Heaven together with the *Simchas Torah* dancing on earth! Can you imagine how much joy there is in the world when both Heaven and earth dance on *Simchas Torah?*"

Then the rebbe of Rizhin nodded for the procession with the *Torah* to begin.

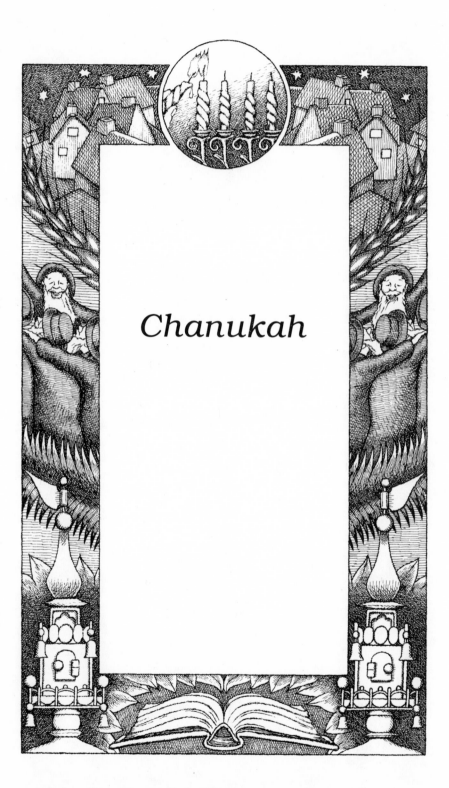

Chanukah

hanukah commemorates a particular historical event that took place in *Eretz Yisrael* while the Jewish people were subjects of Greek rule. In their ambition to conquer the known world during the second and third centuries before the common era, the Greeks spread their culture over their subjects by imposing their pagan ways upon them. Mattathias, the High Priest, and his son, Judah Maccabee, initiated the revolt of the Jewish people against Greek tyranny and successfully expelled them from their land. As they cleansed the Holy Temple from pagan defilement, completely throwing off the influence of the alien Greek culture, they found one purified flask of oil with the seal of the High Priest. It was enough to last but one night. Miraculously, the oil lasted eight.

The rabbis who witnessed the miraculous victory of the few (Jewish people) over the mighty (Greek conquerors) ordained an eight-day festival, *Chanukah*, beginning on the twenty-fifth day of *Kislev*.

Each night for eight nights, we light one candle or cupful of oil in the *chanukiyah*, the eight-branched *menorah*. We begin with one flame on the first night and add one more each succeeding night, until eight flames glow on the eighth night.

Playing *dreidel* (spinning top) is a popular pastime during *Chanukah*. Four Hebrew letters are engraved on the four sides of the *dreidel*: *nun, gimmel, hay, shin.* The letters stand for, "A great miracle happened there."

Latkes (potatoe pancakes) and *sufganiyot* (donuts) are two special foods that enhance the meals of *Chanukah*.

Torah Thoughts

Special *Chanukah* Oil

Secrets of our past are the links that mold our present and become the bridges to our future. These secrets are steeped in Jewish tradition; one of them is the mystery of the special *Chanukah* oil that Judah Maccabee found when he rededicated the Holy Temple.

The mystery begins with Noah. He sent a dove from the ark to see if the waters had abated. The dove flew in the direction of *Eretz Yisrael* from Mount Ararat in Turkey, where the ark had rested. When the dove reached *Eretz Yisrael*, it plucked an olive branch—a symbol of new growth and the renewal of life—from an olive tree[1] and returned to the ark with the branch in its beak.

Noah took the olive branch and snipped the olives. He pressed the olives into oil and sealed the oil in a flask. Noah wanted the flask of oil to represent light and truth. When he saw that his son Shem was following in his footsteps, he bequeathed the flask of oil to him, for he was certain that righteousness would endure through Shem.

[1]*Eretz Yisrael* was not affected by the waters of the flood. *Shir Hashirim Rabbah* 1:65, Pirkei D'Rabbi Eliezer 23.

Shem established a school of *Torah* learning in Shalem (Jerusalem), where he transmitted the light and truth he learned from his father to his grandson Ayver. Our patriarch Abraham studied in the school of Shem and Ayver. Being their most promising student, they passed the flask of oil to him.

Abraham entrusted it to his son Isaac. Isaac entrusted it to his son Jacob. When Jacob fled from Esau, he carried the flask of oil with him. It was with this oil that Jacob anointed the stone that supported his head as he slept and dreamed of the angels going up and down the ladder.[2]

That little flask of oil sustained Jacob for the twenty years that he lived with his father-in-law, Laban, until he returned to *Eretz Yisrael* with his wives and children.

Jacob transmitted the little flask of oil, the light and the truth, to Joseph. When Joseph descended to Egypt, he carried it with him. It guided him to establish another school of *Torah* learning in exile, in preparation for the arrival of the remainder of his father's children.

The little flask of oil inspired the yearning for redemption. Moses carried it out of Egypt and transmitted it to Joshua; Joshua transmitted it to the elders; the elders transmitted it to the prophets. The prophet Samuel anointed two kings, Saul and David, with this oil. The oil in the little flask was always replenished.

When King Solomon built the first Holy Temple, he placed the little flask of oil in the cornerstone, in perpetuity for future generations. None of the foreign conquerors who set foot in Jerusalem knew about the little flask of oil. Only the high priest knew the secret and transmitted it to his successor just before he died. Judah Maccabee, descendant of the priestly family, knew the secret of the oil. When he marched victoriously into Jerusalem to rededicate the Holy Temple after it had been defiled by the Syrians, he searched for the little flask of oil that was hidden in the cornerstone. He used this oil, this symbol of light and truth, to rekindle the light in the Holy Temple.

[2]Genesis 28:18.

The Miracle of Renewal

In the long history of the Jewish people, many miracles occurred that saved them from the hands of their enemies.

The judge Gideon, leading three hundred men armed only with *shofars* and lanterns, overthrew the oppressive Midianites.[1]

Samuel the prophet subdued the Philistine menace.[2] Sancheriv, King of Assyria, and his mighty army succumbed to a mysterious plague when they attempted to capture Jerusalem, the holy city.[3]

None of these miraculous events was commemorated with a festival. Only *Chanukah* was "established for eight days, for all generations, to express thanks and praise to Your Holy Name."[4]

What did our Rabbis see in the miracle of *Chanukah* that led them to ordain a special festival?

The miracle of *Chanukah* was not only in the victory over

[1]Judges 7:15–21.
[2]Samuel 7:10–14.
[3]II Kings 18:13–26, 19:1–36.
[4]*Al Hanisim*, the special *Chanukah* prayer.

the Syrians. More important, the miracle lay in the rekindling of the oil and the rededication of the Jewish people to the way of God and His commandments.

"What is the reason for the celebration of *Chanukah*? When the Syrians entered the Holy Temple, they defiled all the oils therein, and when the Chashmoneans defeated them, they found only one cruse of oil, which was sealed with the insignia of the high priest. It contained sufficient oil for one day. Yet a miracle was wrought, and they lit the lamps for eight days."[5]

From this passage in the Talmud, we understand the emphasis that our Rabbis placed on the study of *Torah*, for they equated the miracle of the oil, the rekindling of the light in the Holy Temple, with the rededication of the Jewish people to the word of God, which brings light to the world.

Even though many miracles were witnessed by the Jewish people prior to the miracle of *Chanukah*, none had the significance of rededication. Had the Syrians succeeded, they would have destroyed the *Torah* and the Jewish people. When the oil was rekindled in the Holy Temple, a new light was created. Every time we study *Torah*, we draw strength from the light of *Chanukah*.

[5]Talmud, *Shabbbos* 21b.

Chanukah Lights

Did you ever wonder why it is a custom to kindle the *Chanukah menorah* in the doorway or by the window?

Reflect upon the reason for celebrating *Chanukah*. Compare *Chanukah* 2,000 years ago with Jewish life today. The Maccabees fought a valiant battle to rededicate the Jewish people to the *Torah* way of life, for Antiochus Epiphanes attempted to impose his alien ways upon our people. Many Jews lost their way and adopted Hellenism. The *Torah* way of life was in danger of being lost.

Today, many of our young people are assimilating into the American culture at the expense of Judaism. When we kindle the *Chanukah* lights in a doorway or window, we beckon our young people who have lost their way to follow the glow of the little flames. The flames serve as a guide, bringing our children back to us.

This may also be the reason why we don't have a *Chanukah* festive meal similar to the *se'udah* (festive meal) on *Purim*, for while waiting for the return of a lost child, how can one eat?

Three Letters, Three Words, Three People

Lamed chet mem is *lechem*, bread.
Chet lamed mem is *cholem*, dream.
Lamed chet mem is *lochem*, fight.
Some people fight for bread.
Some people dream of fighting.
Some people fight for their dreams.

Gemar Chasemah Tovah

I recently met some *chasidim* who told me that their custom is to wish their family and friends, *"Gemar chasemah tovah"* ("May you be inscribed and sealed for good")[1] all the days of *Chanukah*, but particularly on the eighth night. I asked one of them to explain this most unusual custom. This is what he said. "There is a talmudic passage in which rabbis from the school of Hillel argue with rabbis from the school of Shammai over the procedure of kindling the *Chanukah* lights.[2] Basically, the position of the school of Hillel was that one flame is kindled on the first night, two the second, increasing the number daily until eight flames burn on the eighth night.[3]

"The school of Shammai had an opposing viewpoint. Its position was to kindle eight lights on the first night and gradually

---

[1]This greeting is generally used between *Rosh Hashanah* and *Yom Kippur*.

[2]Talmud, *Shabbos* 21b.

[3]The reasoning behind the position of the school of Hillel was the principle that the level of holiness increases by adding.

decrease each night until one light remained. They based their reasoning on the precedent that the animal sacrifices offered in the Holy Temple in Jerusalem during the festival of *Sukkos* decreased each ensuing day of the festival.[4]

"Keeping in mind the reasoning of the school of Shammai," my chasidic friend continued, "it is easy to associate the festival of *Sukkos* with the festival of *Chanukah*.[5] Now, most people recognize the fact that the last days of *Sukkos* officially close the High Holiday period, the penitential period. It is as if the Almighty grants us an extended period of time after *Yom Kippur* as a grace period, wherein He inscribes and seals us for a good year. But it is necessary that an agreement be signed by both participants. For our part, we like to examine the agreement and think it over for a few months. We go over it word by word, line by line, for the two months between *Sukkos* and *Chanukah*. Finally, during *Chanukah*, we are ready to sign the agreement. As we *chasidim* sign the agreement, we wish our friends, *"Gemar chasemah tovah."*

---

[4]On the first day of *Sukkos*, thirteen bullocks were sacrificed, on the second day, twelve, on the third day, eleven, gradually decreasing each day of the festival (Numbers 29:12).

[5]During *Sukkos*, the animal sacrifices diminished in number. On *Chanukah* the lights diminished in number, according to the school of Shammai.

The Little Flames

The flame in the *Chanukah menorah* is so small, so simple. Only one little candle, one drop of oil, fulfills the *mitzvah* of kindling the *Chanukah* light. In the simplicity of fulfilling the *mitzvah* of kindling the *Chanukah* lights, there is great profundity. Each night we increase the number, one, two, three, four, five, six, seven, eight. Each night, as we increase the candles or oil, the light from the flames increases and illuminates the darkness.

We place the *menorah* in the window, facing the dark street, or in the doorway of the hall, so passersby can see the reflection of the little lights in the darkness. The Jewish people are confident that real life is reflected in the light of the *menorah* and in what the *menorah* represents; they set it in a place in their home that can be seen by the people in the street.

The *Chanukah* light can shine into the darkest corners of the soul. As the lights burn, it is a custom to do no work, for these precious moments are an opportunity for individual introspection:

Who am I?
Where do I belong in the scheme of creation?

How can I introduce the light of truth to a world that is filled
   with so much darkness?

What can I do to make certain the glow of the little flames in
   the *Chanukah menorah* continues to grow stronger and
   brighter?

Stories

The Light of a Small Candle Shines in Valley Forge

The number of Jews who migrated to American shores in pre-revolutionary times was very small. Yet most of those Jews joined in the fight for freedom against Britain and fought on the side of the Continental Army in the war for American independence.

I remember that difficult winter well. It was December 1777. Shortages of food, inadequate clothing, and raging illness caused untold suffering and tremendous hardship for the troops loyal to General George Washington and the revolutionary cause.

In the winter quarters at Valley Forge, the troops sat and waited for an extra blanket or for a crust of bread. They sat and wondered whether General Washington would be able to force a British retreat. Morale was low.

I never doubted the outcome of the war, for men have always struggled against tyranny in the cause of justice. My father had told me about his personal struggle against tyranny, how he fled religious persecution in Germany and migrated to the American colonies, how he hoped to build a new life in the new world.

When I joined the Continental Army two years ago, he gave me a *Chanukah menorah* and candles. I remember him telling me, "These candles are a symbol of man's struggle against tyranny. Light them each *Chanukah*. They will direct you toward the path of freedom."

I carried the *menorah* and the candles in my knapsack wherever I went.

Tonight was the first night of *Chanukah*. I removed the *Chanukah menorah* from my knapsack and walked away from where my comrades sat. I wanted to be alone when I lit my *Chanukah menorah*. I placed the *menorah* in the center of a small mound of snow. I inserted one candle and the *shamash* (candle used to light the other candles). I struck my one remaining flint, lit the *shamash* and the first candle, and recited the blessings. Tears welled up in my eyes as I imagined my father lighting his *Chanukah menorah* in front of the parlor window in our New York apartment.

I sat down in the snow to watch the little flickering lights. From time to time, I cupped my hands over the flames, protecting them from the wind.

Suddenly, I felt that I was not alone. A man was standing over me. I looked up and recognized General George Washington. He spoke softly. "Soldier, are you lost? Why are you so far away from your comrades? I noticed the flickering lights of your candles, and I walked over here to see if you were in any kind of trouble. Why did you light two candles so far from the campsite?"

I could hardly speak. I hastily jumped to my feet. General Washington waited patiently for me to organize my thoughts.

"I am a Jew," I began haltingly. "Tonight is the first night of *Chanukah*, our festival of freedom. *Chanukah* celebrates the Maccabean victory over Greek tyranny more than eighteen hundred years ago. When I joined the Continental Army, my father gave me this *Chanukah menorah*. He told me to light the candles, that they would help me remember the cause of freedom. I wanted to be alone when I lit the candles, so I walked away from the campsite. I know that your soldiers will also win their freedom, just as my people did long ago. I hope that we will build a new land together.''

I could distinguish a smile on General Washington's face in the soft glow of the candlelight. He stood with me for a few minutes, watching the reflection of the nearly extinguished candles. When the flames died out, he shook my hand and walked away. I sat down again near the mound of snow and remained there for a long time that night.

When the Revolutionary War ended, General George Washington was chosen to be the first president of the United States. I was certain that he forgot the incident of the *Chanukah* lights at Valley Forge, but it was imprinted in my memory forever.

As years passed, I settled on Stone Street, adjacent to the Dock and South wards facing the East River. Each year during *Chanukah* I placed my *menorah* on the front windowsill, as I remembered my father had always done. The glow of the candles was noticed by all passersby.

One *Chanukah* night, I answered a knock at my door and found President Washington standing in the entranceway. For the second time, I could hardly speak. President Washington did not wait for me to organize my thoughts. He initiated the conversation. ''I was riding this way, and I saw your *Chanukah* lights bringing hope to all passersby. I remembered the *Chanukah* lights at Valley Forge, and I recalled your inspiring words. I took a chance by knocking on this door, hoping that you were the soldier who had inspired me. I have been searching for you all these years. I am glad that I found you, for I have carried this Medal of Honor with me. Please accept it as a symbol of my thanks.''

I extended my hand and accepted the box with the special Medal of Honor. Inside the box lay a small, engraved *Chanukah* *menorah* with the words, ''Thank you for the light of a small candle.''

A *Mitzvah* Gives Life

Rebbe Areleh Roth was the son of a poor tailor who grew up in chasidic circles, in Satmar, Hungary, around the turn of the last century. He realized that the *chasidim* with whom he studied and prayed were not the kinds of *chasidim* whom the Baal Shem Tov envisioned when he founded the chasidic movement. The Baal Shem Tov taught, "When joy reigns within the body of an individual, it also brings joy to the soul, for sadness is the greatest impediment to one's service of His Creator."[1]

In the *shtibels* (small, simple *shtetl shuls*) where Areleh prayed, the service was decorous, but it did not fulfill his dreams or the visions of the Baal Shem Tov, so he decided to form his own *shtibel,* his own *minyan.*

The service was prayed intently, with complete attention to the nuances of every word, and with joy. Sometimes, the *Shabbos* morning service lasted until four o'clock in the afternoon. It was an "experience" to pray with Rebbe Areleh Roth and his *chasidim.*

[1]*Moray Hadoros. Last Testament of the Besht.*

He made *aliyah* (immigrated to *Eretz Yisrael*) in 1939 and settled in the Meah She'arim section of Jerusalem. There he taught his philosophy of Judaism, "Blessed be He and Praised be He for crowning the Jewish people with *mitzvos*," for twenty years, until he was seventy-five years old.

As he aged, his strength ebbed. He grew weaker and weaker until finally he was confined to his bed. His family and disciples thought he was dying, so they gathered at his bedside and remained with him continuously.

It was the first night of *Chanukah*. Rebbe Areleh Roth's family and disciples were concerned about him. One disciple asked, "Rebbe, could I possibly do anything to make you more comfortable?"

Rebbe Areleh answered, "Please, just lift my head a little from this pillow." It seemed that Rebbe Areleh became a bit stronger after his disciple had fulfilled his request, so another disciple was encouraged to ask, "What more can I do for you, Rebbe?"

"Please, help me sit up," requested Rebbe Areleh. Soon, Rebbe Areleh was sitting, then his feet hung over the edge of the bed, then he motioned to two disciples to help him stand. Gradually he inched along, faltering, but each step he took made him stronger because he wanted desperately to light the *Chanukah menorah* one more time before he died. Finally he reached the table in front of the window where the *Chanukah menorah* was prepared and he stood up, ready to fulfill the *mitzvah* of lighting the *Chanukah* candles.

Rebbe Areleh hummed a soft melody, preparing to kindle the lights. He paused and whispered, "Maybe I won't even be able to finish reciting the first word of the blessing." A disciple struck a match to the *shamash*. Rebbe Areleh began, weakly, "*Baruch!*" He felt a little stronger. "Maybe, I can manage the second word," he uttered. "*Atah.*" With each word, Rebbe Areleh felt a little bit stronger.

He whispered the third word, "*Adonai*," and he grew stronger and stronger with the recitation of each word of the blessing. "*Eloheinu melech ha'olam*" echoed in the silent room.

"*Asher kiddeshanu b'mitzvosav v'tzevanu*" resounded joyfully. Then Rebbe Areleh shouted, "*L'hadlik ner shel Chanukah.*" With each word of the blessing Rebbe Areleh felt stronger
and stronger. The *Chanukah* lights restored his soul.

He felt so strong that he began to dance around the *Chanukah menorah.* After the first hour, Rebbe Areleh paused and
said, "Everything I have ever taught you about *Chanukah* and
the kindling of the lights is true, namely, that the lighting of the
menorah is not just to commemorate the Maccabean victory.
The commandment rekindles the light in the soul of each Jew
and literally restores life."

Rebbe Areleh danced that first night of *Chanukah* for eight
hours. He was blessed to live another ten years.

My Father's *Tefillin*

Tefillin are holy. They are precious when they are used by a holy master. Can you imagine how precious the *tefillin* of the *maggid* of Mezeritch were?[1]

The *maggid's tefillin* were inherited by his son, Rebbe Avraham the Malach, who passed them down to his son, Rebbe Shalom Schachna, who passed down the precious *tefillin* to Rebbe Yisrael Rizhiner, the first of the chasidic rebbes to live like royalty.

When Rebbe Yisrael Rizhiner passed away, his sons gathered to divide his wordly possessions. As they were sitting around a table, trying to decide how to proceed, Rebbe Moshe David, one of the brothers, said, "I relinquish my rights to any of our father's possessions that may fall into my hands. I only want to inherit his *tefillin,* which were passed down from our grandfather and our great-grandfather."

Upon hearing this, the brothers decided to cast lots to divide their father's possessions, because each of the brothers desired

[1]Rebbe Dov Ber, the *maggid* of Mezeritch, succeeded Rebbe Yisrael ben Eliezer, the Baal Shem Tov, the founder of the chasidic movement.

the *tefillin* in addition to other possessions. Rebbe Moshe David was the winner, and the other brothers realized that he was the most deserving to inherit their father's *tefillin*.

Afterward, the brothers moved to different *shtetlach* and formed separate chasidic communities. Rebbe Moshe David moved to Putik, Rebbe Avraham Yaakov moved to Sadagura, and the others went their own ways.

Two years passed. Rebbe Avraham Yaakov of Sadagura had just finished kindling the *Chanukah* lights. He sat down at a table and beckoned his students to join him. He began discoursing on the deliverance of the Jewish people from their enemies and the miraculous rededication of the Holy Temple. He rambled on a bit and then said something unconnected to his theme. "I'm envious of my brother, Moshe David," he said, "because he has the privilege of donning my father's *tefillin* every day."

Two students exchanged glances, and their faces paled when they heard Rebbe Avraham Yaakov's rambling. They did not know whether to speak or to remain silent. Finally, without waiting for Rebbe Avraham Yaakov to finish his thought, one of them interrupted and confessed in a trembling voice, "We did what we did because of our devotion to you."

Rebbe Avraham Yaakov's curiosity was aroused. "What did you do?" he asked.

"One night," the student said, "we went to your brother's house, crept stealthily into his study room, and found his *tefillin*. We removed the original *parsheyos*[1] from the *batim*,[3] replaced them with different *parsheyos*, sewed the *batim* back together, and hid the original *parsheyos* until we had the opportunity to give them to you. No one saw us. Here are the original *parsheyos* from your father's *tefillin*." He laid them on the table.

The other students couldn't believe what they saw. One exclaimed, "How could Rebbe Moshe David not know that the

[2]*Parsheyos* — the parchment upon which four sections of the *Torah* are inscribed and inserted into the black boxes of the *tefillin*.
[3]*Batim* — the outer black boxes of the *tefillin*.

parsheyos in his *tefillin* are not the original *parsheyos* from the *tefillin* of the *maggid* of Mezeritch?"

Another snorted, "If he doesn't know that there is something wrong with his *tefillin*, then he doesn't deserve the privilege of donning the *maggid's tefillin* every day!"

A third shouted over the confusion, "How did you two have the nerve to remove the original *parsheyos* and replace them, anyway?"

A fourth noticed Rebbe Avraham Yaakov's reaction. "Quiet," he hissed, raising his hand for silence. "Quiet!"

Rebbe Avraham Yaakov had gently lifted the *parsheyos* from the table, examined them carefully, kissed them, and wrapped them in a handkerchief. He said, "Please don't discuss anything that you have seen or heard here tonight. After *Chanukah* we will visit my brother Rebbe Moshe David in Putik."

After *Chanukah*, Rebbe Avraham Yaakov gathered all the people who witnessed the confession, and they set out for Putik. When they arrived, Rebbe Moshe David greeted the travelers warmly, even though he was surprised by their sudden, unannounced visit.

Rebbe Moshe David made his guests comfortable and then asked his brother Rebbe Avraham Yaakov to join him in a special room for the afternoon prayer service.

The next morning, when Rebbe Avraham Yaakov entered that same room, he noticed three pairs of *tefillin* spread out on a table. Among the three pairs were the *tefillin* from his great-great-grandfather, the *maggid* of Mezeritch.

Rebbe Moshe David picked them up, began to wrap himself in them, but then removed them. He donned another pair of *tefillin* and prayed the morning prayers. Afterwards, Rebbe Avraham Yaakov asked his brother why he did not pray wrapped in his great-grandfather's *tefillin*.

Rebbe Moshe David answered, "From time to time, I try to don those *tefillin* that were an inheritance from our father, but somehow I don't feel their holiness. It must be that I am not worthy to use them." Upon uttering these words, tears formed in Rebbe Avraham Yaakov's eyes.

Rebbe Avraham Yaakov gulped and stuttered. "My precious brother," he said, "please don't suspect yourself of being unworthy. You don't feel the holiness of the *tefillin* because the original *parsheyos* have been removed. Here, I have brought them to you."

Rebbe Moshe David didn't ask any questions. He took the *parsheyos,* inserted them into the *batim* after removing the other *parsheyos,* and sewed up the *batim*. From then on, he used those *tefillin* daily, locking them up in a secret hiding place each morning after he finished praying.

When Rebbe Moshe David passed away, the precious *tefillin* were inherited by his son, Rebbe Yisrael. Rebbe Yisrael moved to Tshortikov.

Years elapsed, and World War I engulfed central Europe. The people of Tshortikov fled to Vienna. Among the refugees were Rebbe Yisrael and his family. In the haste of their departure, Rebbe Yisrael left all his possessions behind, including the precious *tefillin*. As soon as the rebbe and his family had escaped the city, the enemy entered his house, searched for valuables, removed them, shredded the furniture, and set the house ablaze. Each house in the village was set ablaze in turn. Looking back, Rebbe Yisrael saw his village consumed in fire.

Rebbe Yisrael thought that he would have to remain in Vienna only a short time, but the war dragged on for four years.

When peace was restored, Rebbe Yisrael sent a trusted disciple to Tshortikov to investigate the possibility of returning to his home. He also beseeched him to try to locate the precious *tefillin* in the ruins of his house.

The disciple spent two despairing weeks in Tshortikov, trying to find Jews who had survived the conflagration, searching through the ruins for the precious *tefillin*.

When he returned to Vienna and told Rebbe Yisrael that the village had become a heap of ashes, the rebbe said, "Bricks and trees burn, but the *tefillin* of my great-grandfather do not burn. I will never give up the hope of having them returned to me."

One day a Russian Jewish soldier, bedraggled and dirty, entered the anteroom of the rebbe's home. The rebbe's *gabbai* (appointment secretary) asked how he could be of help. The soldier answered, "I have to see the rebbe immediately." The *gabbai* looked at the soldier and told him that the rebbe had set hours for receiving guests and asked him to return later that day. The soldier was insistent upon seeing the rebbe that moment, so the *gabbai* asked him to wait, entered the rebbe's study, and inquired what to do. The rebbe told the *gabbai* to send the soldier in immediately.

The soldier walked into the rebbe's study. He did not say a word. He simply opened his knapsack, removed a pouch containing a pair of *tefillin,* and placed them on the table.

Then he spoke. "I found these *tefillin* in the rebbe's house," he said, "and now I am performing the *mitzvah* of returning lost property."

The rebbe picked up the *tefillin* and kissed them, tears streaming down his cheeks. "I know," he said quietly, "that these *tefillin* were returned to me because of the merit of my holy forebears. Please, sit down and tell me how you happened to find them."

The soldier sat down and began to tell his story.

"I grew up in a village, not far from Tshortikov. My father used to take me there to celebrate holy days with the rebbe. When I was old enough, I was drafted into the army. I was stationed outside of Tshortikov. I saw the enemy plunder the village and set it ablaze. When the flames died out, I walked through the rubble. I went into the rebbe's house, walked from room to room, and cried at the total and utter destruction. Then I stopped short in my tracks, for I saw that the holy books in the rebbe's study were strewn all over but were intact. I began to search for something . . . anything . . . and I found these *tefillin.* I put them in my knapsack and decided to carry them with me wherever I went. I vowed that if I came back safely from the war, I would return these *tefillin* to their rightful owner. Shortly thereafter, I was captured by the enemy and placed in a prisoner-of-war camp. I did not see much fighting on the front. I guarded these *tefillin* carefully all the years of my incarceration. I believe I was saved because of these *tefillin.*"

Rebbe Yisrael sat, entranced by the story of his visitor. When the soldier finished his tale, the rebbe said, "You should know that these *tefillin* were once donned by my great-great-grandfather, the *maggid* of Mezeritch. Neither the hand of an enemy soldier nor fire could damage them in any way. You were especially chosen for this *mitzvah* of restoring lost property to its rightful owner. In the merit of your having fulfilled this deed, I bless you that the Almighty should further protect you and return you to your family in peace."

Rebbe Yisrael continued, "Please wait here while I go to the next room to bring you some money to purchase civilian clothes." He walked out of his study and was gone only a minute. When he returned, the soldier had disappeared. The rebbe sent the *gabbai* to look for the soldier. He sent his children to search the neighborhood and the marketplace. Two hours passed. Two days passed. They searched the synagogues. They searched the entire city of Vienna—in vain. No one ever saw the soldier again.

The rebbe realized that Elyahu Hanavi had returned his great-great-grandfather's *tefillin* in the disguise of a Russian Jewish soldier.

A Jew's Story

The Polish-Russian border proposed at the Paris Peace Conference in 1919 awarded large parts of eastern Poland to Russia. Poland insisted on the restoration of her 1772 borders.[1] War broke out between Poland and Russia. The war raged for two years, until Poland drove Russia out of her land. Part of the newly created Polish state was made up of ethnic minorities: Germans, Belorussians, Ukranians, Lithuanians, and Jews. The new Polish government treated the minority populations inequitably.

Those years were especially difficult for the Jews. The atmosphere was permeated with hatred and jealousy. Pogroms abounded. The Jews became the scapegoats for the ills of the Polish government. During these pogroms, the Jews hid behind bolted doors and sealed windows. They dared not wander outdoors, even in the daytime. While the opposing forces clashed, the commander-in-chief of the Polish army issued an order imposing a curfew on the civilian population. Not only did every

---

[1]Poland was partitioned by Russia, Austria, and Prussia in 1772.

man, woman, and child have to be indoors after dark, but no illumination of any type was permitted inside the houses.

The first night of *Chanukah* was rapidly approaching. Many Jews decided to disregard the ordinance in order to kindle the *Chanukah* lights. They considered the Almighty's *mitzvah* more important than the government's ordinance.

Tears flowed freely down the cheeks of those Jews who turned a ritual of joy into a mortal risk. Yet, throughout the *shtetlach,* the flames of the little candles flickered without anyone noticing.

One Jew, however, lived on the outskirts of a *shtetl* near the border. He, too, was aware of the ordinance. He, too, decided to disregard it. After dark, he set his *menorah* on his windowsill. He inserted one candle and the *shamash* into their places. He struck a match and kindled the first candle. Basking in the light of the small flame, he hummed a *Chanukah* melody. Then he sat down at his kitchen table to study.

A Polish lieutenant happened to pass the little house on the outskirts of the *shtetl.* He was in charge of guarding the area from enemy infiltration. He noticed the flickering light. He burst into the little house and shouted charges at the Jew, accusing him of signaling messages to the enemy camped nearby. He shackled the Jew and dragged him to the temporary barracks that served as a military prison. Sneeringly, he yelled, "You will be brought before the military court and charged with treason. You will be sentenced to death!"

News of the Jew's arrest spread swiftly through the *shtetl.* The next morning, a mob gathered outside the barracks to watch the trial of the Jew and to jeer at his execution.

It was difficult for the general to maintain order inside. The mob pushed and shoved, taunting voices pitched in a screaming crescendo, "Shame on the Jew! Shame on the Jew! Death to the Jews! They are all traitors." Soldiers and police, untrained in crowd control, lashed out with whips at the unruly mob, trying to maintain order.

Inside the makeshift courtroom, the general arose and announced, "It is the judgment of this court that you have betrayed your beloved fatherland by signaling the enemy with the light of a flickering candle. I condemn you to death for treason. You will be taken immediately to the place of execution and shot."

Two soldiers grabbed the prisoner. Five policemen walked in front of him, five, behind, trying to push the mob aside. The mob ranted and raved, spitting, cursing. The Jews of the village hid, fearing for their lives, praying that another pogrom would not follow the execution of their brother. They knew they were powerless to help.

When they reached the village square, the place of execution, the general raised his hand for silence. The mob simmered down. He repeated the charges. "You have been sentenced to death for treason, for betraying your beloved fatherland. The candle you lit on your windowsill revealed to the enemy our position. You have endangered this entire area. Prepare yourself for death!"

The Jew was pulled against a wall and blindfolded. A young recruit was handed a rifle. It was clear that he was agitated. He had never pulled the trigger before. He crossed himself, kneeled, and cocked the rifle, ready to shoot. He waited for the command to fire.

Suddenly, galloping horses were heard approaching the village square. Faces turned toward the oncoming horses. Proudly astride the lead horse rode the commander-in-chief of the area's military forces. He was gesticulating wildly, shouting at the top of his voice, "Wait! Wait! I have brought you two more Jews from a neighboring village!"

The bloodthirsty mob became silent. They thought they would witness the execution of three Jews.

The commander-in-chief raised his hand. He turned toward the two Jews who sat shivering astride a single horse. "Jews," he demanded, "did you disregard the government's ordinance and kindle lights in your windows last night?"

One of the Jews meekly opened his mouth to speak. He whispered, "Yes, I kindled a light in my window last night."

"Why did you do this?" demanded the commander-in-chief. "You knew that it was completely contrary to the blackout order that was imposed on this area for the protection of its citizens."

The Jew began to stutter, "Please, let me tell you my story. We have a very important commandment to observe at this time of the year. In order to remember the miraculous deliverance of our forefathers from the Syrian tyrant King Antiochus, to recall the victory of a few Jews over the mighty Syrian army, and to celebrate the rekindling of the light in the defiled Holy Temple that stood in Jerusalem, we kindle lights, adding one each night for eight nights."

"When were these battles?" the commander-in-chief asked.

"These battles were fought more than two thousand years ago," replied the Jew, dropping his voice.

The commander-in-chief was clearly agitated. In a shaking voice, he asked, "Do you know that the miracle did not only happen to your forefathers? Let me explain what I mean. Last night another miracle occurred. My troops and I were surrounded by the enemy. There was barely any moonlight. We could not see anything ahead of us. The terrain is very unfamiliar. We feared we would be trapped. Then we saw two lights twinkling from the windows of your homes. The reflection of those two lights in the darkness guided our steps. We were able to extricate ourselves from the enemies' trap. Thanks to you and your *Chanukah* lights, our lives were saved."

The three Jews were released from their shackles. Although the bloodthirsty mob was disappointed, the decent citizens of both villages rejoiced over the modern miracle of the little *Chanukah* lights.

The Fiddler

He looked like a chasidic rebbe, outfitted with black hat and coat, surrounded by loyal disciples. The only difference between a chasidic rebbe and himself was the black fiddle case he carried with him whenever he traveled. He was never seen without his fiddle; it was always in one hand, his *tallis* and *tefillin* in the other. People affectionately called him "Shlomo the rebbe, the fiddler."

When he was certain that his hiding place was out of the enemy's range, he played his fiddle and sang melodies of joy that echoed through the trees of the forest. His music lifted the heavy hearts of those partisans who hid from the Nazi beast. He was the leader of a group of brave guerrilla fighters, staked out in the forest, fleeing from cave to cave, trying to hinder the advancement of the enemy.

Many of their raids were successful. They had captured blankets and clothing to shield them from the approaching winter's cold, food to sustain their bodies, ammunition to maintain a campaign of sporadic harassment against the enemy, and unity of purpose that kept them from sinking into despair.

Then another partisan group joined Rebbe Shlomo's group. Their leader was Yosel. At first Rebbe Shlomo was very happy that another Jewish partisan group had joined his, but his happiness was short-lived, for Yosel's personality was opposite his own. Yosel was hot-tempered, excitable, usually grim, and almost always cross. Often the two groups were at odds with each other. Rebbe Shlomo exerted tremendous energy trying to keep peace between them.

One night, about two weeks before *Chanukah,* Rebbe Shlomo summoned every partisan to an urgent planning meeting. When they had gathered in the largest cave in their part of the forest, he did not waste time with formalities. Rather, he began speaking. "Our numbers have grown larger," he said. "We are in short supply of food, clothing, blankets, and ammunition. I propose that two of you join me in the very dangerous mission of trying to round up supplies. I'm asking for two volunteers to go with me to infiltrate Nazi territory. Maybe we can get close enough to pilfer adequate supplies to help us survive the oncoming winter months."

Immediately, every hand shot up. Shlomo hushed the commotion of everyone arguing over who should accompany him. Some of the partisans even wanted him to remain in hiding.

"You are too important a leader," they agreed. "You remain here, and we will go. We know that if, God forbid, you are caught, the Nazis will torture you to take revenge on all the partisans."

But Shlomo refused to heed their plea.

"No," he insisted, "I am the leader, and I will lead this mission."

The partisans knew they would not be able to convince him to remain in the forest. He put his arms around two friends, as if signaling them that they were the ones he wanted to accompany him.

Rebbe Shlomo opened his fiddle case. He tuned the strings, plucked a *Chanukah* melody, and whispered, "Before I leave, I will play *Ma'oz Tzur* (*Rock of Ages,* a *Chanukah* song) for you. When I leave, I want you to continue singing. Sing it until *Chanukah.* Every time you sing, I want you to remember my prom-

ise: I will return in time to kindle the first *Chanukah* light."
Shlomo played *Ma'oz Tzur* three times, then put his fiddle back
in its case, motioned to his two friends, and disappeared with
them into the night.

The next morning, Yosel called a meeting of the remaining
partisans. He lost no time with formalities.

"If you ask me," he said loudly, grimacing, "Shlomo is
never going to return. He has left us here to die of cold and starva-
tion. I know. Had he planned on returning, he would not have
taken his fiddle with him!"

Anger and surprise overcame Shlomo's loyal friends. When
they recovered from their shock, they proclaimed together,
"Shlomo always carries his fiddle with him! He does marvelous
things with that fiddle. You have only been with us a short while.
You could not possibly know what Shlomo does with his fiddle.
The best thing you can do is sit quietly, keep your mouth shut,
and wait patiently for him to return!"

"That is all idle talk," sneered Yosel. "I can't stick around
here any longer. I am going to follow Shlomo's tracks. Who
wants to come with me?"

Immediately, Yosel's friends moved to his side. Yaaki, who
was from Shlomo's group, pleaded, "If you leave, you are acting
irresponsibly. You will be endangering all the partisans hiding in
this forest. Please be patient and wait out the two weeks until
Chanukah. Shlomo promised to return in time to kindle the first
Chanukah light. I know he will keep his promise."

But Yosel could not be persuaded. He motioned to his
friends, and they left.

Four days passed; the partisans remained hidden in the
cave. On the fifth day, around noontime, the calm broke. Breathless, dirty, with dried blood on his arms, one of Yosel's friends
fell exhausted at the cave's entrance. One of the partisans carried him deep inside the cave to safety and revived him with
water.

"I don't know where to begin," he blurted out. "Yosel and I
followed Shlomo's trail to an inn. The next day, we watched from
outside the frost-covered windows. Sitting inside, half drunk,

was a batallion of Nazi soldiers. Standing on one of the tables, Shlomo fiddled and danced, leading the merriment, encouraging them to drink." He paused, then continued in a sullen tone. "Now do you believe that Shlomo will never return?"

The partisans did not speak. Yaaki answered, "Indeed, you bring us a strange story, but you only saw one side. I am certain that Shlomo will return. I am also convinced that he will be able to explain his actions. He has risked his life so many times for us. He will return to kindle the first *Chanukah* light." Yaaki lowered his voice. "By the way," he asked, "where is your leader Yosel?"

"I really don't know," he replied. "The last time we were together, we were running from a Nazi scouting party, and we each fled in a different direction. We had succeeded in stealing some food. We were carrying it in a sack. When the scouting party sighted us, we dropped the sack and fled."

Yaaki was no longer calm. "What if you did not cover your tracks?"he demanded. "What if the Nazi scouting party followed you here? They will discover the cave that has provided sanctuary for us for a long time. I promised Shlomo we would not move. Now, we might no longer be safe here!"

Suddenly, footsteps echoed through the cave, nearer and nearer. Yaaki was the first one to recognize the intruder as one of the two friends who had accompanied Rebbe Shlomo.

"I returned temporarily, with a message from Shlomo. He found out how stupidly Yosel acted. He told me to tell you that you are all in grave danger. He wants you to head for the Hungarian border immediately. There," he said, "you should find another cave, large enough to accommodate all of you. He also wanted me to repeat his promise: he will return in time to kindle the first *Chanukah* light with you." Then he disappeared.

It was very difficult to move a group of people and their remaining meager supplies through the forest undetected. They were forced to outwit Nazi scouting parties and sniffing hound dogs. Carefully, checking to make certain that they left no trail, they reached the Hungarian border three days before *Chanukah*. They found another hiding place and settled in to await Shlomo's arrival. The days dragged on. To keep their spirits from wavering, Yaaki insisted they sing *Ma'oz Tzur* every time they gathered to pray or to eat.

On the eve of *Chanukah,* Yaaki asked for a volunteer to go out in search of Shlomo. Without hesitating, Moshe immediately took his rifle in hand and set out. Daring to climb the hills in the clearings, Moshe peered into the distance. Searching for Shlomo's silhouette, he was alarmed by what he saw and fled back to the shelter immediately.

"We are doomed," Moshe shouted breathlessly. "A battalion of Nazis and bloodthirsty hunting dogs are approaching— closing in on us—not five kilometers from here." He sank down on the ground in despair.

Yaaki shouted, "We will not sit back and worry. We will survive! We will fight with every ounce of strength. We will kindle the *Chanukah* candles tonight."

The sound of the barking dogs grew nearer. The partisans prayed and aimed their rifles, waiting.

Suddenly, amidst the sound of the barking dogs, a tune from Shlomo's fiddle was audible. There were trumpets, shouting, barking, commotion, and merriment fading in the background, growing fainter and fainter. Then all that could be heard was the sound of Shlomo's fiddle.

The faith of the partisans hung between hope and despair. Was this a trap? Had Shlomo betrayed them? Was he leading the Nazis to their new hiding place? Unable to move, they waited.

Then Shlomo's *Chanukah* melody echoed from the strings of his fiddle. Ten minutes later, he appeared in the clearing, followed by his two friends.

The partisans rushed to him, puzzled.

"Later, I'll explain," he said. "Now it is time to kindle the first *Chanukah* light."

The flame of that first little candle restored their hope. The melody that echoed from Shlomo's fiddle lifted their heavy hearts.

The flame of the first *Chanukah* candle flickered its shadow across the wall of the cave. The partisans were sitting around Rebbe Shlomo.

"Now," he began, "I will tell you what happened. We were on our way back when we ran into a Nazi battalion. We had to keep cool. I hid our sacks of supplies in the bushes, undetected. Then we continued to amble along our path, pretending innocence. While we ambled, I played my fiddle. The Nazi battalion was the same one I had entertained in an inn two weeks ago. Then, they danced, drank, and made merry to the sound of my music. They wanted a repeat performance in the forest. So I played. The more I played, the more they danced, the more they drank, the more tired they became. Soon they were all dead drunk, dropping along the roadside, one by one, to sleep it off. When the last one dropped, we backtracked, picked up our sacks of supplies, and ran to find you. I promised you I would return in time to kindle the first *Chanukah* light with you." Shlomo paused, removed his fiddle from its case, tuned up the strings, and started *Ma'oz Tzur*. The partisans silently thanked God for the miracle that happened, not only to their forefathers, but to them as well.

Purim

Purim commemorates a historical event that occurred in the Diaspora and affected Jews dispersed throughout the known world of that time. After the destruction of the first Holy Temple, the Jewish people were driven into exile by their Babylonian conquerors. Soon after, the Babylonians were conquered by the Persians. During the seventy years of the exile, before the rebuilding of the second Holy Temple, they were threatened with total annihilation by Haman, prime minister to the Persian King Achashverosh. Haman had persuaded the king that the Jewish people were no asset to his nation. "There is a certain people scattered abroad and dispersed among your provinces. Their laws are different from other peoples'. They do not observe even the king's laws; therefore it is not befitting the king to tolerate them."[1]

Lots were drawn to choose the day of annihilation, followed by a decree circulated throughout the empire.

Unbeknown to both Haman and King Achashverosh, Queen Esther was Jewish. Under the influence of her uncle Mordechai, leader of the Jews living in Shushan, the capital city, Esther pleaded before the king for her people. Haman's plot to destroy the Jewish people was exposed, and he was hanged. The decree of annihilation was rescinded. Esther and Mordechai proceeded to write the facts of the miraculous deliverance of their people for posterity in a scroll, called *megillas Esther*. *Purim*, meaning lots, is celebrated on the fourteenth day of *Adar* each year.

The ceremonies of *Purim* include: *Ta'anis Esther*, a fast day commemorating Esther's fast as she prepared to plead for her people before King Achashverosh; reading the *megillah*—

---

[1]*Megillas Esther* 3:8.

the story of *Purim*—twice, on the evening of *Purim* and in the morning; *matanos l'evyonim*, distributing charity to the poor; *shalach manos*, sending two gifts of food to a friend; *seudas Purim*, sharing a festive meal with family and friends.

The *gragger*, a noisemaker, stamps out the name of Haman during the reading of the *megillah*, a reminder of the *Torah* injunction to erase evil from the world.

The most popular food during *Purim* is *hamantaschen* (Haman's pockets), a three-cornered, filled pastry.

Torah Thoughts

The Symbolism of Wine
for *Purim*

Most of our festival meals begin with *kiddush,* the sanctification of wine. During the Passover *seder,* we drink four cups of wine. Yet, it is only on *Purim* that "a man mellows himself with wine until he cannot tell the difference between 'cursed be Haman' and 'blessed be Mordechai.' "[1]

The association of *Purim* merriment with drinking begins with wine imagery in *Megillas Esther* (the Scroll of Esther).

> On the seventh day, when the heart of the King was merry with wine, he ordered . . . the seven chamberlains . . . to bring Queen Vashti before him.[2]
>
> The King and Haman sat down to drink.[3]
>
> So the King and Haman came to feast with Queen Esther.[4]

[1]Talmud, *Megillah* 7b.
[2]*Megillas Esther* 1:10.
[3]*Ibid.,* 3:16.
[4]*Ibid.,* 7:1.

They were to observe them as days of feasting and gladness.[5]

This wine imagery is used so many times that it must have symbolic significance. The wine imagery contrasts the profane and the holy.

King Achashverosh became intoxicated. His wife Vashti was degraded and executed. Achashverosh profaned the use of wine.

Mordechai and Esther decreed a feast of merriment and joy to celebrate the miraculous deliverance of the Jewish people. They sanctified the use of wine.

The contrast is obvious. In a profane, intoxicated state, one loses his inhibitions: secrets disappear, speech becomes imprudent, innermost thoughts are revealed, propriety is forgotten, evil decrees are promulgated, near tragedy occurs.

When wine is sanctified, the drinker has the opportunity to reflect on his innermost thoughts, to take stock of his actions, to discover his depth, to rise to that level of holiness that expresses gratitude to the Almighty "for the miracles wrought for our ancestors in days of old, and at this season."[6]

[5] *Ibid.*, 9:22.
[6] *Shehecheyanu.*

Shalach Manos

There are four *mitzvos* associated with the celebration of *Purim*: the reading of the *megillah* evening and morning, distribution of charity to the poor, a festival meal, and *shalach manos* (sending two gifts of food to a friend).

Three of the four commandments are practiced at other times in the Jewish calendar year, and they are not unique to *Purim*. There is one exception: we do not send *shalach manos* on any other holiday except *Purim*.

Why did Esther and Mordechai decree *shalach manos* as a unique observance of *Purim*?

The answer lies within the context of the story itself. As the story of the *megillah* unfolds, we read about the Jews wining and dining at a lavish party, hosted by King Achashverosh. Reading between the lines, commentators on the *megillah* point out that the level of Jewish religious commitment in Persia was so low that the Jews did not hesitate to feast in the court of a pagan king. Carefully following the plot of the story, we encounter the appearance of Haman, who threatens to annihilate the Jewish people. Toward the end of the story, the Jews are so thankful for their miraculous deliverance from their arch-enemy Haman, that "*kemu v'keblu,*"[1] they "confirmed and took on themselves and their posterity the laws and commandments that they had confirmed and undertaken at Sinai long before."[2]

This reaffirmation of the laws and principles of *Torah* is expressed in *shalach manos,* sending two gifts of food to a friend.

According to Rabbi Akiva,[3] the commandment to "love your neighbor as you love yourself"[4] is the fundamental principle and essence of *Torah.* Therefore we reaffirm our commitment to the fundamental principles of the *Torah* that we had undertaken at Sinai long before by sending *shalach manos* to a friend.

The concept of sending two types of food expresses the hope that love between human beings and commitment to the spiritual values of Jewish life will double, blossom, and flourish.

[1]*Megillas Esther* 9:22.
[2]Talmud, *Shabbos* 88a.
[3]*Midrash, Sifra, Kedoshim.*
[4]Leviticus 19:18.

The *Purim Se'udah*

Generally, the festive joy of *Shabbos* and the holidays is enhanced with a *se'udah* (a special meal) shared by family and friends. Yet, only on *Purim* is the *se'udah* considered one of the four required *mitzvos* of the day: reading the Scroll of Esther, sending two food items to a friend, gifts to the poor, and the *se'udah*.

The scroll of Esther itself provides a clue to our understanding of the importance of the *Purim se'udah* for the major episodes of the story in the *megillah* unfold through parties.

The first party takes place in the palace of the king in Shushan, the capital city: "In the third year of his reign (Achashverosh), he made a (lavish) feast for all his officials and servants."[1] The result of this party brought about the downfall of Queen Vashti.

The second party was celebrated in honor of the coronation of Esther, chosen to replace Vashti as queen of the mighty Persian empire: "And the king loved Esther . . . and she found favor

---

[1]*Megillas Esther* 1:3.

with him . . . so he set the royal crown upon her head. . . . Then the king made a great feast . . . the feast of Esther.[2]

Esther's elevation to the throne brings Mordechai and the Jews into sharp focus, for Mordechai stations himself outside the gates of the palace and incurs Haman's fury for refusing to bow down to him. Now it is up to Esther to plan another party to trap Haman: "And Esther said to the king: if it pleases the king, let the king and Haman come today to the banquet that I have prepared. . . ."[3] Esther's party is indeed successful, for it provides the proper atmosphere for her to petition the king to save her people from total annihilation.

After justice is meted out to Haman, Mordechai records the events for posterity: "And Mordechai recorded these events and sent letters to all the Jews throughout the provinces decreeing upon them to observe . . . the days on which they gained relief from their enemies . . . the month which had been transformed for them from one of sorrow to gladness, from mourning to festivity. They were to observe them as days of feasting and gladness."[4]

Now it is apparent why the emphasis of the *mitzvos* of *Purim* revolves around the *se'udah*: through the feasts, the imminent suffering was transformed to joy, mourning to a holiday.

Mordechai and Esther recorded the saga of their people and the celebration which followed for all future generations. Why were they so insistent that *Purim* be commemorated for all future generations?

Mordechai and Esther had prophetic vision.[5] They knew that "even if all the festivals should be annulled, *Purim* would never be annulled."[6]

Therefore they wrote into the *megillah* the four *mitzvos* by which we celebrate *Purim*, emphasizing the *se'udah*, because the real celebration of *Purim* is in the *se'udah*. Reading the *me-*

[2]*Megillas Esther* 2:17, 18.
[3]*Megillas Esther* 5:4.
[4]*Megillas Esther* 9:20–22.
[5]Talmud, *Megillah* 7a.
[6]*Midrash Mishlay* 10.

gillah retells the story of the miraculous deliverance of our people from the threat of total annihilation; exchanging *shalach manos* and gifts to the poor reminds us of our love for mankind. Only the *se'udah* emphasizes that *Purim* is the festival of transformation. The banquets in the *megillah* symbolize the tragedy that could have befallen the Jewish people. Therefore, we celebrate *Purim* with a *se'udah* that symbolizes the transformation from suffering to joy. However, the redemption in Shushan was temporary. Each year, we partake of the *se'udah* with faith in the ultimate redemption.

Stories

The Jewish People Had Light, Gladness, Joy, and Honor

The town of Worms, in the Franco-Germanic lands, was typical of towns during the Middle Ages. It was ruled by a feudal lord, in this case Duke Adolphus. He was crueler, more vicious, and more hateful than any duke who had preceded him. He ruled Worms with an iron fist; no one dared challenge his word. There was no recourse against his cruelty; robbing and plundering were facts of life, while heavy taxes guaranteed his control of his subjects. The miserable peasants who suffered under his thumb had no control over their lives.

The Jews of Worms were the object of severe persecution. Many of them provided essential services for the duke in their role as merchants. The duke hated them because he was dependent on them, yet he permitted them to live in his town, because no one else could supply him with the services he needed.

There was not much activity to keep him occupied in those days, so Duke Adolphus used to sit on his throne trying to figure out how to make people suffer. One day, while searching through his family records, he discovered that he was descended from the wicked Haman, the villain of the *Purim* story.

"Aha!" shouted Duke Adolphus gleefully. "Now I understand why I enjoy tormenting Jews. I think I will prohibit them from celebrating this coming *Purim*. After all, for fifteen hundred years they have celebrated the downfall of my great-great-grandfather. This year they won't do it! This year, I will prohibit the celebration of *Purim*! This year they will suffer!"

Duke Adolphus ordered his guards to the Jewish section of Worms. "Bring the elders of the Jewish community to the castle at once," he shouted.

They trembled as they entered the throne room. They could not imagine how their situation could be worse, what other form of suffering the cruel Adolphus could possibly inflict upon them. They were totally unprepared for his announcement.

"You Jews! You are the descendants of the people who were responsible for the downfall of my great-great-grandfather Haman, the honored prime minister of the mighty Persian Empire. Every year you celebrate his downfall with festivity and glee. This year you will not celebrate. You will not read the *megillah* publicly. You will not whirl your *graggers* (noisemakers) at the sound of my great-great-grandfather's name. You will not have your festive meal. I have called you here to inform you that I am abolishing the celebration of *Purim*. Any Jew who dares disobey my decree will be punished by death."

The elders of the Jewish community were stunned by this new decree. One of them dared speak. "Please, your honor," he pleaded, "we have celebrated *Purim* for fifteen hundred years. We celebrate to remember the miraculous deliverance of our people from total annihilation. *Purim* is one of the truly joyous festivals of the Jewish calendar year. We have so little occasion to celebrate. Please, do not impose this decree. Please, let us celebrate *Purim*."

Duke Adolphus' voice was high-pitched and uncontrolled. "You Jews have the audacity to challenge my decree! It is only out of the kindness and goodness of my heart that I permit you to live here. I won't change my mind. No amount of pleading will cause me to rescind this decree. You will not celebrate *Purim* anymore. This meeting has come to an end."

He lifted his hands, pointing them in the direction of the door.

The elders of the Jewish community sadly shuffled out of the throne room.

They returned to the synagogue, called for all the Jews to come for an important announcement, and informed them of Duke Adolphus' new decree.

The next day was *Ta'anis Esther*,[1] commemorating Esther's fast as she prepared herself to appear before King Achashverosh.

The Jews of Worms gathered in the synagogue to observe the fast day and to pray for mercy, but at nightfall they returned to their homes without the public reading of the *megillah*. The synagogue was dark, the door, bolted.

They gathered in small groups in a few private homes to chant the *megillah*. Rather than the usual joyful melody, they chanted the melody of Lamentations.[2]

Duke Adolphus went for a walk that night. He wanted to make sure that no Jew disobeyed his decree. When he saw the darkened synagogue, he gloated over his victory. He decided to celebrate with a lavish feast. Returning to his castle, he ordered preparations for a banquet the next day.

He invited his favorite nobles. The tables overflowed with meat and wine. They drank and drank. The nobles became boisterous, Adolphus, inebriated. He fell into a drunken stupor. Suddenly, he began screaming, "Help me! If you were truly my friends, you would help me."

The noise subsided as the nobles looked at each other. They had no idea what was troubling Adolphus. He became angrier and angrier. "Out cowards, out idiots," he shouted at them. "If you are not helping me, leave me alone!"

The nobles struggled to their feet and staggered out.

Adolphus was having a nightmare. A band of Jewish chil-

---

[1] *Ta'anis Esther*, a day of fasting, is observed on the day preceding *Purim*.
[2] Lamentations is read on *Tisha B'Av*, the national day of Jewish mourning.

dren was attacking him with *Purim graggers.* The noise was deafening, and his head was about to explode from the pain of the *graggers* beating down upon him. Mordechai walked at the head of the procession carrying the largest *gragger* Duke Adolphus had ever seen. Mordechai raised his *gragger,* about to strike Adolphus.

"Please, don't hit me, don't hit me. Tell me who you are. Tell me what you want!" screamed Duke Adolphus.

"I am Mordechai the Jew, you wicked man. I never bowed to your great-great-grandfather Haman because a Jew does not bow down. For this reason, your great-great-grandfather wanted to destroy my people, but he met his downfall just as all the enemies of Israel meet their downfall. Fifteen hundred years ago, I proclaimed the holiday of *Purim* for every future generation. Last night, my people could not read the *megillah* publicly because of your decree. Therefore, you shall be tongue-tied as a punishment for decreeing this proclamation against my people."

Duke Adolphus sat upright, startled. He was completely awake. "That was no nightmare! Mordechai is standing in front of me," he stammered. "Please, have compassion on me. I did not mean any harm against your people," he wailed.

"Hah! Compassion for such a wicked man! No compassion for the likes of you. Furthermore," Mordechai said as he lowered his voice, "if you want to save your life, you will immediately summon the elders of the Jewish community and inform them that you have decided to rescind your decree."

Mordechai and the band of children disappeared.

Duke Adolphus was terrified. He did not want to die. He did not want to stammer the rest of his life. He immediately summoned the elders of the Jewish community. They rushed to the castle, fearful that more decrees might be imposed.

"I have decided to rescind the decree against your celebrating *Purim,*" he stammered. "I know that the time has passed for you to publicly read the *megillah,* but I have no objection to your enjoying a *se'udah.*"

The elders looked at each other in disbelief. They breathed a sigh of relief, thanked him politely, and ran from the castle before he had a chance to change his mind. They wondered why he stammered, but no one bothered to ask.

Arriving back in the Jewish section of town, the elders shouted joyfully, "Duke Adolphus has rescinded his decree. We can have our *Purim se'udah!* We can celebrate *Purim!*"

Purim was celebrated that year in the Jewish community of Worms as it had never been celebrated before. "The Jewish people had light, gladness, joy, and honor,[3] so may we celebrate *Purim* in that spirit for all future generations."

---

[3]*Megillas Esther* 8:16.

Frankfort *Purim*, 1614

Frankfort-au-Main was an important commercial center and port in central Germany during the latter Middle Ages. It held fairs twice yearly and attracted both merchants and vendors from surrounding areas. It was also one of the sites of royal residences, and often it hosted coronation ceremony pageantries honoring emperors.

Frankfort-au-Main was one of the important centers of Jewish life during this historical time period. It had a central synagogue, a cemetery, a bath house, a house for migrants, a hospital, and a Jewish population of approximately three thousand. The rabbi of this community was the foremost religious authority in all of Germany.[1]

In 1462, a specially constructed section of the city was segregated as the Jewish neighborhood; it was called "the ghetto." It was surrounded by gates and walls. True, the ghetto walls kept the undesirable mobs out, but it also caused severe physical

[1]The head of the *yeshivah* in Frankfort-au-Main at this time was Rabbi Yaakov Schiff, father of Rabbi Mayer Schiff—the famous authority on Jewish law and author of commentaries on the Talmud.

hardship for the inhabitants, since there was no room for expansion. Growing families were forced to live in more crowded and dilapidated quarters.

Nevertheless, life inside the ghetto revolved around the intensity of talmudic learning and *Torah* observance. Scholars were esteemed and accorded the highest respect. The closely knit community provided a support system for both the joyous occasions and tragedies that are part of the ordinary life cycle. *Shabbos* and holidays were shared family events, and a wedding, *bris* (circumcision), *pidyon haben* (redemption ceremony of the first-born son), and *bar mitzvah* provided an opportunity for all the inhabitants of the ghetto to participate in the festivities. The Jews of Frankfort-au-Main adhered to the talmudic dictum, "Every Jew is responsible to care for every other Jew."[2]

Outside the ghetto, economic and social antagonism simmered between the wealthier non-Jewish guild craftsmen and petty traders, bakers, butchers, blacksmiths, and tailors, who were in debt to the Jewish merchants and money lenders living inside the ghetto. The Jewish merchants and bankers provided vital economic functions in a city that was a thriving commercial center. Thus, the emperor understood the importance of protecting his Jewish subjects, for he had imposed heavy taxes upon them. The tax money provided substantial financial revenues for his treasuries. Only if the emperor's Jews were protected could their revenues augment his treasury. He therefore placed the Jews under his private protectorship; they were considered the emperor's "private property." The Jews cooperated with the emperor simply because this arrangement provided a relatively secure place to live.

In 1612, Emperor Matthias ascended the throne. He chose Frankfort-au-Main to be the site of his coronation ceremony pageantry and notified the mayor of his decision. He assigned the mayor the task of chairing a committee empowered to arrange the coronation with great pomp and ceremony for the summer of 1614.

---

[2]Talmud, *Shavuos* 39a.

The mayor convened the first organizational meeting of the coronation committee. When he arose to speak, he discussed the honor bestowed upon Frankfort-au-Main by the emperor's choice for his coronation ceremony and the financial advantages as a result of hosting visiting royalty and dignitaries from surrounding territories. The members of the committee listened intently and nodded their heads in agreement.

Only one person disagreed. Vincenz Fettmilch, the head of the baker's guild, rose to his feet and shouted vehemently, "Benefit? Benefit for whom? Only the Jews will benefit from the money spent by the dignitaries and tourists who will crowd the city for the coronation ceremony pageantry."

Vincenz Fettmilch was a known anti-Semite, a recognized rabble rouser. He was always surrounded by a group of loyal followers. Most of the time they were drunk. Whenever they walked along the streets, people hid in fear, for they always attacked the weak and defenseless; it was their way of amusing themselves.

Sometimes, they broke into the ghetto, plundered the homes and shops, and assaulted the inhabitants. The police were too afraid to act against Fettmilch and his gang, even though they chanced the wrath of the emperor if harm were to befall his "protected" subjects. The Jews finally organized a self-defense unit that operated within the walls of the ghetto. When Fettmilch and his gang dared penetrate the ghetto, the defenders were ready to fight back. They surprised their attackers with a beating they would never forget. Fleeing the wrath of the ghetto defenders, Fettmilch vowed to take revenge when the opportunity presented itself.

Fettmilch haughtily continued his diatribe. "I will instruct my bakers not to participate in the preparations for the coronation ceremony pageantries!"

Commotion erupted in the room. The coronation committee members were thunderstruck. They began shouting at each other. "How can we make visiting royalty and dignitaries comfortable without bread and pastries?"

The mayor hammered his gavel to restore order. It was apparent that he would have to appease Fettmilch to gain his cooperation. He turned to the head of the baker's guild and asked him his price in exchange for his cooperation.

Fettmilch was prepared with his answer.

"The Jews," he screamed, "have too many privileges. They have taken away our ability to earn a livelihood. We have to pass laws to prohibit them from certain trades, crafts, and businesses. We have to raise the taxes on the profits of their merchants and bankers. We have to deny residence permits to other Jews who want to move into the ghetto. And since the ghetto is so over-crowded, we have to expel half of its population!"

The organization committee turned into a violent mob. The committee members joined Fettmilch in his demand to notify the emperor of their grievances against the Jews. They empha-sized how the Jewish presence in Frankfort-au-Main harmed the non-Jewish community.

In response to their demands, the emperor curtailed the "privileges" of the inhabitants of the ghetto and imposed an ad-ditional tax of fifteen hundred florins on each inhabitant for the privilege of remaining in the ghetto. But he worried that his ac-tions would diminish the revenues of his treasury.

Meantime, these measures did not appease Fettmilch. He incited other people to join him in his war of revenge against the Jews. Fettmilch's followers increased in number. When he thought he had enough henchmen, he ordered them to storm the ghetto. The Jews were totally unprepared to fight back. The en-tire ghetto was plundered. The synagogue was set afire. The in-habitants fled out of the ghetto for safety; most of them were murdered on the streets of Frankfort-au-Main. Those who es-caped fled empty-handed in the face of the enemy. Not one Jew remained!

Eventually, the news of the destruction of the Frankfort-au-Main ghetto reached the attention of the emperor. He was furious that his "private property" had been laid to waste. He investi-gated the circumstances and concluded that Fettmilch and his loyal followers were guilty of treason. He sent a special emissary to the mayor, demanding that Vincenz Fettmilch be arrested and brought before him in chains. The emperor sentenced this modern-day Haman to death on the day which corresponded to the twentieth day of the Hebrew month of *Adar*, six days after the festival of *Purim*.

The emperor asked the surviving Jews to return to their hometown. He promised them financial help in rebuilding their residences and businesses.

The Jews of Frankfort-au-Main set aside this day as a second *Purim*, "*Purim* Frankfort," commemorating the downfall of a modern-day Haman.

Happy Are We

One *Purim* the rebbe of Rizhin sat, preoccupied with thought, his eyes closed, his mind ten thousand miles away. The *chasidim* surrounding the rebbe were seated at banquet-laden tables, humming happy tunes, trying to lighten the mood, trying to get the rebbe to smile. Even Yossele Broder, the jester, who always succeeded in making the rebbe smile, who always brought joy and laughter to the court of Rizhin, could not change the rebbe's mood this particular day.

The *chasidim* were puzzled because they knew that the rebbe hated sadness. "A sad *chasid*," the rebbe always said, "represents the world of Satan: a joyous *chasid* brings the Divine Presence to this world."

So why wouldn't the rebbe smile? Especially on *Purim*? Especially on *Purim* when everyone laughs?

Usually, on *Purim*, when Yossele Broder arrived at the *Purim se'udah*, the rebbe would break into hearty, shrill laughter almost as soon as he saw him. The rebbe taught that raucous laughter, sarcasm, ridicule, and derision, while not being accepted Jewish values during the rest of the year, were permitted on *Purim.* On *Purim* the rebbe wanted to fool Satan, so he acted like him by laughing. If Satan thought that the Jewish people were like him, he would become confused and not be able to inflict evil upon them. The rebbe believed that on *Purim* a Jew had to laugh and drink wine until "he did not know the difference between cursing Haman and blessing Mordechai" in order to confuse Satan.

But this year was different. Nothing Yossele Broder did or said could bring a smile to the rebbe's face. The *chasidim* suspected that the only conceivable explanation for the rebbe's sadness was his knowledge of an impending evil decree being promulgated in Heaven against his people.

Yossele Broder gathered all his energy. He was determined to make the rebbe laugh. He put his hands on his hips, jumped into the air, and landed with all his weight in front of the rebbe. The rebbe was startled for a moment. He began to look around the room, trying to focus his attention on Yossele Broder and his *chasidim.*

Defiantly, Yossele Broder began to speak in a rather loud voice. "We are very disappointed with you, rebbe," he said. "Our lives are more difficult than the lives of any other *chasidim,* both in this world and in the world to come!"

Yossele Broder's nerve astonished the Rizhiner rebbe. Aghast, he demanded, "What do you mean?"

Yossele Broder knew he had the rebbe's attention. "I'll tell you what I mean," he said. "When one of the Ropshitzer *chasidim* used to visit their rebbe, he showed his happiness by extending him a warm reception. He talked to him kindly, hugged him, brought him closer to him. They sang and danced and ate together before the *chasid* departed for home. The Ropshitzer rebbe showed his *chasid* true joy. The joy that he derived from the rebbe's warmth made his life in this world very happy. After the *chasid* passed away, his soul came before the Heavenly Court for judgment. The soul was asked what it did in this world and it answered, 'I was a *chasid* of the Ropshitzer rebbe during my lifetime.'

"The Heavenly Court passed judgment on the soul by saying, 'If you were a *chasid* of the Ropshitzer rebbe, you must have been a good man. You are therefore admitted directly to Heaven.' In other words, a Ropshitzer *chasid* had both worlds: the joy of this world and the joy of the world to come.

"However, when we come from the outlying districts to visit you, you extend to us one finger in greeting. If we happen to arrive during the morning prayer service, the only thing you allow us to do is put on *tallis* and *tefillin* and pray in the same room with you. There is no warmth. There is no joy. In addition, you did not smile or laugh this *Purim*. We have neither happiness in this world nor joy in the next."

Yossele Broder's voice became more agitated.

"When we depart for home, you raise another finger and tell us to travel in peace. You don't look at us. You don't know us. When one of us dies, and our soul appears before the Heavenly Court, it is asked what it did in this world. It answers, 'I was a *chasid* of the Rizhiner rebbe.' The soul hopes to gain entrance to Heaven immediately, but that is not the case.

"The Heavenly Court says, 'The Rizhiner was a very holy man,' but how do you compare yourself to him? He is in Heaven, but his followers do not merit to be with him."

Yossele Broder stopped breathlessly. The Rizhiner seized the opportunity to ask, "If it is so bad here, why don't you go to a different rebbe?"

Yossele Broder did not hesitate. He shouted emphatically, "It is better to be your *chasid* without the benefits of joy in this world and the next than to be a *chasid* of any other rebbe."

When the rebbe heard Yossele Broder's reply, he began to laugh. He laughed and he laughed. Then he raised his eyes Heavenward and said, "You see, Almighty, Master of the World! We have no joy in this world, yet we would rather serve You than anyone else. Even when we are in exile, persecuted and degraded, we do not change You for any other god. What nerve to decree against such faithful servants! How dare there be an evil decree against Your loyal children! Happy are we, Your people, whose portion is with You. Happy are we, Your people, whose God is the Lord."[1]

---

[1] Psalms 144:15.

Then the Rizhiner laughed again. Yossele Broder laughed. Yossele Broder had made the Rizhiner rebbe laugh! The *chasidim* laughed. All of Rizhin laughed. There was joy in the whole world. Satan was confused. The evil decree promulgated against the Jewish people was nullified. It was the happiest *Purim* the Rizhiner *chasidim* ever celebrated.

A *Purim* Story!
L'Chayim Yidden!

Before Moshele Shabosker became a rebbe and holy master, he needed a job to sustain himself and his family. He searched for a job where he could work a little, study *Torah* a lot, and earn a decent weekly salary at the same time.

One day he heard that the owner of a large whiskey factory was advertising for a manager. He was not trained in business management or whiskey production, but he decided to apply for the job anyway. He made an appointment for an interview.

The owner of the factory wanted to know the usual information from job applicants. He was satisfied with Moshele Shabosker's answers. Then he asked the critical question. "Moshele, what experience have you had managing a whiskey factory?"

Moshele Shabosker answered, "You must trust me. I have had lots of previous experience. I'm really a famous whiskey factory manager. It's just that right now I am unemployed, and I need a job to support my family."

The owner was not really convinced of his ability.

"I'll tell you what I'll do," he said. "Since I desperately need a new manager, and you desperately need a job, I will hire you on a probationary basis. I'll hire you for four weeks. If you prove your ability and if my factory prospers, then I will hire you permanently."

Moshele Shabosker agreed to the conditions.

The next day he arrived at the whiskey factory just before daybreak. Under his arm he carried a stack of holy books, his *tallis,* and his *tefillin.*

"I am the new manager," he told the night watchman, who was still on duty. "Please direct me to the office that the previous manager used."

Following the pointed finger of the night watchman, he entered a small room. He placed the holy books on the desk, arranged them neatly, and moved a chair near the window. He then selected a book from the top of the pile, sat down, opened the book, and began to study. He usually studied for at least an hour before he davened the morning service.

The commotion caused by the workers arriving for work did not distract him. He heard the workers shouting at each other to move the casks, to add water to the grains, to be careful with the measurement of peat needed to cure the malt. He kept studying.

It did not take long for him to be interrupted. There was an urgent knock on his office door. "Sir," shouted one of the workers through the closed door, "there is a problem on the production line. One of the machines is not capping the bottles properly."

Moshele Shabosker answered from behind his closed office door, "Has this same problem ever occurred before?"

"Yes," answered the agitated worker.

"What did the previous manager do to correct the problem?" Moshele queried.

The factory worker spelled out the details of the previous manager's solution.

Moshele Shabosker listened to the details, and then he said, "That sounds like a good solution. Since I am new on this job, why don't you do what the previous manager did, until I learn all the technicalities of this job?"

Satisfied, the factory worker walked away.

Every time there was a problem in the whiskey factory, Moshele Shabosker handled it the same way: he instructed the workers to do what the previous manager had done. Meanwhile, he kept studying in his office, the closed door separating him from the factory workers.

At this point, it is necessary to stop the narration to explain that Moshele Shabosker was not collecting a salary from the owner of the whiskey factory for nothing. From the moment he moved into the manager's office, business increased five hundred percent. The bottled whiskey that was packed in boxes for delivery to old-time customers tasted like it had been distilled in the Garden of Eden. There was such an increased demand for the whiskey from this particular factory that the workers had to work overtime in order to fill the orders.

After one month, the owner of the factory told Moshele, "I am so happy with the way you are managing my business that I have decided to hire you on a permanent basis. Do you have a special secret recipe for the way you blend the whiskey?"

Moshele did not have any secret recipes. He only continued to study *Torah* in the manager's office. Every time a problem arose, he solved it the way the previous manager solved it.

The factory owner grew more and more confident in Moshe's ability to manage the whiskey factory. He was lavish with his praise and with his raises in salary. He made it a habit of stopping by the factory every afternoon. The two men learned to respect each other, both for their business ability and their *Torah* wisdom, for the factory owner himself was quite scholarly, and they found that they had a lot in common.

The factory owner was a very hospitable man. He liked to have guests for *Shabbos* and holidays. He invited his new manager and his family to be his guests for *Shabbos,* but Moshele Shabosker always refused the invitation.

Then, one Friday afternoon, the factory owner said to Moshele Shabosker, "You constantly refuse my invitations for *Shabbos.* I understand that you want to be with your family.

However, won't you consider coming to the *melave malke* (the farewell feast to the *Shabbos* Queen) tomorrow night? You will really honor me with your presence."

Moshele Shabosker could not refuse the invitation. Sitting around long tables, singing soft, haunting farewell melodies, exchanging *Torah* thoughts, he was very happy that he attended the *melave malke*. He enjoyed himself so much that he accepted the invitation to return week after week. He became part of the group of men that met every week after *Shabbos* at the factory owner's house to sing farewell songs to the *Shabbos* Queen.

One week, Moshele's place at the *melave malke* table was vacant. The factory owner was very worried that some ill had befallen his manager, so he excused himself from his guests and ran to Moshele's house to see if there was anything wrong.

He rushed up the path leading to the house. Except for the glow of a candle, the entire house was dark. He peered into the window. He saw that Moshele Shabosker sat at the table, studying with a stranger who looked like he came from a different world.

Realizing that the sight was not meant for ordinary eyes, he rushed back to his waiting guests. He tried to put the sight he had seen out of his mind, but his curiosity was aroused. He could not sleep.

The next morning, he sent word to the factory that he would like to see the manager in his house. When Moshele arrived, he said, "Last night, I was concerned about your welfare when you did not show up at the *melave malke*. I left my guests and went to your house. I wanted to be certain that there was nothing wrong. When I arrived at your house, it was entirely dark, except for the soft glow of candlelight. I peered into the window and saw that you were sitting at your table, studying with a person who looked like he came from a different world. Maybe my eyes were not meant to see your guest, but I am very curious. Can you tell me who he was?"

Moshele Shabosker was taken aback for a few moments. He had no idea that anyone had seen him studying with another person.

"I'll tell you the truth," he said in a low voice. "My guest was King David."

This time the factory owner was astounded. He realized that he must be worthy himself to be privileged to see King David, so he persisted in asking, "What did King David tell you?"

Moshele Shabosker hesitated. He knew that he could not keep any secret from the man who had had enough confidence in his ability to give him a job and had befriended him, so he said, "King David told me that it was time to reveal myself to the world as a rebbe and holy master. He told me to stop working in the whiskey factory. He told me that tomorrow, at exactly twelve noon, thousands of people would come to me to ask for my blessings."

The factory owner gulped. He realized that indeed he had hired Moshele Shabosker to manage his whiskey factory on a temporary basis.[1]

---

[1]*L'chayim Yidden* means "To life, Jews!" It is the traditional way we bless our friends when we share a drink. In this story, Rebbe Moshele Shabosker dedicated his life to study. He believed that livelihood would inevitably come from God. When we wish each other *"l'chayim,"* we hope that our lives will emulate the rebbe's, a life of study filled with faith in God's benevolence.

Authors' note: This story was told originally by Rebbe Chayim Halberstam, the Sanzer rebbe, the Divray Chayim. One of his students repeated it to the Bobover rebbe, who told it to his students. One of them told it to Rabbi Shlomo Carlebach. He told it to us. It is being retold here for those who understand what *"l'chayim Yidden"* is all about on *Purim*.

Good *Purim*! Good *Purim*!

Moshele the water carrier, meek, downtrodden, poor, wanted desperately to wish his rebbe, Yisrael Haupstein, the Koshnitzer *maggid*, "Good *Purim*."

He shuffled his tired feet all the way from the marketplace to the rebbe's house, his head bent low. He was hungry and downcast, aware that another working day had passed in which he had barely earned enough to provide his large family with bread and water.

He entered the study where the Koshnitzer *maggid* sat, receiving *chasidim* who bore baskets of *shalach manos* (gifts of food) and sheepishly whispered, "Good *Purim*, rebbe."

The Koshnitzer *maggid* looked at the water carrier with dismay and said, "Moshele, how could you come to wish me Good *Purim* without bringing *shalach manos*? Don't you know that on *Purim* friends exchange gifts of food in honor of the holiday? How could you wish me Good *Purim* with such a sad voice? Don't you know that you are supposed to shout with joy and ecstasy, 'Good *Purim*, Good *Purim*'?"

Moshele did not take his eyes off the ground. "Rebbe," he

whispered, "I owe the grocer money, I owe the baker money, I owe the tailor money, I owe the shoemaker money. Where am I going to get money to buy *shalach manos* for you?"

The Koshnitzer *maggid* said gently, "Moshele, when you learn how to say 'Good *Purim*, Good *Purim*,' everything will go your way. Then you will come back here, bringing *shalach manos* fitting for a gift from one friend to another."

Moshele left the rebbe's study, still shuffling his feet, his head still bent low. He shuffled all the way to the grocery store, trying to figure out how to obtain *shalach manos* for his rebbe.

As Moshele shuffled into the grocery store, he suddenly remembered what his rebbe said. He straightened his shoulders, held his head high, danced a step or two over to the spot where the grocer stood, and said cheerfully, "Good *Purim*, Good *Purim*!" The grocer had a different reaction when he saw Moshele. "What's he doing here?" he thought. "He owes me so much money. It's been many months since I have seen him. I hope he doesn't think that he can buy more groceries on credit."

"Good *Purim*! Good *Purim*! my friend," said Moshele in a happy voice.

The grocer was shocked by Moshele's greeting. He had never heard Moshele speak in such a positive voice. The grocer forgot that Moshele owed him money.

"What can I do for you today?" he asked.

Moshele answered, "Today is *Purim*. I have to bring my rebbe *shalach manos*. I need cakes, candy, honey, and wine. Please put the food in a basket and the amount of money it costs on my bill."

The grocer was so stunned by Moshele's assertiveness that he did exactly as requested. Moshele walked out of the grocery store with a basket of *shalach manos* in his arms, his head high, and he danced all the way back to his rebbe's house.

This time Moshele walked into his rebbe's study with pride. He greeted the rebbe with the happiest Good *Purim* the rebbe had ever heard. "Good *Purim*, Good *Purim*, rebbe," Moshele called out in a ringing voice. "I came to wish you Good *Purim*, and I brought you *shalach manos*."

The Koshnitzer *maggid* stretched out his hand to accept Moshele's *shalach manos* basket. Then he said, "Moshele, my friend, you are really learning how to say Good *Purim*. Do you know that today there is no evil in the world? Do you know that Haman and Amalek[1] have been eradicated? Do you know that today is a wonderful day?"

Moshele agreed with his rebbe that this *Purim* day was a wonderful day. He left his rebbe's study and started homeward, thinking about the lesson his rebbe had taught him. He realized that he was having a wonderful day, but his family was not enjoying such a happy *Purim*. They hadn't eaten a holiday meal in a very long time. So Moshele went back to the grocery store.

The grocer had not expected Moshele to return. When Moshele walked into the store, humming a cheerful tune, shouting "Good *Purim*, Good *Purim*" at the top of his voice, the grocer obliged Moshele's request for food for his family. He filled another box with fish, wine, *challos*, honey, and cakes.

"Thank you, thank you," sang Moshele. "Put the amount of money I owe you for this food on my bill. Good *Purim*, Good *Purim*. Today is a wonderful day. Haman and Amalek have been destroyed. There is no evil in the world!"

With a joyful lilt, Moshele started homeward once again, his hands filled with the box of holiday food for his children. He danced along the road, rethinking the lesson his rebbe taught him. "Before I go home," he thought, "I might as well stop at the tailor's shop. My children haven't had any new clothes in such a long time. I will find them clothes for *Purim*."

Moshele stopped at the tailor's shop. The tailor hadn't seen him in ten years. "Moshele," said the tailor, "I'm so surprised to see you. The last time you were in this shop, you bought a suit, and you still owe me money."

"I know," answered Moshele, "but what difference does that make? Today is *Purim*. Good *Purim*. Good *Purim*."

The tailor was stunned by Moshele's cheerfulness. He said, "Yes, today is *Purim*. What can I do for you?"

[1]Amalek was the grandson of Esau. He led his people in battle against the defenseless Jews camping in Refidim a short time after the Exodus from Egypt (Exodus 17:8–16).

Moshele replied, "I want my children to have a good *Purim*. I want shirts and pants, skirts and blouses for them."

The tailor went into the back of the shop, removed pants and shirts, skirts and blouses, and a dress for Moshele's wife from the shelf, packed them into a box, and brought them to Moshele. Moshele asked the tailor to put the cost of the clothing on his bill. Then he thanked the tailor. Shouting "Good *Purim*, Good *Purim*," laden with groceries and clothing, Moshele started homeward again.

Moshele's wife expected her meek, downtrodden husband to return empty-handed. Imagine her surprise when Moshele walked in shouting, "Good *Purim*, Good *Purim*." Imagine her surprise when Moshele walked in laden with boxes of food and clothing. Shouting "Good *Purim*, Good *Purim*," Moshele placed the box of holiday food on the table and lined up his children to distribute the clothing. As he gave his children their new clothes, he patted their shoulders, whispered in their ears how much he loved them, straightened their heads so they stood tall, and kissed them. Moshele taught his children how to say, "Good *Purim*, Good *Purim*."

"Today is *Purim*," he said. "There is no evil in the world! Good *Purim*, Good *Purim*!"

Later that afternoon, he walked into town, went directly to the bank, inquired after the owner, and asked for an appointment to see him. Sensing a disturbance in the normal business routine, the owner stepped out of his office, demanding to know who Moshele thought he was.

"I'll tell you who I am! I am Moshele the water carrier. I don't want to be a water carrier all my life. I want you to lend me money so I can start a business. Today is *Purim*. There is no evil in the world. Good *Purim*, Good *Purim*!"

Because of Moshele's joy, the banker lent him the money.

Moshele started a business. He became a very wealthy man. He repaid all his debts. His home was always open to the meek, the downtrodden, and the poor. Each *Purim*, the Koshnitzer *maggid* sent his *chasidim* to Moshele's house to learn the meaning of "Good *Purim*, Good *Purim*!"

Purim, Buchenwald, 1943

Kiddush Hashem (martyrdom), death, and conversion were not the choices of those incarcerated in Hitler's concentration camps. Rather, *kiddush hachayim* (the sanctification of life)— living with dignity as Jews for whatever time they were permitted to live—was uppermost in their minds. This striving towards *kiddush hachayim* was a most dynamic form of resistance, for it temporarily thwarted the evil plan of the Nazi beast that stood face to face against the stubbornness of the Jew in his battle for survival.

This resistance took many forms in the concentration camps that scarred the face of the European continent. Stories abound about people reduced to human skeletons who bartered their bread rations for raw flour so they might secretly bake *matzos* to fulfill the *mitzvah* of *Pesach*; emaciated souls who scraped the pat of margarine from their bread crusts and used it to make candles for *Chanukah*; ravaged creatures who smuggled a prohibited pair of *tefillin* from bunker to bunker so that all might recite the blessing, thinking silently as they passed them, "Thank you Almighty, Master of the Universe, for not having created me like one of them!"

This story is about salvaged scraps of paper and a *Purim megillah.*

Among those incarcerated in Buchenwald was a teenaged boy named Nachum. He was determined to continue conducting morning and evening prayer services in a hidden pit, deep in the bowels of the earth, as he had done prior to his arrest in his *shtetl.* The pit looked like a manhole. It was located behind the cluster of bunkers, covered over with cement block, wooden planks, and gravel. No one seemed to pay much attention to the hidden pit except Nachum. Following a rumor that a pit existed in the area from the days of World War I, Nachum explored the area, risking his life after night roll call, until he stumbled on it. He found that it was deep enough to accommodate the height of an average person and wide enough for fifteen men to cling together in the thick darkness. He also found a ladder descending from the top of the pit to its bottom.

Now that he had found a place to hold his prayer service, Nachum passed the word to his friends. Rising before the break of dawn, long before roll call, they slipped silently behind the bunker, lifted the cement block and wooden planks, scraped away the gravel, and slipped down the ladder, one by one, until they stood, squashed together in the pit, ready to hold the morning service. They did this for weeks and weeks, reciting the psalms and supplications they remembered by heart. Surprisingly, no one bothered them.

As the days preceding *Purim* approached, Nachum became more daring. He contemplated the possibility of his prayer group reading the *megillah,* celebrating the festival of "good overpowering evil" together. He only had one problem; no *megillah* was available in Buchenwald.

Nachum reflected on how to solve this problem. He could not sleep. He became obsessed with finding a way to read the *megillah* in his makeshift *shul,* his hidden prayer room.

After several sleepless nights, Nachum could not hold his head up straight. He finally dozed off into a fitful sleep. He dreamed about his *Purim* celebration. In his dream, Nachum stood in the center of a whirlwind. As it swirled around him, he recognized scraps of paper that were inscribed with the names of the characters of the *megillah*. Very clearly, he read the names of Haman, Esther, Mordechai, Achashverosh. The whirlwind did not abate. Nachum continued to read, "And it came to pass in the days of Achashverosh, the Achashverosh who reigned from Hodu to Kush over one hundred and twenty-seven provinces. . . ."[1]

He awoke, startled, trying to find the meaning of the swirling pieces of paper. The next morning, standing in the exercise area during roll call, Nachum noticed that the Nazi guards were discarding gum and cigarette wrappers, old messages, and torn newspapers. The Jews would be forced to clean after them. The discarded scraps danced around the open area, swirling in the gentle March breeze. Suddenly, Nachum understood his dream.

Immediately, he passed the word to save the discarded papers. When questioned about what to do with them, he answered, "Pass them to anyone who knows any line from the *megillah* by heart. I have a pencil stub. We will write the parts of the *megillah* we remember on the scraps. I will save the scraps on my bunk; they don't search too carefully on the top level. Just before *Purim* we will put all the scraps together. Maybe we will have a completed *megillah*. We will read the *megillah* together in our *shul*."

Nachum created an air of expectation in Buchenwald around *Purim* in 1943. There existed a sense of unity, of purpose, of a goal, of dignity. Word spread through most of the camp: Jews were going to read the *megillah* in Buchenwald!

They waited for the silence of night that *Purim*. Then Nachum, his friends, and their friends, and those who dared risk breaking the rules slipped out of the bunkers and headed toward the hidden pit. Looking behind him, Nachum saw that the number of people far exceeded the space in the pit, so he decided to read his makeshift *megillah* right there, behind the bunkers.

[1]*Megillas Esther* 1:1.

"Hush," whispered Nachum. "Tonight is *Purim*, but we cannot yell 'down with Haman!' We can only think it in the deepest recesses of our minds and silently stamp our feet to erase this modern evil that afflicts us. As you know, I have put together a makeshift *megillah*. It is missing words, phrases, whole sentences, but it is enough that we are standing here together, able to listen to the story of the miraculous deliverance of our people from the enemy. I will read very slowly whatever I remember, whatever I can see from the light of the moon that reflects upon the words written on the scraps of paper. Think the words with me as I read. Never forget this *Purim* night in Buchenwald!"

The night after *Purim*, special S.S. stormtroopers burst into the bunker and dragged Nachum down from the top level, pulling him by the hair. The beasts forced him across the exercise area to a waiting truck, the motor revved up to move quickly. They must have known who was infusing *kiddush hachayim* to the incarcerated, who was encouraging them to meet for prayer, who had arranged the *Purim* celebration.

Nachum's friends swore that if they survived, they would repeat his story every year on *Purim*. They further swore to instill it into their yet unborn children, so they might transmit it to theirs for posterity.

Pesach

Pesach, one of the three pilgrim festivals when the Jewish people ascended to Jerusalem to worship in the Holy Temple, celebrates the beginning of the Jewish nation. It was on *Pesach* that the Jewish people were redeemed from Egyptian bondage.

The name of the holiday means "pass over," because the Almighty passed over the houses of the Jewish people when He struck Egyptian first-born sons during the tenth plague.

Of all the holy days during the Jewish calendar year, *Pesach*, observed from the fifteenth through the twenty-second day of *Nissan*, is the richest in symbols. Each year, the symbols of the *seder* table serve to remind us of slavery and freedom.

Matzah (flat cakes of unleavened bread) is a reminder of the haste in which our ancestors departed from Egypt.

Salt water is a reminder of the tears of slavery.

Karpas (greens, parsley, celery, and potatoes) are a reminder of the meager diet our ancestors ate in Egypt and an omen of the coming springtime.

Marror (bitter herbs, horseradish) and *chazeres* (romaine lettuce) are reminders of the bitterness of slavery.

Zeroa (roasted shankbone) is a reminder of the *paschal* sacrificial offering.

Beitzah (roasted egg) is a reminder of the festival sacrificial offering.

Charoses (a mixture of nuts, apples, and wine) is a reminder of the clay bricks our people built for Pharoah in Egypt.

Four cups of wine and the cup for Elyahu Hanavi are a testimony to redemption, not only from Egyptian bondage, but from all the exiles in which the Jewish people are dispersed.

The purpose of the symbols is that we may taste, feel, and experience the exodus each year.

The word *seder* means order; the ritual of the *seder* follows a fifteen-step prescribed order from *kiddush*, the sanctification of the wine—the first step—to *nirtzah*, a prayer that our *seder* service be accepted by the Almighty — the last step.

The ritual of the *seder* is explained in a *hagadah*, a book in which the entire exodus story is retold. The root of the word *hagadah* is "to tell": the *seder* fulfills the *Torah* injunction of telling our children the story of the exodus.

Pesach is also called the festival of springtime. It is the time of year when the rebirth of nature parallels the birth of the Jewish people, so we add a special petition for dew to the prayer service on the first day of *Pesach*.

Torah Thoughts

The Egg

Eggs are a very important part of the *seder*. Have you ever wondered why most of us begin our *seder* meal with hard-boiled eggs?

The answer lies in the essence of the egg, which defies the general laws of nature. Everything created in this world is created in its complete form: babies become adult humans, kittens become cats, puppies become dogs, calves become cows. All of these are born smaller in size but completely formed at birth. Not so a bird: first the egg is laid, then the fledgling emerges, clearly a two-stage process.

The exodus from Egyptian bondage, celebrated each year on the *seder* night, reminds us of the dual process that molded the Jewish people from a nomadic band of slaves into "a kingdom of priests and a holy nation."[1]

The Jewish people's incubation period was the exodus from Egypt. Then, the emergence of the fledgling (completion) for the Jewish people took place at Sinai seven weeks later, on *Shavuos*,

---

[1]Exodus 19:6.

with the revelation. The nomadic band of slaves stood at Sinai and reiterated, "All that God has spoken we will do."[2] Just as the fledgling develops in two stages, so the Jewish people developed in two stages.

This dual process emphasizes that the fight for freedom needs to be goal-oriented. It is not enough to achieve freedom. Rather, the goal of freedom must be the service of God, the highest attainment of man.

Eating the egg at the *seder* table reminds us that the exodus was but the first step in the process of redemption. True freedom was attained only in the second step of the process, the revelation at Sinai.

[2]Exodus 19:8.

Tal—Dew

During the *musaf* prayer[1] on the first day of *Pesach*, we recite a special prayer for *tal* (dew). Ever since our patriarch Isaac blessed his son Jacob, *tal* has been associated with *Pesach*, for Isaac said, "May God grant you the dew of Heaven."[2]

According to our sages, this blessing was bestowed on *Pesach*, the day of the future redemption of Jacob's children from Egyptian bondage, the day when *hallel*, songs of praise, would reverberate throughout the world.[3]

Pesach is a unique festival. Spiritually, it symbolizes the beginning of redemption, freedom, and *Torah* after the harsh winter of Egyptian enslavement; physically, it symbolizes the rejuvenation of nature after a harsh winter of slumber. Therefore, *Pesach* is an auspicious time to recite the prayer for dew, since the moisturizing effect of dew renews both man and nature.

[1]The morning prayer service is divided into three parts on holy days: *shacharis*, the reading of the *Torah*, and *musaf*.

[2]Genesis 27:28.

[3]Eliyahu Ki Tov, *Sayfer Haparsheyos*, Jerusalem: Aleph Publishers, 1962, pp. 494, 500.

Dew is a blessing because it gently quenches the thirst of nature. We cannot see it fall, we cannot feel it, yet we know that it covers the ground each morning. Dew is constant, steady, invisible. We pray for its blessing even though we cannot see or feel it lest we come to take it for granted.

The accepted explanation of the prophecy of Isaiah, "For Your dew is as the dew of light," compares the moisturizing effect of dew to the rejuvenation of the Jewish people through the light of *Torah* and its commandments. *Torah* is constant, steady. It is the dew, the life-giving force for the Jewish people. It accompanies us through joy and sorrow from exile as we return to our homeland. It is the fulfillment of our patriarch Isaac's blessing.[4]

[4]Rashi, Isaiah 26:19.

The *Seder* of Life

Celebration of the *Pesach* festival is synonymous with the *seder*.

The Hebrew word *seder* means order; the order in which we observe the various rituals, the specific steps from *kiddush* to *hallel-nirtzah*.

The *hagadah* explains the rituals of the *Pesach seder*. Many hagadic interpreters explain the *seder* to be equivalent to the *seder* of life, i.e., the *Pesach seder* is a microcosm of the life of a Jew.

What can we learn about the *seder* of life, the passage between life's stages, from the steps enumerated in the *hagadah*?

Kadesh—Sanctifying the Wine

The *seder* begins with *kiddush*, the sanctification over the first of the four cups of wine. The word *kiddush* means holy. The word for marriage is *kiddushin*. Marriage begins with holiness. "You shall be holy, for I, the Lord your God, am Holy."[1]

---

[1]Leviticus 19:2.

The holiness of marriage, the purity of the Jewish family, precedes the birth of a child, the first passage of life, thus setting the goal toward moral human perfection. This is the first step in the ladder of the stages toward attaining holiness through life.[2]

U'rechatz—Washing the Hands

Washing the hands symbolizes the purification of the body in preparation for participation in the *seder* ritual.

In the *seder* of life, *u'rechatz* is the symbol of purification of the the male body—the covenant of circumcision—a visible reminder of submission to carry out the Divine Will of the Creator. Judaism does not split body and soul and does not deny the sensuous. Rather *bris milah,* the covenant of circumcision, prescribes moral limits as a requisite for leading a holy life.[3]

Karpas—Dipping the Vegetable in Salt Water

The blessing is recited over a simple vegetable, expressing gratitude to the One Who created the fruit of the earth.

In the *seder* of life, a blessing recited over even the simplest food teaches the child, from early infancy, to thank God for everything. "And you shall teach your children (inculcate into them) and speak to them (about the word of God)."[4]

Yachatz—Breaking the Middle Matzah

The larger portion of the *matzah* is hidden for the *afikomen.*

There are two parts to the *seder* of life, the spiritual and the

---

[2]Rabbi Pinchas ben Yair explains the ladder of stages reaching toward moral perfection, the purpose being to teach that holiness is dependent on manners, morals, and a specific way of life (Talmud, *Avodah Zarah* 20b).

[3]According to Rabbi Shimshon Raphael Hirsch, the female guides the direction of the home. The female has an innate feeling for what is morally correct; therefore she does not require a physical sign of the covenant. A child must have both an Abraham for a father and a Sarah for a mother in order to transmit the holiness of a people (Hirsch Commentary, Genesis 17:10–16).

[4]Deuteronomy 6:7.

material. *Matzah* represents the spiritual. *Chametz* (leaven) represents the material. *Matzah* is flat, it is not blown up; it has not risen out of proportion like *chametz*. We hide the larger part of the *matzah* to stress that the spiritual values of life should be our primary concern. Although life is a struggle between the spiritual and the material, the emphasis should be on that portion of life consecrated to the service of the Almighty rather than on that portion dedicated to the care of our mundane needs.

Maggid—Reciting the Hagadah, the Story of the Exodus from Egyptian Bondage

We not only recite the story; we enact it through discussion and tasting the various *seder* symbols. This part of the *seder* ceremony is derived from "And you shall tell it to your children on that day."[5]

The basis of the *seder* of life is learning, teaching, and explaining the heritage of our people.

Rachtzah—Washing the Hands and Reciting the Blessing

This ritual hand washing is to prepare for the eating of the *seder* meal.

A talmudic dictum provides a clue for connecting this ritual with the *seder* of life: "For anyone who takes lightly the ritual washing of hands, it is as if he has uprooted himself from his place in the world (as if he has disregarded the words of the Rabbis)."[6]

As the child matures, he/she is admonished to guard his/her actions; that the dealing of his/her hands be above reproach in his/her relationship with peers. Just as the ritual hand washing is preparation for the *seder* meal, so the admonition to deal uprightly with peers is preparation for life's later challenges.

[5]Exodus 13:8.
[6]Talmud, *Sota* 4b, *Tosafos.*

Motzi—Reciting the Blessing over the Matzah

The *matzah* is used in place of the *challos* used on *Shabbos* and other holy days.

Matzah—Reciting the Special Blessing to Fulfill the Command-ment to Eat Matzah

Eating the *matzah* during the *seder* ritual makes us aware of the difference between the loaves of risen *chametz* and the flat cakes of *matzah*.

As we pass through the *seder* of life, we are confronted with many questions. There are no easy answers, but keeping in mind the difference between *chametz* and *matzah* helps. *Chametz* and *matzah* each have three letters; two of the letters in each word are identical. One of the letters in *chametz* and one of the letters in *matzah* are shaped slightly differently. Although both letters seem to be shaped like a three-sided rectangle without a base, the letter in *matzah* is slashed on the side. This letter is called *hay*. *Hay* is also an abbreviation of one of the names of the Almighty. This suggests that the answer to man's search for meaning might be in the opening of the *hay*, allowing the Divine Presence to enter into our struggle with life.

Marror—Eating the Bitter Herbs

Applying better herbs to the *seder* of life teaches us that the *marror* will pass from those people whose lives have been embit-tered by sorrow. "A person is obligated to recite a blessing for what seems evil just as he/she recites a blessing for good."[7]

Marror reminds us never to abandon our belief in the good-ness of God.

Korech—Sandwiching Bitter Herbs between Two Pieces of Matzah

The *seder* of life apportions both bitterness and joy. In order to learn from these experiences, we must sandwich together those

---

[7]Talmud, *Berachos* 54a, *Mishnah*.

who need help (bitter) with those who can provide help (joy), thereby fulfilling the talmudic dictum: "Every person is responsible to care for every other person."[8]

Shulchan Orech—Sharing the Seder Meal with Family

The festival table symbolizes the altar, and the Jewish home symbolizes a miniature Holy Temple. It is the miniature Holy Temple that focuses upon the unity of the Jewish family, the meeting place of parents and children.

*Tzafun—Eating the Afikomen, the Larger Portion of
the Matzah, Hidden at the Beginning of the Seder*

Passing through the *seder* of life, we are cognizant that we are storing much spiritual wealth during our lifetime.

Barech—Reciting Grace After Meals

*Hallel—Giving Thanks for the Gift of Life, for Freedom, and for
Future Redemption*

*Nirtzah—Hoping that Our Seder Service Be Acceptable to
the Almighty*

The formal *seder* ritual concludes with psalms of thanksgiving, followed by, "May we celebrate this *seder* ritual and this *seder* of life next year in the rebuilt holy city of Jerusalem."

The *seder* of life has merged with the ritual *seder*. We are secure in our belief that "He is near to all who call upon Him in truth,"[9] that His Way is the source of abundant blessings.

[8]Talmud, *Shavuos* 39a.
[9]Psalms 145:18.

Stories

The Baker's Lad

Prague was shrouded in darkness. Two people walked along two different streets, destined to meet where the streets crossed.

Rabbi Yechezkel ben Yehuda Landau, the Noda B'Yehuda —the famed halachic authority—had just emerged from the Altneuschul[1] on Maiselova Street. He was returning home after davening the evening service.

As he walked along, he heard the uncontrolled sobbing and frightened whimpering of a thin lad, clad in rags, trodding along Parizska Street, heading toward the Charles Bridge, which spanned the Ultava River. The lad carried empty baskets slung across his shoulders.

Rabbi Landau stopped him and asked, "Why are you crying? How can I help you?"

The lad hesitated for a moment. He was surprised that this Jew should stop to help him. Feeling that he could trust the stranger, he blurted out his story amidst the sobs.

"My father is a baker. When my mother died, he remarried.

[1]See footnote 1, page 33.

His wife is cruel and vindictive. Each morning, winter and summer, rain, snow, sleet, and fog, she forces me to take baskets of
bread and rolls to the Jewish quarter to sell. If I do not sell all my
wares by the end of the day, and I return home with less money
than she expects, she beats me without pity.

"Today," his voice faltered, "I sold all of the bread and rolls.
I earned ten *rhenish* (monetary exchange). I was relieved that I
would not be beaten. But as I was heading home, I put my hand
in my pocket to feel the money. It was gone! Either someone
picked my pocket, or I lost it. I have been wandering around the
streets of the Jewish quarter for hours, afraid to return home. I
don't know what to do."

The lad started wailing again.

Rabbi Landau didn't hesitate one moment. Comfortingly,
he put his arm around the lad.

"What is your name?" he asked.

The lad answered in a faint voice, "My name is Wenceslaus."

"Wenceslaus," the rabbi said, "please come with me. I will
take care of you."

Gently, he led the lad to his home. He asked his wife to prepare a meal for him. After Wenceslaus finished eating, Rabbi
Landau gave him ten *rhenish*. "Return home now, Wenceslaus," he said. "Tonight you will not be beaten!"

Wenceslaus' eyes sparkled. He could not believe that a Jew
had helped him.

"Before I leave," Wenceslaus said gratefully, "I want to
swear to you that someday I will repay this good which you have
done for me."

The lad disappeared in the darkness of night.

Many years later, at about two in the morning, on the eighth
day of *Pesach*, the Jews of Prague slept peacefully, having eaten
their fill of *matzah*. Only Rabbi Landau sat and studied by the
thin ray of light reflecting from the lantern of his table. His
thoughts were disturbed by an urgent rapping on his door. Startled, he stood to open it. He found a tall, lanky man standing in

the doorway. He was peering into the darkness, his eyes darting first to the right, then to the left, then behind him. Having made certain that no one followed him, he motioned to the rabbi to let him in.

"Are you alone?" he queried.

Rabbi Landau moved away from the doorway, and the young man entered, closing the door firmly behind him. The two men faced each other. Then the intruder spoke.

"Rabbi, don't you remember me? I am Wenceslaus, the baker's lad, the one you comforted and cared for the night I lost my money, the night I was too frightened to return home lest I be mercilessly beaten. Remember, when I left your house, I swore I would repay your kindness. I have never forgotten my promise. I waited and waited for an opportunity to present itself, so I might fulfill my oath. I sneaked into the Jewish quarter at great risk. If my family finds out that I told you what I am about to reveal, they would kill me immediately. I want you to know that there is a plot afoot that will endanger the lives of every Jew in the Prague ghetto."

Wenceslaus stopped the rushing words to catch his breath. Rabbi Landau's face paled in the shadow of the dim light. Wenceslaus continued.

"My stepmother is the leader of the baker's guild. She called a meeting of all the bakers, and together they hatched a plot to poison all the Jews of Prague. They plan on putting poison in all the loaves of bread that will be sold tomorrow, the day after your holiday. They are so hateful that they want to rid Prague of its Jewish community. They know that all the Jews buy bread from non-Jews on the day after the holiday. They even planned a party to celebrate their success. Whatever you do to avert the tragic consequences for the Jewish community, make certain that no one knows that it was I who revealed this information to you."

Rabbi Landau thanked Wenceslaus. He slipped quietly out the door, ran stealthily through the Jewish quarter, across the Charles bridge, to his home on the other side of the river.

Rabbi Landau returned to his table. Deep in thought, he had to find, without incriminating Wenceslaus, a plausible reason for the Jews not to purchase bread the following day.

He stood and paced the floor; forth and back, back and forth. Soon the Jews of Prague would gather in the Altneuschul for the morning prayer service of the eighth day of the *Pesach* festival.

As the dawn broke, Rabbi Landau hit upon a plan of action. After the *Torahs* were returned to their places in the ark, he ascended the *bimah* (the center pulpit) and stood before the *omed* (the prayer leader's desk). He raised his hands to get the attention of the worshippers.

"Silence! I have a very important announcement to make," he began. "It is so important that every Jew must listen to what I have to say. If any of you seated here has any member of your family missing, go and bring them. I will wait."

A puzzled hush spread over the *shul*. Some men looked around at the women's gallery. Not finding their wives and children, they went home to fetch them.

The *shul* was packed wall to wall. Bystanders, not understanding the urgency in Rabbi Landau's voice, milled around outside.

When the commotion quieted. Rabbi Landau spoke firmly and clearly. "With the authority vested in me as the religious leader of this community, I decree upon every single Jew in Prague, man, woman, and child, not to eat bread tomorrow, according to your calculations, the day after *Pesach*. You see," he explained, "I miscalculated. Tomorrow is actually the last day of the holiday. Tomorrow is still *Pesach*."

Rabbi Landau descended the pulpit and returned to his seat at the front of the *shul*.

That year, the Jews of Prague celebrated *Pesach* for nine days. Not one Jew dared challenge the rabbi's authority. Not one Jew bought a loaf of bread that day.

The bakers, however, not knowing of Rabbi Landau's decree, gathered early on the ninth day in front of the Prague ghetto, laden with freshly baked, poisoned bread. They waited for the Jews to purchase their wares, but the hours of the day dragged on, and no customers approached. Wenceslaus' step-mother, leader of the bakers' guild, motioned to a few of her ac-complices for a conference. "Let us go to see the mayor," she suggested defiantly. "Those Jews who did not purchase our bread, as is their usual custom, have caused us to lose a great deal of money."

The mayor summoned Rabbi Landau to his office. When he arrived, he was greeted by the bakers, who demanded an expla-nation as to why the Jews did not purchase bread from them as they did each year. They waited impatiently for his answer, ready to pounce upon him.

Rabbi Landau was prepared to deal with the mayor and the mob. Replying to the mayor's inquiry, he unhesitatingly said, "We of the Jewish community are prepared to pay the bakers the sum of their loss."

The bakers ran helter-skelter to retrieve their merchandise. When they returned with the other bakers and their wares to the mayor's office, Rabbi Landau announced, "Yes, we are prepared to pay the bakers the sum of their loss, but first I want to examine the quality of the bread they are offering for sale."

Confusion reigned in the mayor's office. Quick as a wink, the bakers picked up their baskets of bread and fled for their lives.

The Jews of Prague rejoiced that the wisdom of their rabbi, who had decreed the observance of *Pesach* for nine days, had saved them from total annihilation.

A Different *Seder*

The Baal Shem Tov wanted to see *Eretz Yisrael*, to walk the length and breadth of the land where his ancestors walked, where he could discover his past, the roots of his people. He attempted the hazardous trip many times but never reached his destination; once, the axle of his carriage broke just as he reached the outskirts of Medziboz, once the boat upon which he had booked passage to *Eretz Yisrael* sailed from the harbor without him. But he did not give up hope.

One day an unusual opportunity presented itself. He could be in *Eretz Yisrael* for the coming *Pesach* if he sailed on the next boat from the port city of Odessa. Hurriedly, he made preparations, packed, and arranged his affairs; a long overland journey awaited him between Medziboz and the port. "I will be in *Eretz Yisrael* for *Pesach*," sang the Baal Shem Tov excitedly. "Hurry, Udel," he said to his daughter, "hurry, for we must not miss the boat again." He did not know, in his great excitement, that he was not destined to reach *Eretz Yisrael*.

The overland journey was wearisome, but the Baal Shem Tov did not tire. He was too excited, contemplating the thought of doing what his ancestors had done before him. He was making *aliyah*—he was ascending to Jerusalem for *Pesach*.[1]

They arrived in Odessa in plenty of time, went down to the pier, and boarded the boat. They settled themselves comfortably and waited for it to sail from the harbor.

One day out to sea, the beautiful spring weather changed. Cool winds blew, the clouds overhead filled the sky in one gray mass, thunderclaps echoed all around, and lightning streaked across the sky.

The Baal Shem Tov sat in his chair on the deck, clutching a book of Psalms in his hands. He prayed fervently that he reach *Eretz Yisrael*, that he might have the privilege of setting his feet on the soil of the Holy Land, that he might pray at the western wall, the ancient symbol of Israel's glory.

The stormy weather continued. After a few miserable days at sea, the captain announced briefly, "If this weather does not abate, we will dock at Istanbul, the next port city, and wait out the stormy weather. It is too hazardous to continue on to Palestine in this weather."

The trip had taken much longer than the Baal Shem Tov calculated. The boat docked in Istanbul on the twelfth day of *Nissan*, two days before *Pesach*. The Baal Shem Tov was distraught. He knew his plans had been thwarted again, and he did not know how he would observe *Pesach* in a strange land.

His happy mien turned quickly to depression. Usually, his reputation preceded his arrival in a strange town, and many people recognized him. But here, so far from his home and so distraught, no one paid much attention to the depressed newcomer who shuffled around in their midst. No one recognized the famous rebbe who had arrived in Istanbul for *Pesach*.

On the day before the holiday, the stormy weather subsided somewhat. The Baal Shem Tov walked sadly through the town,

---

[1]In ancient times, the Jews living in *Eretz Yisrael* ascended to Jerusalem three times each year, during the pilgrim festivals: *Pesach*, *Shavuos*, and *Sukkos*.

toward the synagogue. He had no solution to the problem of where to spend *Pesach*.

"Maybe," he thought, "if I spend the day in the study hall, someone will recognize me and invite Udel and me to be their *seder* guests."

When her father left for the study hall, Udel went down to the river's edge to wash his tunic. She wanted to do something to prepare for the approaching festival. As she stood on the river's edge, pounding the tunic clean, she thought bitterly about their predicament. "A *seder* for two in the inn, lonely, despondent. I wish we were back home in Medziboz." Picturing the beautiful *seder* table at home, she could not remove the sad thought from her mind. Unable to control herself, filled with self-pity, she started to cry.

A passerby noticed Udel standing at the river's edge, red-eyed and mournful.

"Why are you crying?" he asked.

At first she refused to answer. She did not recognize the man. But he persisted.

"Please, let me help you. If you tell me why you are so sad, maybe I can help."

Udel could not contain herself any longer. She blurted out the entire story.

"My name is Udel. I am the daughter of the Baal Shem Tov. My father has tried to go to *Eretz Yisrael* many times but has been unsuccessful. A few weeks ago, a marvelous opportunity presented itself. We thought we could be in *Eretz Yisrael* for *Pesach*, but storms on the seas forced the captain into this port. We don't know anybody here. We will be forced to spend *Pesach* by ourselves in the inn."

Udel wept uncontrollably.

The man said, "My name is Don Yosef. I am so happy you told me your troubles. I am one of the leaders of the Jewish community of Istanbul. I insist that you be my guest for *Pesach*. See that big house in the distance? That is where I live. Find your father immediately. Go back to the inn and put your belongings together. I will send my servant with my carriage to pick you both up in a short while."

Udel rushed to find her father. Excitedly, she told him what had happened. The Baal Shem Tov's face lit up.

"Udel," he said, "again my plans were thwarted. We will not be in *Eretz Yisrael* for *Pesach,* but we will not be alone either."

They were ready when the carriage arrived at the inn. As they approached the house in the distance, they saw that the house was a magnificent mansion. Don Yosef was gracious. He welcomed them warmly and gave them the best rooms in his house.

"Please," said the Baal Shem Tov, "I am very tired from my journey. I would like to rest before the *seder*."

The Baal Shem Tov lay down on the bed and fell into a deep sleep.

The hours passed. Don Yosef went to synagogue to pray the evening service, returned home, and waited patiently together with his family for the Baal Shem Tov to rouse from his sleep, to start the *seder.* Eight o'clock, nine o'clock, ten o'clock. Don Yosef looked quizzically at Udel, and she shrugged her shoulders, not being able to explain why her father was still sleeping.

Anxiously, he took a lighted candle, cupped the flame with his hand so it would not be snuffed out, and carried it upstairs to the room where the Baal Shem Tov slept.

Stealthily, he tiptoed into the room and shined the light over the sleeping form of the Baal Shem Tov. He saw that tears streamed down his closed eyes. Suddenly, the Baal Shem Tov screamed a piercing shriek and awoke.

He was startled by Don Yosef's presence. He washed his hands, walked over to the side of the room, and prayed the evening service.

When he finished, he turned to the waiting Don Yosef and said, "Later I will explain. Now we must begin the *seder*."

The two men went downstairs to the dining room, where Don Yosef's family and Udel waited patiently. The Baal Shem

Tov conducted the *seder*. He explained the significance of the *seder* symbols, he lovingly interpreted every word of the *hagadah*, he sang, he told parables, he literally fulfilled the commandment, "Teach your children what happened on that day."[2] Don Yosef and his family had never participated in such a *seder*.

Near dawn, Don Yosef turned to the Baal Shem Tov and said, "We have just about finished our *seder*. Can you please tell me now why you were crying in your sleep and screamed as you awoke?"

All eyes turned to the Baal Shem Tov.

"This is what happened," he said. "As I slept, I felt my soul ascending. I approached the Heavenly Court. I overheard an evil decree being promulgated against the Jews of this city. I began to plead for mercy with the Heavenly Court, but no heed was paid to my pleas. Finally, in desperation, I offered my life in exchange for the lives of my brothers and sisters who reside here in Istanbul. When the Heavenly Court heard my offer, it granted mercy and informed me that not only would the decree be nullified, but my soul would be returned also. My tears were from the pleas before the Heavenly Court. The scream was my relief that my offer had been accepted. During the morning prayer service in the synagogue, someone will come to corroborate what I have just told you. Now I understand why I did not reach *Eretz Yisrael* for *Pesach*. The Heavenly Court wanted me to be in Istanbul."

Just as the Baal Shem Tov had said, his story was corroborated the next morning, near the end of the prayer service.

Normally, the Jews of Istanbul waited for their leaders before they started to pray. That first day of *Pesach*, they waited and waited, but two people were still missing. They realized that they could wait no longer, for the *Sh'ma* (affirmation of faith) must be recited before the first quarter of the day is over. The leaders arrived after the reading of the *Torah*.

They greeted the worshippers with grave, somber voices. "Good *yom tov*, Good *yom tov*," they said softly.

[2]Exodus 13:8.

Don Yosef went over to them and asked them why they were so late. They ascended the pulpit, and one said, "Please listen carefully. We have something very important to tell you." The worshippers crowded around the pulpit, hushed in silence.

"We heard that a decree against the Jews of Istanbul had been promulgated by the sultan. It seems that one of his officers, who hated Jews, convinced him that we were responsible for a plot to overthrow his majesty. As leaders of this community, we went directly to the sultan to plead with him to rescind the decree, to try to convince him that the plot had no substance, that the officer had invented it as a pretext to perpetrate an evil decree against us. We succeeded. The sultan tried the officer for treason because he had endangered the safety of his loyal Jewish subjects. The officer was found guilty and has been imprisoned. The danger has passed. We can truly wish each other *"chag same'ach"* (a joyous holiday).

The Baal Shem Tov remained in Istanbul for the remainder of *Pesach*, then returned to Medziboz.

Redeemer of Israel[1]

In a little *shtetl*, near the outskirts of Kolbesof, a Jewish tenant named Moshe leased a liquor store from the local *poretz* (landowner). He barely eked out a living, thereby finding it extremely difficult to pay the monthly rent.

As time went on, Moshe found it increasingly difficult to pay, for business deteriorated more and more every day. One month he earned no profit at all from his liquor sales.

The *poretz* sent his deputies to remind Moshe that he was negligent in paying his debt. They stormed into the liquor store and demanded, "The *poretz* sent us to collect the back rent! He wants the money now!" Moshe shrugged his shoulders, raised his hands toward Heaven and wailed, "I don't have the money. I simply don't have it!"

They returned to the *poretz* empty-handed. "Go back to Moshe," he yelled, "and tell him that I will punish him, evict

---

[1]This story was told every year by Rebbe Avraham Yaacov Sadigura on the night preceding *Pesach*, the night we search for leaven.

him, jail him . . . tell him anything . . . tell him I must have my money now."

But Moshe had no money to pay the rent.

Early on *Shabbos Hagadol* (the Sabbath before *Pesach*) the *poretz* ordered his deputies to go to Moshe's house. He instructed them very clearly. "Teach that Jew a lesson. Raid the house. Tear up the floors, rip the window coverings and the furniture, dump the *cholent* pot, turn over the tables, throw the chairs outside the house, trample everything."

The *poretz* thought this would surely force Moshe to pay his back rent. He could not believe that the money simply was not available.

Moshe, accustomed to praying alone in his house, was in the midst of the *Shabbos* morning prayers when the deputies broke in. He stood horrified and helpless as they tore through his house. When they were satisfied with the havoc they had created, the deputies left.

Rather than cringe with fear or sink into a state of depression like the rest of his family, Moshe decided to walk to the town to hear the rebbe's sermon.

The rebbe of Kolbesof at that time was Rebbe Avraham Yehoshua Heschel, the Apter rebbe, the same rebbe whom people affectionately called *Ohev Yisrael,* the lover of the Jewish people. When Moshe entered the crowded synagogue after his very long walk, the rebbe was in the midst of delivering his sermon. The worshippers were standing, sitting, squeezing together, trying to hear his words.

Moshe tiptoed into a corner in the back. He heard the rebbe say, "I want all of you to know that we recite two blessings for redemption, with similar sounding words. The first blessing, 'Who redeemed Israel', is recited daily in the introduction to the silent devotion and in the *hagadah.* It is pronounced in the past tense. The second blessing, 'Who redeems Israel', is recited during the silent devotion. It is pronounced in the present tense. The first blessing is said to remind us of the exodus from Egyptian slavery. The second blessing is recited to make us aware that the Almighty redeems Israel, even a tenant whose house has just been destroyed by the *poretz's* deputies.''

When Moshe heard the rebbe's words, he was overcome with joy. He began to sing and dance, shoving aside the people who surrounded him in the crowded synagogue. He danced and sang, ''He is redeeming Israel, He is redeeming Israel,'' all the way to the door, down the path of the synagogue, all along the road, until he reached his home.

Late that afternoon, the *poretz* sent his deputies back to his tenant's house to see how he was faring after his home had been turned into a shambles. The deputies tiptoed up to the broken front window and peered inside. They saw that Moshe was danc- ing and singing, ''He is redeeming Israel, He is redeeming Israel!''

The deputies wondered how Moshe could dance and sing after he had suffered such a beating. They thought that he had lost his mind. They returned to the *poretz* and reported what they had seen.

That night, the *poretz* sent his deputies once again to his tenant's house and ordered them to bring him to his manor. Moshe became very frightened when he saw the deputies but re- alized that they could cause no more damage than they already had.

''Maybe they have come to kill me,'' he thought.

But he refused to let that thought get the better of him. He continued to dance and sing, interrupting himself only to ask in the same rhythmic beat, ''What do you want? Didn't you cause enough trouble already? He is redeeming Israel, He is redeeming Israel.''

The deputies snarled, ''The *poretz* wants to see you now. Follow us!''

The deputies walked to the manor, but Moshe sang and danced all the way. He sang and danced even as he stood in front of the *poretz.*

''Moshe, Jew, you unfortunate wretch! Stop singing and dancing already! You are so poor. You have no reason to sing and dance. You will never be able to pay the rent you owe me!''

Moshe answered diffidently, "What can I do about it, my master?"

The *poretz* thought a moment, and then he said, "Moshe, take this purchase order with my signature to the liquor distributor in the city. Tell him I said to sell you liquor on credit. Buy all you need. When you sell it, you will have earned enough profit to pay me what you owe me. You should even have enough money left over to repair your house."

Moshe did as he was told. He went to the liquor distributor and bought cases of liquor on credit. Suddenly, his business picked up. Customers came from near and far to patronize Moshe's liquor store.

That year, the first *seder* was on Friday night. Moshe had six business days to earn enough money to pay the rent, repair his house, and purchase all the necessities for *Pesach.* By Thursday, he had earned enough to pay his debts. He even had some money left over.

On Friday morning, the eve of the holiday, Moshe joyfully walked the road between his home in the *shtetl* and the synagogue in Kolbesof. He wanted to give his left-over money to the Apter rebbe to distribute to the poor.

Moshe knocked on the door of the rebbe's study. The Apter rebbe opened the door himself.

"Rebbe," Moshe said, "I listened to your words last *Shabbos.* I want you to know that your words are true. I brought you this money, for He *is* redeeming Israel. He is the redeemer of Israel."

Watch Your Words

When Naftali Tzvi Horowitz was sixteen years old, he went to
study with Rebbe Mordechai Neschizer. He arrived in Neschiz
before *Purim.* When the rebbe welcomed him, he said, "Naftali
Tzvi, I'm so glad you came here for *Purim.* I want you to experience the real joy of celebrating this holiday with me, but you
must leave here before *Pesach.*"

Naftali Tzvi liked the atmosphere in Neschiz. He did not
want to leave after *Purim.* Seeing the hundreds of people who
flocked to Neschiz for *Purim,* he reasoned that by making himself indispensable as a kitchen helper, he would be able to remain
permanently. Being extremely intelligent and intuitive, he went
to the kitchen and asked the *rebbetzen* (rabbi's wife) if he could
assist her. He calculated that she could always use a helping
hand, particularly between *Purim* and *Pesach.*

The *rebbetzen* became accustomed to his daily appearance
around the kitchen and liked the way he worked.

Two days before *Pesach,* when the work load was heaviest,
Naftali Tzvi timidly approached the *rebbetzen* and said softly,

"I'm sorry to tell you this, but the rebbe told me I have to leave before *Pesach.*"

The *rebbetzen* was aghast. She wailed, "How can you do this to me? How can you leave two days before *Pesach*? I need your help now more than in the past three-and-a-half weeks."

Naftali Tzvi answered gleefully, "If you really want me to stay, you should go and talk to the rebbe. Maybe he will change his mind about my staying."

She went immediately to the rebbe. Standing adamantly, hands on hips, she proclaimed firmly, "We will not be ready for *Pesach* unless Naftali Tzvi stays!"

The rebbe tried to calm his wife and said patiently, "I want you to know that if he stays for *Pesach*, we will have nothing but aggravation."

"If he stays in the kitchen and helps me," she queried, "how much trouble can he cause?"

Naftali stayed in Neschiz.

Can you imagine the ceremony of *bedikas chametz*[1] (the burning of the leaven), the climax of the *Pesach* preparation? The people watched in awe as Rebbe Mordechai Neschizer burned the *chametz* the morning of "*seder* night," for they honestly believed that the *chametz* he burned symbolized arrogance and evil.

When he finished, every person in Neschiz felt cleansed, ready to celebrate the festival of the exodus, the redemption of the Jewish people from slavery to freedom.

Naftali Tzvi didn't have any more chores in the kitchen, so he went to the study hall and started to study Talmud.

Suddenly, the door of the study hall opened. Standing there was a man who appeared to be a beggar. Sadness was written across his face. His shoulders were slumped. His clothes were disheveled. His feet dragged slowly toward the bench where Naftali

---

[1]Because the *Torah* prohibits the possession of leaven during *Pesach*, we search our premises for any crumb that might have been overlooked during the thorough housecleaning preceding the festival. *Bedikas chametz*, the searching ceremony, takes place on the evening of the day before the *seder*.

Tzvi studied. For a while, Naftali Tzvi ignored the beggar man, then looked up. The beggar man was encouraged to speak. He whispered, "I'd like to see the rebbe. Can you please tell me where I might find him?"

Naftali Tzvi did not hesitate to admonish the beggar man. He blurted, "After all the work is done, after all the *chametz* has been burned! Go and cleanse yourself! Do a good deed! How dare you come to see the rebbe the way you are! Get out of here!"

He returned to his studies.

Ten minutes later the rebbe stormed into the study hall. "Naftali Tzvi," he demanded, "has anybody been looking for me?"

Naftali Tzvi raised his head from the page of the Talmud and turned it from side to side.

"Naftali Tzvi, listen to me," shouted the rebbe, "I'm waiting for somebody, not a holy person. Has anybody been looking for me, any human being?"

"Why, yes," recalled Naftali, "a beggar man was here a few minutes ago. I sent him away!"

The rebbe grabbed Naftali by the shoulders and shook him. "Go and find that beggar immediately. Bring him back to me. Don't come back without him!"

Then he lowered his voice and whispered in Naftali Tzvi's ear, "If you don't find him, I never want to see you again!"

Naftali Tzvi ran from the study hall toward the main street of the town. Methodically, he searched all the inns. The beggar man was nowhere to be found. Despondently, he followed the main street to the outskirts of the town, hoping that he would find him at the last inn. With a glimmer of hope, he entered. There the despondent, dejected beggar man sat, drowning himself with liquor, his last drink before *Pesach*.[2]

Naftali Tzvi pleaded with the beggar man. "Please, you must come back to Neschiz. My life depends on it. With all my heart, please come back with me to the rebbe."

---

[2]Liquor is *chametz* (leaven), prohibited on *Pesach*.

The beggar man refused to budge. "It is no use," he said stubbornly.

Since the beggar man was a little bit drunk, Naftali Tzvi saw no point in arguing with him. He picked him up, slung him across his shoulder, stalked out of the inn, and carried the beggar man back to the rebbe.

The rebbe saw the beggar man on Naftali Tzvi's shoulders. He beckoned him to put the man down and motioned him to leave. Then he kissed and hugged him.

"You'll never know how happy I am to see you, my dearest friend," cried the rebbe.

That *seder* night, the beggar man sat on the right-hand side of the rebbe. He had slept off his drunkenness, and now his face was shining. He was clearly content.

After *Pesach,* the rebbe called Naftali Tzvi to his room. "I want to explain to you who the man was who sat at my right-hand side during the *seder,*" he said.

"You see, not too long ago, he was one of my most loyal disciples. His understanding of God and *Yiddishkeit* (Judaism) was exalted. He recognized not only the intricacies of *halachah* (Jewish law) but the mysteries of the hidden secrets of *Torah.* He confided in me and sought my advice on everything.

"Once he erred in judgment. It was a minor error, but he was embarrassed to discuss it with me. Gradually, he withdrew from me. He moved further and further away, both physically and emotionally. I knew he was very disturbed. I saw him become more and more downtrodden, but I was helpless. A long time passed.

"I want you to know that I believe that every *mitzvah* we do, the Almighty also does. On *Purim,* we send *shalach manos* (gifts). This *Purim,* I heard a voice from Heaven call me. "Mordechai ben Fayge, what do you want Me to send you for *shalach manos?*"[3]

"At first I was startled. Then I began to plead, 'Master of the

---

[3]The contemporaries of Rebbe Mordechai Neschizer believed that he had the gift of prophecy (divine inspiration).

Universe, please send me back my loyal disciple! Send him back to me now!' "

"I knew he would return to me between *Purim* and *Pesach*. I also knew he was broken and downhearted. He returned conditionally: if he came to the study hall on the eve of *Pesach* and was permitted to see me, then it was a sign from Heaven that he should stay; however, if someone threw him out, then he would never return.

"When you arrived in Neschiz for *Purim*, I envisioned how you would treat him when he returned. Now you understand why I wanted you to go home before you caused any problems. I'm explaining this to you so you will understand who the beggar was. I don't want you to think that you were not welcome here."

Naftali Tzvi Horowitz became the Ropshitzer rebbe.

The Water Carrier's *Seder*

On the first day of *Pesach,* the disciples of Rebbe Tzvi Elimelech of Diniv told him that they knew of no one who conducted a *seder* with as much fervor as the one he had conducted the previous night.

"What do you mean?" he asked them. "Don't you know that Moshele the water carrier conducted his *seder* with even more intensity than I did?"

The disciples looked quizzically at each other, their faces reflecting amazement. They were puzzled by the words of their rebbe. Rebbe Tzvi Elimelech wanted to clear up the mystery, so he asked one of them to bring Moshele the water carrier to him.

Moshele shuffled into the room where Rebbe Tzvi Elimelech and the rest of his disciples waited.

"Good *yom tov,* Moshele," Rebbe Tzvi Elimelech greeted him joyfully. "I wanted you to come here so you could tell us about your *seder.*"

"Oh, rebbe," moaned Moshele, "please don't make me tell you about my *seder.* I'll never do it again. I promise, I'll never do it again."

Rebbe Tzvi Elimelech said gently, "Please, Moshele, tell me about your *seder*. Tell me what happened at your *seder* last night. You don't have to be ashamed. You don't have to be afraid."

Moshele's hands and feet trembled. His lips quivered. He stammered as he began to tell the rebbe what happened at his *seder*. Moshele began.

You assuredly know, rebbe, that I am the town drunk. Sometimes, after I finish delivering water, I buy liquor instead of food for my family. I have drunk myself into a stupor many times, more times than I can count.

Yesterday, just before *Pesach*, I realized that I would not be able to drink for eight days, since liquor is *chametz* (leaven). I decided to drink enough to last me all the days of the festival. I sat in the inn and drank until I could drink no more. Then I shuffled out the door, tripping and staggering all the way home. I'm not sure exactly how I reached my house, but I must have passed out nearby. Someone could have dragged me to the doorstep, for that is where my wife found me. She did not know how much I had drunk, so she pulled me into the house, laid me on my bed, and hoped that I would recover my senses in time for the *seder*.

The day grew shorter. As the sun began its descent, the men walked slowly through the streets toward the synagogue for the evening prayer service. The women set festive *seder* tables. I was stretched out on my bed, unable to distinguish between night and day.

My wife tried to awaken me. I begged her to let me sleep a little longer. She shook me an hour later. I pleaded with her for a little more time.

When her patience came to an end, she screamed at me, "Aren't you ashamed of yourself? Everybody in this whole *shtetl* has already started their *seder*. Your children are waiting for you to begin. Where is your pride?"

She shook me, poked me, and screamed frantically every hour on the hour. I was dead to the world. When the sun finally came up, I sat up in my bed. I was filled with remorse, for I knew that it was too late to begin the *seder*. Tears streamed from my red swollen eyes. I called out to my wife. "Please," I begged, "wake the children and bring them to my bedside. I know it is too late to begin the *seder*, but I have something I want to tell them."

Normally, she tried to shield the children when I drank myself into a stupor, but she must have detected the urgency in my voice, because she did as I requested.

The children trudged sleepily across the room and stood around the foot of my bed. I began to speak to them in a very low voice. "My precious children," I said shamedly. "I want you to know that I've been drinking all my life, but I swear to you I will never touch another drop of liquor again. Nothing will ever prevent me from making a *seder* for you again . . . as long as I live. I am truly sorry that we did not eat *matzah* and *marror* (bitter herbs), but now I want to tell you why we celebrate *Pesach*. Please give me your undivided attention.

"First, I want you to know that there is One God Who created the world. The people of the generation of the flood destroyed it, but the patriarchs Abraham, Isaac, and Jacob, and the matriarchs Sarah, Rebecca, Rachel, and Leah rebuilt it. Jacob and his children were enslaved in Egyptian bondage, but the Almighty set us free on this night a long, long time ago. It is possible that we will live through more Pharoahs, but you must believe that the Almighty will always redeem us. That is the most important part of the *seder*. We did not recite it last night, but I want to tell it to you now.

" 'And it is this that has stood by our fathers and us'; for more than one has risen up against us to destroy us, but in all ages they rise up against us to destroy us, and the Holy One, Blessed be He, rescues us from their hands.[1]

"The Almighty who redeems us, He is the One to Whom we pray. He answers prayer. Tonight the gates of Heaven are open to receive your prayers. Swear to me that you will always remember that you are Jews. Swear to me that you will always keep in

[1]*Hagadah.*

mind that the Almighty is the redeemer of Israel. I want you to promise me that no matter what happens to the Jews in the world, you will always be loyal to your people."

I finished those words. Then my head fell back on my bed, and sleep overpowered me once more.

Moshele the water carrier paused. Tears streaming down his cheeks, he said in an agitated voice, "Rebbe, I promise you that I will keep my word. I will never drink another drop of liquor again. I will never be prevented from making a *seder*."

Rabbi Tzvi Elimelech put his hands on Moshele's shoulders. He turned to his disciples, who stood awestruck, listening to the water carrier's story, and asked them, "Did you ever attend a *seder* where a father instructed his children so clearly about God? Just one time in my life I wish I could be privileged to transmit *Yiddishkeit* (Judaism) the way Moshele the water carrier transmitted it to his children. I wish I would have been privileged to have been a guest at Moshele's *seder*."

Only God Helps

Moshe, a poor tailor, lived with his wife and children in an isolation *shtetl*. He served the surrounding area, sewing for the farmers and innkeepers, trying to eke out a meager living. They affectionately called him "Moshke," for they like his homey, cheerful disposition.

He worked all week, leaving his dilapidated hut in the *shtetl* early Sunday morning, carrying his *tefillin, tallis,* and supplies for the week: assorted needles, multi-colored threads, scissors, and a loaf of bread. He returned home early on Friday afternoon in time to prepare for *Shabbos.* The minute he entered his hut, he counted the money he earned, tithed it for the poor of the *shtetl,* and gave his wife the remainder with which to purchase food for *Shabbos* and manage the household for the week.

On Friday night, the worries of the week lifted from his face. His dilapidated hut was transformed into a palace. The candle-light sparkled, and the fragrance of the *Shabbos* food filled the air—he, the king, sitting at one end of the table; his wife, the queen, at the other end; and their children, all princes and princesses, at their sides, together, welcoming *Shabbos.*

That winter was particularly fierce. Near *Pesach* time, snow still covered the ground. The winds blew furiously. Walking between his customers' houses took twice as long as usual. Moshe's earnings for the week before *Pesach* were less than he normally earned. He worried about how he would earn the extra money for wine and *matzah* for the rapidly approaching festival. As he struggled against the wind, he prayed and sang out, "Only God helps, only God helps!"

Suddenly, he heard the jingle of the bells on the *poretz's* (landowner's) carriage. He barely avoided being trampled by the three white horses that pulled the carriage. From inside the carriage, Moshe heard the drunken voice of the *poretz* shouting after him, "Stop! Stop! Come here, Moshke, quickly!"

Moshe's knees trembled; his lips quivered. He did not know what the *poretz* wanted from him. He did not know that the drunken *poretz* wanted to play games.

Moshe peered into the carriage and saw that the *poretz* was clutching a rifle. "Moshke," screeched the *poretz*, "crawl out there in the field. I'm going to practice shooting. You are the target. Quickly, quickly, crawl fast!"

Moshe paled and began to plead, "Mighty *poretz*, have compassion. I have a wife and children!"

The *poretz* was deaf to Moshe's pleas. "Hurry, crawl, don't waste time," the drunken *poretz* demanded. As he sputtered out commands, the *poretz* raised his rifle and prepared to shoot.

Moshe began to move slowly toward the open snow-covered field. Tears flowed from his eyes as he thought about his wife, who would be widowed, and his children, who would be orphaned. He began to utter the words of *Sh'ma Yisrael.*

The *poretz* screamed, "Move faster!"

A rifle shot pierced the air. Moshe breathed a sigh of relief. He was still alive! He began to mutter, "Only God helps, only God helps!"

The *poretz* turned to his wife and jeered, "Why did you move my hand?"

His wife retorted, unafraid of her drunken husband, "Isn't it enough that you frightened the poor tailor to death? Now, go and help him!''

One hour passed while the *poretz* tried to calm Moshe after his brush with death. Then the *poretz's* wife insisted that Moshe ride back to their mansion with them in their carriage. In a conciliatory tone, she said gently, ''I know you are a fine tailor. I have work for you. Please stay in our mansion and sew the clothes that need to be mended.''

Soon, Moshe was sitting in the sewing room in the mansion. His hands busily sewed the garments, but his mouth sang words of thanksgiving from the Psalms.

When he finished his work, the *poretz's* wife paid him generously and asked him to return one day each week. Moshe earned more money working for her for a few hours than he earned working for the farmers and innkeepers all week.

Now that he had the promise of steady employment, he was able to devote more time to prayer and study. He worked for the *poretz's* wife at least one day a week.

He dreamed of paying off his debts, of celebrating *Pesach* in comfort.

The day before *Pesach,* Moshe headed toward the mansion. He thought he could work one more time before the holiday. He did not know that the *poretz's* wife had gone to visit a friend in a distant town. Moshe bumped into the *poretz* as he entered the gates. ''Moshke,'' jeered the *poretz,* ''how is it that you are still alive?''

Moshe answered, ''The Almighty has granted me life. Only God helps, only God helps!''

The *poretz* continued sneering, ''Moshe, do you earn a living?''

Moshe replied, ''The Almighty provides. Only God helps, only God helps!''

The *poretz* continued sarcastically. ''Why do you keep saying, 'Only God helps'? I think my wife provides for you and your family.''

The *poretz* could not restrain his anger when Moshe answered, "Only God helps, only God helps. The Almighty decrees how much every person should earn."

The *poretz* shouted, "Get out of here and don't come back! Let your God provide for you for *Pesach*. I am not giving you another ruble." The *poretz* reached for the revolver in his belt, and Moshe fled as fast as his feet could carry him.

Dejected, the tailor returned to his dilapidated hut. On the night of the searching for leaven, there was no *matzah* and no bread in the house. Suddenly, someone pushed the door open and threw a sack into the dilapidated hut. The flame from the single candle was extinguished by the wind, and the smell emanating from the sack was that of a corpse.

Moshe struggled to rekindle the light. His teeth chattered. This was not the first time a corpse had been thrown into a Jewish home before *Pesach*. Moshe feared the worst—a blood libel.

"I must run immediately to the rabbi," the trembling tailor said to his wife. He turned to put on his torn coat. In a split second, his wife Bayla opened the sack to see what was inside.

"Look, Moshe," she called out, "it is only a dead monkey!"

Moshe was dumbfounded. He could not believe his eyes. He bent to pick up the sack so he could throw it out of his hut. As he bent over and moved it, he heard the sound of clinking coins from inside the sack.

"Bayla," the tailor said, "only God helps, only God helps. The Almighty has sent us a treasure."

Moshe picked up a knife and split the body of the dead monkey in half. He found a treasure of gold coins in the innards of the monkey.

Moshe's *seder* that year was celebrated with great joy. He purchased the best wine and *matzah* and new clothing for his family. He even invited two poor people from the *shtetl* for the entire week of the holiday.

Everyone recited the *hagadah* with deep feeling. Throughout the recitation, Moshe added intermittently, "Only God helps, only God helps!"

After the meal, Moshe thought he heard the sound of wagon wheels approaching. He responded fearfully to the knock at the door. The *poretz* and his wife stood there. Moshe invited them inside. The *poretz* began to speak, gesticulating wildly with his hands. "Where did you get the money to purchase all this *Pesach* food? I thought this house would be gloomy and dark."

Moshe answered respectfully, "Only God helps, only God helps. Let me tell you how God helps."

Moshe then told the *poretz* and his wife how he had found the dead monkey and the gold coins.

This time the *poretz* was dumbfounded. He confessed, "That monkey lived on my estate. It died mysteriously two days ago. I commanded my servant to throw it into your hut as a *Pesach* present. But I don't understand how you found the coins. Something is going on at my estate among the servants."

The landowner's wife knew the truth, so she began to explain. "You know that a few days ago we collected a great deal of rent money. The coins were supposed to be solid gold. Your bookkeeper wanted to examine the weight of the coins, so he bit them. The monkey was watching him and imitated his actions, swallowing handfuls of the coins before the bookkeeper could stop him. The monkey died."

Now the *poretz* began to laugh heartily. He said, "It seems, Moshke, that your God did not abandon you. When the Almighty commands us to give, we give, whether willingly or unwillingly."

The landowner's wife interrupted the *poretz*. "When the *Pesach* holiday is over," she said, "I want you to return to work in the mansion."

Then the *poretz* and his wife backed slowly out the door and departed.

Moshe concluded the *seder*, singing joyfully,

> Give thanks to the Almighty for He is good,
> His kindness endures forever! . . .
> Who alone does great wonders,
> His kindness endures forever![1]

[1]*Hagadah* and Psalms 136:1,4.

Elyahu's Cup

Rebbe Avraham Yehoshua Heschel sat at a book-laden table, deeply immersed in his studies, surrounded by eager students who absorbed his every word. Suddenly, he lifted his head and leaned back in his chair. He relaxed his brow and smiled.

Courteously, one student asked, "Rebbe, what thought entered your mind that distracted you from studying? You were in the midst of explaining a difficult passage. Why are you smiling? Won't you tell us what you are thinking?"

The rebbe sat quietly for a few moments, stroking his beard. It seemed as if he were trying to remember something.

"I was thinking about that wonderful cup of Elyahu," he said.

"Maybe I've told you the story previously. I don't remember. Nevertheless, before *Pesach* it is good to retell the story of Elyahu's cup."

The students moved their chairs away from the table and waited patiently for their rebbe to begin. They loved to listen to his stories.

Once there was a very wealthy man, named Elkana, and his wife, named Penina. They lived in a splendid mansion, according to the standard of their wealth. They owned china, crystal, silver, jewelry, furs. One possession was more precious to them than all the rest: a magnificent, jeweled cup of Elyahu which they proudly used as their table centerpiece each *seder* night.

Elkana and Penina were both God-fearing, hospitable, righteous people. They recognized that the source of all their blessings was the Almighty. In gratitude, they opened their home to the poor of their city and to travelers who passed through.

Sadly, Elkana invested in a few bad business deals. Slowly, he lost much of his assets. In order to cover his expenses, he started to sell off some of his possessions, thinking that future business investments would be profitable. But Elkana's choice of investments continued to be a financial disaster. Years passed, and Elkana and Penina became poorer and poorer. Their sole remaining possession was Elyahu's cup.

Penina never complained. That year, as *Pesach* approached, she wondered how she would be able to purchase *matzos,* wine, and other necessities for the festival. There was simply no money available.

The morning before *Pesach,* Penina gently reminded her heartbroken husband that there was not one ruble in the house with which to purchase *Pesach* food.

"I think," said Elkana, "you will have to take Elyahu's cup to the pawnbroker. The pawnbroker will undoubtedly give you more than enough money to buy food for the holiday."

Until that moment, Penina suffered silently, always hoping that their lot in life would improve, that her husband would invest in a good business that would restore their wealth. She never despaired. But when she heard her husband's suggestion, she could not bear her pain any longer. She cried out in anguish, "What! Sell Elyahu's cup! I will never sell it. It is our one remaining precious possession. There has to be another way. I simply will not part with Elyahu's cup."

Elkana recognized the tone of Penina's voice: she would never change her mind, no matter what he said.

Not knowing how to solve the crisis, he slipped sheepishly out of the house and headed straight for the study hall, the one place where he found solace.

Penina did not know where she would find the money to buy food for *Pesach.* She wandered around alone in the big mansion, walking from one empty room to another. Only a few pieces of furniture were left where once overstuffed sofas stood and exquisite paintings and tapestries hung.

Suddenly, Penina heard a knock at her door. She ignored it at first, not wanting to face anyone, but the intruder persisted. Finally, Penina opened the door. An elderly, well-dressed gentleman stood on her doorstep.

"Is this the house of Elkana and Penina?" he queried. "I have come from a distant town. I have a letter of recommendation from a mutual friend of ours. He told me that your home is always open to travelers. I need a place to stay for *Pesach.* Is it possible that I may stay here for the holiday week?"

Penina could not speak; only tears streaming from her eyes betrayed her emotions.

"Yes," she stammered, "our house was formerly open to the poor of our city and to travelers who passed this way, but my husband has had some business reverses. We have sold most of our possessions to sustain ourselves. Right now we don't even have any money to buy *matzos* or wine for *Pesach.*"

"Money is no problem," said the elderly, well-dressed gentleman politely. "I have plenty of money. I don't want to be alone in an inn for *Pesach.*" With these words, he put his hand into his jacket pocket and withdrew a bag of coins.

"Please, take this money and buy what you need," he continued. "Tell your husband that I will meet him in the synagogue tonight, and I will walk home together with him."

The elderly, well-dressed gentleman walked slowly down the path, leaving Penina dumbstruck.

After she composed herself, she ran to the marketplace to purchase food for the holiday. For the first time in many months, she had plenty of money. She did not stint on her grocery list: *matzos*, wine, apples for *charoses*, horseradish for the *marror*, fish, eggs to dip in salt water, a bone for the *zeroa*, meat, potatoes for the *kugel*. As Penina ran from stall to stall through the marketplace, she hummed one of the melodies from the *seder*, the one she remembered by heart, the one sung just before drinking the second cup of wine: "Therefore it is our duty to thank, to praise, to laud, to glorify. . . Him who performed all these miracles."[1]

Laden with packages, she ran all the way home. The preparations for the holiday went quickly. Penina was so happy.

"Hurry! Hurry!" she kept urging herself onward.

Elkana came home late in the afternoon to see how Penina was. To his surprise, the house was *pesadik*: everything was ready for the *seder*. Penina was shining and joyous.

"Elkana," she shouted incoherently, "there is an elderly, well-dressed gentleman in town. He was here this morning. He wanted to be our guest. He gave me a bag of coins. He said he would meet you in the synagogue."

Elkana changed his clothes in honor of the holiday and went to find his guest in the synagogue. When he arrived, only the townspeople were present. There was no stranger.

He joined in the evening prayer service with the congregation, one eye on the door, waiting expectantly for his guest. The service ended. No stranger came. The townspeople went home to begin their *seders*.

Elkana was puzzled. He sat around the empty synagogue for about an hour, waiting patiently. When no one came, he went home.

Penina and Elkana waited to begin their *seder*. Eight, nine, ten o'clock. They waited until eleven o'clock, but the elderly, well-dressed gentleman did not appear.

Finally Elkana decided to begin the *seder*.

"I'll do everything very slowly,"he thought aloud. "Maybe our guest will show up soon."

[1]*Hagadah.*

Elkana poured the wine for *kiddush*, washed his hands, broke the *afikomen matzah*, and recited the *hagadah*. The guest, however, did not arrive. They ate the meal. Elkana grew sleepy. He managed the grace after meals, then fell asleep at his place at the table . . . at the moment he should have gone to open the door for Elyahu Hanavi.

Penina decided to finish the *seder* herself. She stood, walked to the door, and opened it. The elderly, well-dressed gentleman was standing outside.

"Please, come in," blurted Penina. "Where were you? We waited and waited. Why have you taken so long to come?"

The elderly, well-dressed gentleman nodded his head, walked into the house, approached the table, and looked around. Penina was right behind him.

"Wake up, Elkana, wake up. Our guest has arrived," she said as she bent to gently shake him from his sleep. But Elkana did not move. He slept soundly. When Penina straightened up, the elderly, well-dressed gentleman had disappeared.

The next morning, Penina told Elkana that he missed his guest's visit. He felt sad that he did not meet him.

Elkana passed away soon after *Pesach*. When his soul ascended to the Heavenly Court, it was judged immediately worthy of entering Paradise.

"Welcome to Paradise, holy soul of Elkana," the angels called out in greeting. The holy soul was about to enter . . . but an elderly, well-dressed gentleman blocked its path. He said, "You may not enter Paradise. You wanted to sell Elyahu's cup. You must sit outside and wait."

Elkana's soul waited and waited.

Two years later, Penina passed away. The Heavenly Court judged her immediately worthy of Paradise. The angels came out to meet her soul.

"Welcome to Paradise, holy soul of Penina," they sang.

The soul of Penina was about to enter but noticed something sitting in its path.

"This soul," cried Penina's soul, "was the soul of my husband Elkana. I will not enter Paradise alone. I will not enter without him." She was adamant. The Heavenly Court knew she would never change her mind. The Heavenly Court had no choice. Both souls were permitted to enter Paradise.

Rebbe Avraham Yehoshua Heschel paused for breath and then explained, "As we were sitting here studying, I had a vision. I saw the souls of Elkana and Penina entering Paradise."

A Constable for the *Seder*

In the years preceding the Russian Revolution, when people challenged the Tzar's right to iron-fisted rule and the cries for social justice permeated the land, a new constable arrived in the town.

The Jews did not know how to react to the newcomer. Past experience had taught them to fear government officials. Now they wondered if he was a spy sent by the Tzar's government to ferret out those young Jews who defied the government by joining with the agitators, or if he was just another constable sent merely to keep a semblance of order in these tumultuous times.

The leaders of the Jewish community met and decided to extend a friendly welcome. They hoped they could gain the new constable's sympathy, that he might deal with them even-handedly. They hoped that if he responded to their overtures of friendship, they would have less of a reason to fear the iron-fisted rule of the government.

They chose a regal-looking businessman named Zev Kvirshal to represent them to the constable. They had confidence in Zev Kvirshal, for he did business with Russian busi-

356

nessmen; he mingled with them, he knew their language and their mannerisms.

He felt a tremendous responsibility to the community. He wanted to succeed in showing the new constable that he could count on the friendship of the Jewish community and that they would certainly cause him no problems. With trepidation in his heart, Zev Kvirshal made an appointment to see the new constable.

Surprisingly, the constable turned out to be a very pleasant man. As soon as Zev Kvirshal walked into his office, he served a cup of tea. The two men sat and relaxed, making small talk. Then the constable cleared his throat and began to speak earnestly.

"First," he said, "I want you to know that my name is Captain Gregory Yefetomovitch Ivanov. I am very determined that this town remain quiet. I don't want any problems. I need the complete cooperation of every Jew. I need to know how the Jews earn their living. How do they get along with their non-Jewish neighbors? How do they collect the money to pay their taxes? Have there been any pogroms lately?"

Zev Kvirshal answered the constable's questions as best as he could. When the constable was satisfied with the information, he rose to dismiss his guest.

"Please," he said softly, "I want you to feel free to consult me on any matter that you think my help might benefit the Jewish community. Remember, don't hesitate."

He extended his hand in friendship, and the men parted company.

When Zev Kvirshal reported the results of his meeting with the constable to the leaders of the Jewish community, they were in a quandary. They did not know if the new constable was sincere or if he was trying to gain their confidence on a pretext that they lower their guard against impending trouble.

They had no choice but to adopt a wait-and-see attitude.

After a few months, the leaders of the Jewish community tried again to test the motivations of their new constable.

They asked Zev Kvirshal to bring him an envelope.

Again Zev Kvirshal made an appointment. Again he found the constable to be a very pleasant man. After they drank their tea and chatted awhile, Zev Kvirshal took the envelope from his pocket and handed it to the constable.

"The Jewish community," he said, "knows that your salary is meager. We want you to be able to afford some luxuries. We would like you to take this gift."

The constable was adamant. He said firmly, "My salary is adequate. I have no family to support. My needs are few. I can afford to buy whatever I need. Please, thank the Jewish community for their kindness, but I cannot accept this gift."

Zev Kvirshal returned to the leaders of the Jewish community. They were really puzzled. Most of them believed that the constable refused to take the money because he knew that the government was planning a pogrom, and he did not want to be obligated to help them.

Many weeks passed, and the fears of the Jewish community calmed, for nothing happened to disturb the tranquility of the town. Then, one afternoon, Zev Kvirshal received an urgent message from the constable to come to his office immediately. He ran all the way.

Breathless, panting, he sputtered, "I came as fast as I could. What can I do for you?"

The constable did not waste time with trivialities.

"I called you to come see me in friendship," he said. "You must know that a warrant has been issued for the arrest of four agitators who live in this town. I have already detained two of them, and I am making arrangements to send them to St. Petersburg. The other two are Jewish boys named Laybel Goldberg and Avraham Sasov. I want you to warn them, in my name, to refrain from further anti-government activities, or I will be forced to arrest them and send them to St. Petersburg for trial with their companions. I want you to impress upon them that the government of Russia is not their concern. I did not restrain them because I have compassion for their families."

Zev Kvirshal left the constable and went immediately to the rabbi of the town.

"Rabbi," he said, "I have just come from a meeting with the constable. He told me that Laybel Goldberg and Avraham Sasov are involved in anti-government activities. They will be arrested and sent to St. Petersburg if they don't stop immediately. The Jewish community will become the scapegoats for their adventures. You must warn them."

The rabbi did not hesitate one second. He sent for Laybel Goldberg and Avraham Sasov and their parents. When they arrived in his study, he demanded that they refrain from further subversive activities. He explained that they were not only acting foolishly but they were endangering the entire Jewish community as well.

The boys swore that they would drop out of all anti-government groups. Now the mystery of the constable's intentions intensified. The Jewish community wondered if he were their friend or foe.

Two days before *Pesach*, Zev Kvirshal walked through the marketplace, deeply immersed in thought. He did not notice that the constable was following him. Suddenly, the constable tapped him on the shoulder. Zev Kvirshal jerked backward, shocked and frightened.

"Don't you recognize me?" asked the constable. "Don't you want to recognize me?"

"Please forgive me," sputtered Zev Kvirshal. "I was thinking about the many preparations I have yet to make for the *Pesach* holiday."

"When does your holiday begin?" asked the constable.

"Our holiday begins in two days, in the evening," answered Zev Kvirshal.

"I know," continued the constable. "Doesn't it begin with a festive meal? I just don't remember what it is called."

Zev Kvirshal volunteered the information. "We begin our festival with a *seder*."

"Yes, that's it," mused the constable. "I would like nothing better than to be invited to your *seder*."

Zev Kvirshal stood glued to that spot, astonished at the constable's request. He wondered why the constable wanted to attend a *seder*. He knew that the constable's presence would disturb the family's celebration. He thought that everyone would be uncomfortable.

He hesitated, unsure what he wanted to do. Then he said softly, "It will be my honor for you to attend our family *seder*. My son will come to your office to pick you up before the *seder* begins."

The long *seder* table sparkled. Zev Kvirshal's wife, his sons and daughters, their spouses, and his grandchildren sat smiling all around him. He, the king, reclined towards his left side on an intricately embroidered pillow. He seated the constable next to the son-in-law who spoke the clearest Russian, so that he might explain the *seder* ritual.

Zev Kvirshal and his family proceeded: *kiddush*, washing the hands, dipping the greens or vegetables in salt water, the *afikomen*, *Mah Nishtana* (the four questions), recitation of the *hagadah*.

From time to time, Zev Kvirshal glanced at his guest who sat quietly, rather downcast, his mouth drawn, dejected.

Zev Kvirshal could not understand why the constable had wanted to be invited to his *seder*. "Maybe he likes Jewish food," he thought. "Maybe he came for the festive meal."

But Zev Kvirshal's guess was wrong. After the completion of the first part of the *hagadah*, Mrs. Kvirshal served the gefilte fish, but the constable only picked at his food.

"Don't you care for the fish?" asked Zev Kvirshal gently. "Yes," answered the constable. Without warning, tears welled up in his eyes and streamed down his cheeks. He began to shudder.

Zev Kvirshal was nervous. He knew he had done nothing to offend the constable. The constable stood up from the table. Suddenly, he began to scream in a loud, clear voice, "*Sh'ma Yisrael Adonai Eloheinu Adonai Echad!* (Hear, O Israel, The Lord our God, The Lord is One!). I am a Jew!!"

The Kvirshal family was dumbfounded. "I have to tell you my story," said the constable after he regained composure.

When I was eleven years old, I was kidnapped from my widowed mother to serve in the Russian army. I was sent to a distant outpost where I had no association with my people. Many years passed, and I was promoted from rank to rank. When I reached the rank of lieutenant, I was sent to administer law and order in a big city. I had completely forgotten that I was a Jew.

One day, a strange incident occurred. I found out that a group of farmers from a village outside the big city were planning a pogrom against the Jews of a nearby *shtetl.* I felt it my responsibility to halt that atrocity, so I called for additional policemen to stop the pogrom.

One week later I was demoted to constable and sent to this town with the explanation that Russian officers do not stop pogroms against Jews until after the damage has been inflicted and their property destroyed. Exploiting Jews, I was told, keeps the people's minds off their own problems with the Tzar by providing a scapegoat.

It was then that I remembered that I was a Jew. When I arrived here, I decided that I would do all in my power to protect Jews. I even thought about returning to an observant Jewish lifestyle, but I was so far removed that I did not know where to go for help or how to begin.

It was then that I met you, Mr. Kvirshal. When you began to describe your preparations for this holiday, I imagined my parents' *seder* table. The image was not clear. I must have been nine or ten years old. My father was still alive. I knew that I desperately wanted to be at a *seder* this year.

All during the *seder* ritual, I imagined my mother standing beside me, pleading with me to return to my roots, to my people.

The entire Kvirshal family had been moved to tears by the constable's story. After composing himself, Zev Kvirshal spoke.

"Tonight, my brother, Gregory Yefetomovitch Ivanov, you have ended your life as a Russian constable. From now on you will be called Avraham ben Avraham. Just as our ancestors began a new life on this night of the exodus, so you shall also be redeemed."

"You are right," answered Avraham ben Avraham. "I don't know what my lot in life will be, but I am ready to return to my people."

The festive spirit returned to Zev Kvirshal's table. They ate and sang with gusto and great joy.

After the *seder* ended, Zev Kvirshal and the former constable went off to a room where they planned Avraham ben Avraham's future.

During *chol hamoed,* the intermediate days of the *Pesach* festival, the former constable disappeared.

Only Zev Kvirshal knew the truth.

The Wheat Merchant

Included in our daily prayers is a special petition for rain which wakens the slumbering seeds of the soil to provide food for mankind. "You cause the wind to blow and the rain to fall."[1] This petition for rain is recited both in *Eretz Yisrael* and in the Diaspora, for we are conscious of the necessity for rain in the Holy Land during the winter months.

The early settlers who returned to rebuild the land at the end of the nineteenth century depended upon rain for their very existence.

In the winter of 1915, there was a terrible drought in the land of Yisrael. It seemed as if the windows of Heaven were shut tight. The earth was parched. Instead of the plush golden color of the winter wheat crop, the fallow land lay barren. Fruit on trees shriveled. Branches hung limp. The wind, blowing across the arid land, created a huge dustbin.

Little of the previous year's wheat crop remained, and it was so costly that the ordinary person could hardly afford to pur-

[1]From the *Amidah*, the prayer of silent devotion.

chase it. Famine, hunger, and fear were reflected on the distraught faces of the inhabitants of Jerusalem.

Days turned into weeks, weeks into months. The winter sky dazzled from the glow of the sun, the horizon remained unclouded. *Pesach* was rapidly approaching. The settlers recalled the joyous ceremony in previous years of harvesting the wheat, grinding, milling, and finally baking *matzos* for the holiday. Sadly, this year would be different.

The leader of the Jerusalem Jewish community was Rabbi Yisrael. He had guided his people through many difficulties and assisted them in their personal troubles. He suggested solutions to critical community problems, but never had he faced a dilemma of this proportion. He hoped that some financial help would reach him from the Diaspora[2]—from Jews who felt obligated to support the settlers who were building the land—but as the holiday drew closer, he doubted that any money would reach him in time. He also worried about how he could possibly purchase wheat, even if he did have money. Rabbi Yisrael's face reflected his pain, his heartache, and his helplessness.

Toward evening of one particularly dazzling day, Rabbi Yisrael heard the sound of bells, signaling a wagon approaching his house. Curiously, he stepped to a window and saw an Arab leading the camels that were pulling a wagon laden with sacks of wheat. In a split second, the Arab stood on his doorstep and queried, "Are you the leader of the Jewish community of Jerusalem? I have a wagonload of wheat to sell, and I know that you and your people need wheat for *Pesach*. I thought you would purchase my wagonload of wheat at the fair market price."

Rabbi Yisrael answered, "Yes, we need wheat for *Pesach*, but we have no money to pay for it."

The Arab merchant hesitated for a moment, then spoke gently. "I will wait for the money. I trust you to pay me."

Rabbi Yisrael said, "I will buy the wheat on the condition that you set a date when payment is due."

---

[2]During the years of World War I, Jews living in the Diaspora were spread throughout the countries of the combatants. Turkey controlled the land of Israel and fought on Germany's side. It tried to cut off the funds sent by Jews living in England, France, Russia, and the United States.

The Arab merchant answered, "I will return after the holiday to collect my money." He turned to the workers who had been riding on top of the wagonload of wheat and ordered them to unload the wagons in the storehouse located nearby. Soon, Jews ran from all over the neighborhood to help unload the sacks of wheat.

As the workers unloaded the wheat, dusk descended over the city. Rabbi Yisrael ran home to fetch some lanterns. When he returned to the warehouse, the sacks of wheat were piled neatly inside, and the Arab merchant and his workers had gone.

Rabbi Yisrael rejoiced that the Jewish community would have wheat with which to bake *matzos* for *Pesach* and leftovers to sustain them afterwards, but he still worried that he would not have the money to pay the Arab merchant. So he wrote letters to everyone he knew in the Diaspora, describing the emergency situation and appealing for help. Money began trickling in. Each mail delivery contained marks, dollars, francs, rubles, zlotys, pounds. Before candlelighting time on the eve of the *Pesach* festival, Rabbi Yisrael had accumulated the money to pay the Arab merchant for his wheat.

After the *Pesach* holiday, Rabbi Yisrael waited for the Arab wheat merchant. Days passed . . . one month . . . two months . . . three months. The Arab merchant did not come. Over the years, Rabbi Yisrael guarded the money that rightfully belonged to the Arab wheat merchant, but the merchant never appeared to collect his money.

When Rabbi Yisrael realized that he had not much more time to live, he talked to his son-in-law and told him where he kept the money that belonged to the Arab merchant. He told his son-in-law to keep the money in a safe place for another ten years, in the event that the Arab wheat merchant came to collect the money the Jewish community owed him. "If he does not come in another ten years," said Rabbi Yisrael, "then you may distribute the money to both the Jewish and Arab poor of Jerusalem." The Arab wheat merchant never returned to collect his money.

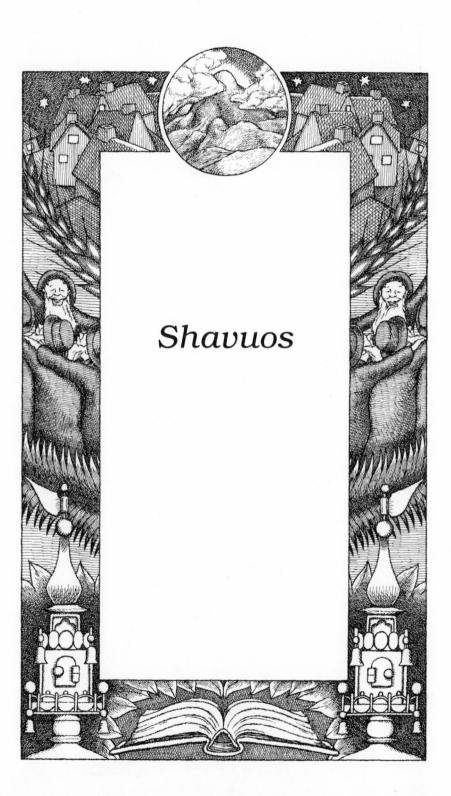

Shavuos

havuos is one of the three pilgrim festivals when the Jewish people ascended to Jerusalem to worship in the Holy Temple.

On *Shavuos*, which falls on the sixth and seventh days of *Sivan*, the Jewish people stood unified under Mount Sinai, ready to receive the *Torah*. It was for this purpose that they were redeemed from Egyptian bondage.

This holy day derives its name from the *Torah's* commandment to count seven complete weeks from the day after *Pesach*, for the root of the word *Shavuos* is "weeks."

The Jewish people were commanded to count seven weeks, day by day, in anticipation of revelation.

Shavuos marks the beginning of Jewish nationhood. Following the exodus, the Jewish people set forth on a long trek through the desert, from Egypt to Sinai, where they accepted the mantle of peoplehood through *Torah*. It was at Sinai that a group of slaves was formed into a kingdom of priests and a holy nation.

Paralleling preparation for receiving the *Torah*, it is customary to study during the entire night of *Shavuos*, for who can sleep when the Almighty is about to reveal Himself to the world?

The tradition to eat dairy foods on *Shavuos* is explained by the fact that prior to receiving the *Torah*, the Jewish people were not commanded to observe *kashrus*, the dietary code.

Shavuos is also called the festival of the first fruits.

Torah Thoughts

The Days of Counting

There are three pilgrim festivals[1] during the Jewish calendar year, *Pesach, Shavuos,* and *Sukkos.*

The *Torah* describes two of these three festivals in terms of the commandments or the historical events that are associated with them. Concerning *Pesach* we read, "On the fifteenth day of that month is the feast of unleavened bread . . . seven days you should eat *matzos.*"[2]

We are commanded on *Sukkos,* "You shall dwell in booths seven days; all Jews shall dwell in *sukkos* because they dwelled in booths when I redeemed them from the land of Egypt."[3]

The third festival, *Shavuos* (the holiday of revelation) is not described as a historical event or in terms of the commandments associated with it. Rather, it is described as the holiday of weeks: "And you shall count, from the day after *Pesach,* seven weeks, until you number fifty days."[4]

---

[1]During the pilgrim festivals, the Jewish people went up from their homes to worship in the Holy Temple in Jerusalem.

[2]Leviticus 23:6.

[3]Leviticus 23:42–43.

[4]Leviticus 23:16–17.

By omitting a description of the commandments or the historical event associated with *Shavuos*, the *Torah* emphasizes a different aspect of the holiday, the significance of the counting of the weeks.

The significance of counting focuses upon the necessary preparation for the betrothal of the Almighty to the Jewish people. It is as if the counting of the days between *Pesach*[5] and *Shavuos* are the days of preparation for the wedding. For on *Shavuos*, through the revelation of *Torah* on Sinai, the Jewish people and the Almighty became one: "the Holy one, blessed be He, the *Torah*, and the Jewish people are One."[6]

The seven weeks resemble the days of a bride and groom's purification before their union. During each day of this waiting period, the days are counted in anticipation of the event:

Today is day one, today is day two,
Today is one week and one day, closer and closer,
Today is three weeks and three days,
Today is five weeks and two days, closer and closer,
Today is six weeks, closer and closer,
Today is seven weeks, the wedding day!

Just as each day draws the bride and groom closer to their wedding day, so each day of counting draws the Jewish people closer to the Sinaitic revelation.

Therefore, the emphasis for the holiday of *Shavuos* is on the counting of the weeks. The preparation for receiving the *Torah* is essential to appreciate the magnitude of the historical event.

[5]The ultimate purpose of the Egyptian slavery and the redemption was the revelation at Mt. Sinai (Rashi, Exodus 20:2). Therefore, the counting period begins with the exodus.

[6]*Zohar, Acharei Mos*, Ch. 73.

A Precious Treasure

When Moshe Rabbeinu (Moses our teacher) ascended the heights of Sinai to receive the *Torah* in order to transmit it to mankind, the ministering angels demanded from the Almighty an explanation for permitting a human to enter the heavenly sphere. They said, "Master of the Universe, what business has one born of woman among us . . . to remove your precious treasure from the heavenly to the human sphere?" The Almighty answered, "Moshe has ascended these heights to receive the *Torah*."

The ministering angels were perplexed and argued, "In the heavenly sphere, we revere *Torah*, we uphold the principles of *Torah*, we honor the *Torah*. Your *Torah* is a precious treasure . . . that was hidden for seventy-four generations before creation. Why do you desire to give it to mankind? 'Your glory is over heaven and earth. . . . What is man that You are mindful of him?'[1] Will man appreciate *Torah*? Will man uphold the principles of *Torah* as guidelines for his life? Will man search for light and truth through the principles of *Torah*?"

[1]Psalms 8:2, 5.

The Almighty turned to Moshe and prodded him into answering. Moshe began to enumerate the reasons for wanting to transmit the *Torah* to mankind by using the ten commandments as the basis for his answer. He began, "The first commandment clearly states, 'I am the Lord your God who brought you out of Egypt from the house of bondage.' "[2] Moshe took a deep breath and demanded of the ministering angels, "Were you slaves in Egypt?" He paused, but continued before they had a chance to respond.

" 'You shall have no other gods before Me.' Do you live among idolatrous nations?"

The ministering angels had no time to retort for Moshe pressed his argument forward.

"It is written, 'Do not take the name of the Lord in vain.' Do you need guidelines where there are no business transactions among you? It is written, 'Remember the Sabbath day and make it holy.' Do you work so hard that you need a day of rest? It is written, 'Honor your mother and father.' Do you have parents to honor? It is written, 'Do not murder. . . . Do not commit adultery. . . . Do not steal.' Is there jealousy or greed among you? Do you have an evil inclination that needs controls? How do you intend to apply the commandments of the *Torah* to the heavenly sphere? Clearly, there is no evil inclination in heaven, so why do you need the *Torah*? People need the *Torah* in their search for light and truth, in their striving from darkness to inner light, for it is the *Torah* that radiates light."

The ministering angels acknowledged their defeat. They were convinced that mankind needed the *Torah* more than they. Therefore, the Almighty, in His Infinite Wisdom, understanding the needs of mankind, and the searching nature of man's soul, gave His precious treasure to the Jewish people, guardians of *Torah*, on the condition that they bring light and truth to the world.[3]

[2]Exodus 20:2.
[3]Talmud, *Shabbos* 88b.

La'asok B'Divrei Torah

We Jews have a blessing for everything. We bless our food, "Who brings forth bread from the earth," and our drink, "who creates the fruit of the vine." We bless the fragrances we smell, "Who creates spices of fragrance." We bless the *mitzvah* of circumcision, "Who had commanded us to bring him into the covenant of our patriarch Abraham." We bless the *mitzvah* of affixing a *mezuzah* to our doorpost, "Who has made us holy with His commandments and commanded us to set the *mezuzah* on our doorpost." We bless in gratitude, "Who clothes the naked." We bless natural phenomena, "Whose strength and power fill the universe."

The words of each blessing specifically and clearly describe the action involved. Curiously, when we study *Torah,* the words of the blessing *la'asok b'divrei Torah* do not describe the specific action clearly. The verb of the blessing should actually be *lomed* (to learn, to study), but *la'asok* is used instead. *La'asok* means to attend to, to engage in, to occupy oneself with, to immerse in, to be busy with, to practice.

The reason for using the verb *la'asok* is that it implies a fine

377

difference in the action involved. Not every person has the ability or time to learn or study on the level that is required by the verb *lomed*. However, every person can attend to, engage in, occupy oneself with, be immersed in, be busy with, and practice *Torah* according to one's ability, time, and need to cling to the word of God.

Wondrous Manna

A curious passage merits explanation: "The *Torah* was given for explication and interpretation only to those who ate the manna."[1] What was so unusual about the people who ate the manna that they were singled out as the repositors of *Torah*? The *Torah*'s description of the qualities of the manna provides an answer: "bread raining from Heaven, sandwiched in between layers of dew, scattered around the camp, and when the dew evaporated, there were little grains all over the surface of the desert; it looked like fine frost on the ground."[2]

In addition, the manna had many different preparation possibilities. "Bake what you want to bake and cook what you want to cook."[3] "The manna was like coriander seed with a pearl-like luster. The people could gather it as they walked. Then they could grind it in a handmill or crush it in a mortar, cook it in a pan, mold it into cakes. It tasted like an oil wafer."[4]

[1] *Midrash Mechilta, B'shalach* 17.
[2] Exodus 16:14.
[3] Exodus 16:23.
[4] Numbers 11:7–9.

According to our tradition, based upon the above text, we can conclude that the manna tasted like whatever food the person wanted to eat at that particular time, fulfilling the desires of each individual. The spectrum of choices encompassed both steak and vegetarian fare, seasoned or bland food, sweet delicacies or salty snacks.

Understanding this, we can construct an explanation for the original midrashic statement, "The *Torah* was given for explication and interpretation only to those who ate the manna." That statement means that the *Torah* has seventy facets or branches extending in many directions.[5] It is studied by *Torah* scholars, by intellectuals, by professionals, by laymen and laywomen, by teens, by children. Each person finds satisfaction in the study of *Torah* according to his level of understanding, just as the possible variations and recipes of the manna satisfied the needs of many different individuals.

The *Torah* speaks to individuals according to their level, according to their understanding, according to their background, according to their ability, according to their need.

[5]Letter of Rabbi Akiva, *Midrash Rabbah* 13.

Ongoing Revelation

The Jewish people had gathered around the foot of Mt. Sinai, breathlessly awaiting revelation, the receiving of *Torah*. This was the historical revelation, approximately three months after the exodus from Egypt.[1]

There was also a spiritual revelation: a "new receiving" of *Torah* in the following days, months, years, generations. Each "new receiving" continues the development of *Torah*, from that first *Shavuos* until this very day.

New receiving—new revelation—means deeper, clearer insight into the words of a living *Torah*, a *Torah* that constantly renews its message for every time, for every place, for every circumstance.

The *Torah* itself provides the framework for this concept. The first four books of the *Torah* were entrusted by the Almighty to the generation of the exodus. They witnessed the historical revelation and then studied under the guidance of Moses our teacher, for the forty years they sojourned in the desert. Thirty-

[1]Exodus 19:1.

381

six days before Moses died,[2] he taught the *Mishne Torah*[3] to the
people who had been born and raised in the desert, so that they
would be more learned in the commandments as their lives un-
folded in *Eretz Yisrael*, the Promised Land. Moses expounded on
the words that the Almighty placed on his lips. For the generation who were about to enter *Eretz Yisrael*, the *Mishne Torah*
was a new receiving—a new spiritual revelation—of the words of
a living *Torah*.

Each generation that followed continued adding to the development of the living *Torah*: Talmud, *agadah*, *midrash*,
Responsa, Codes.

Each one of us is part of this living *Torah*, for it speaks to us
according to our personal circumstances and our level of understanding. When we study *Torah*, we become one with God. Just
as the oneness between man and wife is fulfilled through the
birth of a child,[4] so too the oneness between man and God is fulfilled through the continued "new spiritual revelation" of the
words of living *Torah*. "The Holy One, the *Torah*, and the Jewish
people are One."[5]

[2]Rashi, Deuteronomy 1:3.
[3]The *Mishne Torah* is another name for Deuteronomy, the fifth book of the
Torah. In it, Moses reviewed the first four books of the *Torah*—adding, clarifying,
and explaining specific laws to guide the Jewish people in the future as a nation.
[4]Rashi, Genesis 2:24.
[5]*Zohar, Acharei Mos* 73b.

Stories

The Blessing of the Righteous

Once, Rebbe Zusia and Rebbe Elimelech decided to spend *Shavuos* with Rebbe Dov Baer, the *maggid* of Mezeritch, disciple and successor to the Baal Shem Tov, the founder of the chasidic movement. They wanted to experience the celebration of the holiday of the revelation of *Torah* on Sinai with Rebbe Dov Baer; they had heard that Mezeritch during *Shavuos* was like revelation at Sinai.

Rebbe Zusia lived in Anipoli, and Rebbe Elimelech lived in Lizensk. They planned to meet on the road to Mezeritch, joining with other pilgrims who had the same intention, namely to spend the holiday with Rebbe Dov Baer, *maggid* of Mezeritch.

Suddenly, Rebbe Zusia lurched toward Rebbe Elimelech, and they both stopped short. The distance between them and the pilgrims widened. Rebbe Zusia moved off the mud road toward the trees at the roadside, verdant with the foliage of springtime.

He lifted his hands toward Heaven and began to pray, "Master of the Universe, grant me the power of Aaron the high priest, the power of the priestly blessing for only one hour, so that I will be able to bestow Your Heavenly blessing upon whomever I meet."

As soon as Rebbe Zusia finished his prayer, he felt saturated with the power of prophecy. He knew he would be able to touch people. He knew his blessings would be fulfilled. Rebbe Zusia was overcome with joy: he had one hour, sixty minutes, thirty-six hundred seconds to bestow blessings upon the whole world. But when he returned to the mud road, he was disappointed; the pilgrims were far ahead of him, and there were neither people nor wagons behind him. Upon whom could he bestow his blessings? The precious hour, the precious minutes, the precious seconds were ticking away.

Rebbe Zusia scanned the horizon, searching for people upon whom he could bestow his blessing. The inn where pilgrims usually stayed over on their way to Mezeritch was not too far up the road.

"Hurry, Elimelech," he shouted. "Maybe there will be some people in the inn whom I could bless."

They ran toward the inn.

They hoped that some of the pilgrims might have stopped for refreshment and rest, but when they arrived, the inn was deserted. Apparently, the pilgrims had proceeded to Mezeritch without stopping. Rebbe Zusia and Rebbe Elimelech were alone in the inn. The precious hour of blessing had passed.

Rebbe Elimelech tried to console his distraught brother by saying, "What you prayed for was not in your domain to request. Only the Almighty grants blessings."

Rebbe Zusia was not placated. Body and soul throbbed with pain. He did not understand why he found no one upon whom to bestow his blessing. He was so upset that he thought it wise to remain in the inn overnight to gain control of his emotions before proceeding to Mezeritch for the holiday.

Rebbe Zusia and Rebbe Elimelech made arrangements with the innkeeper and his wife for bed and board. They prayed the afternoon and night service, ate the simple meal that the innkeeper's wife served them, and retired for the night.

The next morning, after prayers and breakfast, Rebbe Zusia

and Rebbe Elimelech prepared to take leave of the innkeeper and his wife.

The innkeeper's wife was sobbing. When Rebbe Zusia asked her why she was sobbing, she groaned, ". . . Because you are on your way to Mezeritch to celebrate the holiday of the revelation of *Torah* with the great Rebbe Dov Baer. But in this inn there is no *Torah*! Only when righteous people pass through on their way to Mezeritch are words of *Torah* heard in this inn. We are simple people. We don't know the words. We only know how to live as Jews. We pray, but our prayers go unheeded. Had the Almighty blessed us with children, words of *Torah* would have been heard in this inn. We could have hired a teacher for our children. We would have heard our children learn the prayers and the words of our holy *Torah*. Children are the guarantors of *Torah*. The Almighty gave the *Torah* to the whole world, but in this inn, there is no *Torah*."

By the time she blurted out the reason for her unhappiness, the innkeeper's wife was hysterical. "Her pain is so much greater than mine was yesterday," thought Rebbe Zusia. He turned to his brother and said to him, "Elimelech, you go to Mezeritch to spend the holiday with Rebbe Dov Baer. I will remain here in this inn with the innkeeper and his wife for the *Shavuos* holiday."

The brothers parted company.

The innkeeper and his wife were happy that Rebbe Zusia had decided to spend the holiday in their home.

On the eve of *Shavuos* in the *shul* of the great Rebbe Dov Baer of Mezeritch, his disciples and their families and Rebbe Elimelech prayed with great joy, but their prayers were chanted more slowly than usual.

At the same time in the inn, on the outskirts of Mezeritch, Rebbe Zusia prayed with the innkeeper and his wife. He said the words, and they repeated them in broken Hebrew. Only Rebbe Elimelech understood why Rebbe Dov Baer was chanting the prayers so slowly.

After the holiday meal that evening, the people of Mezeritch returned to the *shul* for all-night study with their rebbe. They were preparing to receive the *Torah* the following morning.

After the holiday meal in the inn, Rebbe Zusia sat with the innkeeper and his wife. He taught them the fundamentals of the Hebrew alphabet.

The next morning in Mezeritch, the prayers were the culmination of the all-night study session. By the time the *Torah* was read, Mezeritch was like Mt. Sinai, with thunder, lightning, the trees rustling, the mountains shaking.

The *Torah* reader trembled as he read, "I am the Lord your God who brought you forth from the land of Egypt from the house of bondage. . . . You shall have no other gods before me."[1] The Jews of Mezeritch left Egypt. They were on their way to Mt. Sinai.

In the inn, there was no *minyan* (quorum of ten males) nor was there a scroll of the *Torah*. Rebbe Zusia sat with the innkeeper and his wife, praying slowly, chanting each word, repeating the sounds of the Hebrew alphabet he had taught them the night before. Then Rebbe Zusia thought, "I have no *Torah* scroll, but I have a *chumash* (Bible). I will teach the holiday *Torah* reading to the innkeeper and his wife." He opened the *chumash* to the verses for the festival of *Shavuos,* and he read slowly, explaining the nuances of each word and idea.

"In the third month after the children of Israel left Egypt, that same day they came to the Sinai desert. . . . Now, if you will listen to My Voice and Keep My Covenant, then you will be My own treasure from among the peoples of the earth . . . and you shall be a kingdom of priests and a holy nation . . . and the people answered: 'All that the Almighty has spoken, we will do. . . .' "[2]

As he was explaining the meaning of "we will do," Rebbe Zusia pondered upon the importance of learning the *mitzvos* (commandments), in order to do them, in order to transmit them.

The second day of *Shavuos* was special for *chasidim;* it marked the *yahrzeit* (the anniversary of the death) of the Baal

---

[1]Exodus 20:2, 3.
[2]Exodus 19:1–8.

Shem Tov as well as the *yahrzeit* of King David, the sweet singer of Israel.

In Mezeritch, the *Torah* reader chanted the Book of Ruth. The people followed the story from the description of the harvest to Ruth's acceptance of the commandments and her meriting to be the great-grandmother of King David.

In the inn, the innkeeper, his wife, and Rebbe Zusia prayed with a melody that the world had not yet heard. It seemed as if the air reverberated with the sound of music. All of creation joined in Rebbe Zusia's symphony orchestra: the birds chirped the words while the wind rustled the melody. The prayers of the innkeeper and his wife floated to the gates of Heaven as if plucked on the strings of a harp.

After the *Shavuos* holiday, a messenger from Rebbe Dov Baer arrived at the inn, inviting Rebbe Zusia to come to Mezeritch. Rebbe Zusia refused the invitation. Instead he sent a return message to Rebbe Dov Baer saying, "I will not move from this inn until I receive word of a Heavenly decree that a child will be born to this family."

The messenger returned to Rebbe Dov Baer with Rebbe Zusia's message. Rebbe Dov Baer said to the messenger, "Go back to the inn. Tell Rebbe Zusia that I know that his prayers were answered."

Rebbe Zusia did not need to wait for the messenger. As soon as Rebbe Dov Baer uttered his words in Mezeritch, Rebbe Zusia heard them in the inn, so he began to review what had transpired during the past three days. Rebbe Zusia visioned the power of prophecy returning to him. He visualized the prayers of the innkeeper and his wife crashing the gates of Heaven. He felt the music echoing all around him. He realized that the harp was King David's harp, that the innkeeper and his wife were direct descendants of King David.

Rebbe Zusia turned to the innkeeper and his wife and said, "The Almighty has heard your prayers. I bless you. Next year at this time, you will be the parents of a baby boy. Name him David."

The blessing of the righteous Rebbe Zusia was fulfilled.

God's Partner

"Rebbe, did you hear what happened?" asked Yoel David. "Chanale, the woman who was barren for so many years, the one who lives in that house by the brook, gave birth to a baby girl last week. She is telling everyone that Yankele Kretchmer, the innkeeper, blessed her last year."

A few days later, Chaim slid over on the bench where he sat in the study hall and whispered in his rebbe's ear, "Rebbe, I heard that Berel the tailor—the one who has his shop at the edge of Apt and who had such difficulty eking out a living—received a big order for suits from the owner of a large clothing store. When I asked him why he thought his luck changed, he told me that Yankele Kretchmer blessed him."

The following month, the Apter rebbe heard that a very sick man, who was not expected to live, had fully recovered. He went to visit the man. During their conversation, the man volunteered the information that he believed he would never have recovered had it not been for the blessing of Yankele Kretchmer.

"Who is this Yankele Kretchmer?" mused the Apter rebbe. "Imagine, if only I had the power to bless as he does, I could help so many people. I have to find out who Yankele Kretchmer is, what good deeds he has done, and what he does to merit that all his blessings are fulfilled. If I know what he does, I could emulate his actions. I could be a source of blessings also."

There were so many things that took the rebbe's time that temporarily he pushed the stories of the wondrous blessings out of his mind. But the rumors about the fulfillment of Yankele Kretchmer's blessings persisted. The Apter rebbe kept wondering what the source of his power was. Finally, unable to contain his curiosity any longer, he decided to go to the inn to personally investigate the source of Yankele Kretchmer's blessings.

Since he was well-known in the vicinity, he disguised himself as a merchant. He did not want the innkeeper to recognize him. He arranged to stay for three days, thinking that in that amount of time, he certainly would be able to find out the secret of Yankele Kretchmer's blessings.

He observed the innkeeper carefully, but he couldn't figure out why he merited that his blessings be fulfilled. The innkeeper spoke gruffly to the customers who patronized the bar in the inn. He ate without manners at times, stuffing the food into his mouth. He prayed the morning and evening services by himself, never taking the time to attend a *minyan* in the *shul.* The Apter rebbe noticed that he mispronounced every other word. It was obvious that Yankele Kretchmer was a boor. Yet people stood in an endless line, outside the inn, waiting to see him. They stood in line with hunched shoulders and heavy hearts, some scowling, some crying, pain clearly marked across their faces, but when they emerged, their faces shone. The Apter rebbe was puzzled.

"Maybe," thought the Apter rebbe, "the innkeeper performs righteous deeds at night, after the working day, when he is alone. I will sneak into his bedroom and hide under his bed. I have to find out the secret of his blessings."

That night, the Apter rebbe lay under Yankele Kretchmer's bed. As soon as he lay down, he fell into a deep, sound sleep and snored loudly. The Apter rebbe waited for something to happen. In the middle of the night, Yankele woke up. From under the bed, the Apter rebbe heard him go into a room at the end of the hallway, shut the door, and bolt it. He stayed for about an hour, returned to his bed, and immediately started to snore again.

The Apter rebbe could not contain himself any longer. In the morning he decided to tell Yankele Kretchmer who he was, hoping that he could find out the secret of the blessings.

"I am the Apter rebbe," he began. "I have been watching you for the past three days. I came here to try to find out the secret of your blessings. Truthfully, I haven't noticed that you do anything differently than any other ordinary Jew. I am stymied. Please tell me the secret of your blessings, so I could emulate your actions. I could help so many people."

"Rebbe," answered Yankele Kretchmer modestly, "indeed I am flattered by your visit, but I have no secret. I have no special powers."

The Apter rebbe persisted.

"I have heard rumors about your blessings for months. I have heard that a barren woman gave birth to a child, that a penniless tailor is now making a living, that a very sick man has recovered. Please tell me why your blessings are fulfilled."

The innkeeper saw that the rebbe would not leave without knowing the secret of the blessings, so he explained.

I will tell you what happened. First of all, I want you to know that I believe that everything that happens in this world happens because the Almighty decrees it. I have always placed my trust in Him. Many months ago, I received an urgent message from the *poretz* (landowner) of this *shtetl* to come to his mansion immediately. I knew what he wanted. I owed him three months' back rent. I did not have the money to pay him, but I knew I had no choice but to answer his summons. On the way, I decided to pass through the town. I thought I could borrow the money from the bank. However, as I walked along, I thought, "Why should I borrow money from a total stranger? Why should I make a total stranger my partner?" I turned in prayer to the Almighty and said, "Master of the World, if you give me what I need now, I promise You that I will make You my partner."

No sooner had I finished praying than I heard the jingling bells of a horse-drawn carriage trotting swiftly beside me. The horses came to an abrupt stop at my side. Two fashionably dressed men alighted from the carriage. One spoke. "Are you Yankele Kretchmer? We have been looking for you. We have heard that you are an honest businessman. We are about to embark on a business venture to another continent, to South Africa. We have quite a bit of gold with us from our last venture. We do not want to take it with us. We would like to commission you to hold it for us until our return. You may use any part of it on the condition that you return the original sum to us after our trip."

I agreed to their proposition. They gave me the bag of gold, climbed back into their carriage, and disappeared into the distance.

Rebbe, do you know what? I knew that my partner was working already. Joyfully, I counted the gold coins that they entrusted to me.

I ran to pay the *poretz* the back rent and returned to the inn.

I wanted the agreement with my partner to be effective immediately. I returned home, divided the money into two boxes, and locked them up in the empty room at the end of the hall.

Each business day I keep an exact accounting of the money I earn. Every night, I enter the empty room and put half of the money in one box and half in the other box. I use the money that I put into my box to sustain my family. I use the money that I put into my partner's box to sustain the needy of this *shtetl* and to support worthy students who devote themselves to the study of *Torah*. Ever since I have contracted this partnership, I have prospered. You may have noticed that I eat very quickly. Sometimes I gulp down my food. I do this because I do not want to take time from the business day for myself, since I do not want to cheat my partner. I fall asleep as soon as I go to bed so I will have strength to work, because I know that my partner is depending on me.

Yankele Kretchmer's voice faltered. He had never told anyone his secret before.

"Now that I have told you the secret of the blessings, I want you to swear to me that you will not repeat this story again to anyone while I am alive."

The Apter rebbe promised. He understood why Yankele Kretchmer's blessings were fulfilled.

After the innkeeper passed away, the Apter rebbe told his story every year on his *yahrzeit*. He always concluded the story with these words: "Is it any wonder that Yankele Kretchmer's blessings were always fulfilled, for who can compare to Yankele, God's partner?"

The Real Jew

From the day of the revelation on Sinai, it was an accepted fact that Jews lived according to the *mitzvos* of the *Torah*. But Mendele Sokolover was not satisfied with the mere observance of *mitzvos*. He was searching for more than that. He was searching for what he called a "real Jew."

Mendele Sokolover had grown up and had been educated in Kotzk, where he learned what a real Jew was capable of doing. He spent all of his formative years trying to find such a person. He traveled around the Pale of Settlement, from *shtetl* to *shtetl*. The people he met were fragmented; something was missing. True, he found Jews who were observant of every detail of *halachah* (Jewish law); he found Jews who studied day and night; he found Jews who were dedicated to *mitzvos*; he found Jews who devoted their lives to acts of kindness. But somehow, none of these Jews measured up to his image of a real Jew. They did not portray what he knew a real Jew was capable of doing.

One day, he found Moshele, a poor, illiterate, downtrodden water carrier. This is the story that Mendele Sokolover told about Moshele the water carrier, the real Jew.

I was passing a dilapidated hut one night. As I peered into the window, I noticed a lone man clutching a worn volume of Psalms. He seemed to be praying fervently. I stood outside the window for a long time, watching. I did not want to intrude. He never raised his eyes from the pages: his lips never ceased moving.

I returned many nights and found the same scene each time. One night, I hesitantly knocked on the door. I wanted to talk to him. I wanted to find out if he had that special quality, that spark of holiness for which I was searching.

He opened the door. I asked him his name. He told me, "My name is Moshele the water carrier."

I tried to draw him into conversation, but he shook his head from side to side. I asked him how he was and he answered, "Good, thank God."

I wanted to get close to him. I tried, but I could not get him to say more than, "Good, thank God."

Many years passed, and I became the rebbe of Sokolov, the *shtetl* where Moshele the water carrier lived.

One night, as I walked, I saw that Moshele was not reciting Psalms, as he usually did. There was a party in his dilapidated hut. The *shtetl's* shoemakers, tailors, and water carriers were dancing around Moshele. It seemed to me as if the Divine Presence radiated from his face.

I wanted to know why everybody was celebrating, so I walked in. Moshele was the first one to notice me.

"Rebbe," he asked, "what are you doing here?"

"I was walking by," I said, "and I saw that you were having a party. I wanted to find out why everybody was celebrating." At first, Moshele refused to answer my question, but I persisted. Finally, he began.

This is my story, rebbe. I was orphaned at a very young age. I remember neither my father nor my mother. I grew up on the streets of this *shtetl*. I had very little education. There was an old man who took a liking to me, and he taught me how to recite Psalms. I married a most beautiful girl, but she is not beautiful anymore. We had seven children. They were born angels, but we can't bear to hear them crying anymore. It is impossibly difficult to eke out a living as a water carrier. Most of the time we go to sleep hungry. Since I can't sleep when I am hungry, I spend the night reciting Psalms, the only prayers I know.

A week ago, I ran to the *shul* in the middle of the night. I could not bear to hear my wife and children crying anymore. I stood before the Holy Ark and I pleaded from the depths of my soul: "Master of the Universe! I can't stand to see my wife and children suffering so much anymore. Please help me. Give me enough money to ease their pain."

I did not know if the Almighty heard my prayer.

Two days ago, I was delivering water to my usual customers. I carried two buckets attached to a yoke across my shoulders. From the weight, my shoulders were stooped, and my eyes gazed at the ground. As I passed the *shul*, I noticed one thousand rubles lying on the ground. I picked up the money and lifted my head in thanksgiving. "You do listen to prayers, Almighty, don't You!" I exclaimed gratefully.

I vowed to keep my good fortune a secret for two days. I returned home after I finished my deliveries. My wife appeared to be as beautiful as she was on the day I married her. My children seemed to be angels again. I was bursting with joy.

That evening, I returned to the *shul* for the evening prayer service. As I approached the entrance to the *shul*, I found Channale, the widow of one of the water carriers, standing in front of the *shul*, crying bitterly.

She was crying because she lost the one thousand rubles the water carriers collected for her when her husband died. I didn't go into the *shul* to pray. I ran to the other side of the street, and I began screaming at God.

"Why did You have to give me Channale's rubles?" I demanded. "Couldn't You find one thousand rubles someplace else for me? What kind of compassionate God are You anyway? I don't want to have anything to do with You anymore."

I ran home sullenly. I hated the whole world. I was angry at God. I lay on my bed for a whole day. I cried and I cursed. I ranted and I raged. I was heartbroken and distraught.

Suddenly, I was in touch with my soul.

"What happened to you?" my soul asked. "All your life you prayed. Why did you stop praying now?"

I swear, Rebbe. I heard my soul talk to me. It said, "The soul that stood on Mount Sinai, the soul that swore we will do and we will listen . . . this soul is capable of keeping the widow's money?" My soul continued talking to me. "Return the money to Channale," it said.

I ran out of my hut and searched the entire *shtetl*, trying to find Channale. I found her, sitting at a broken-down table in her dilapidated hut. She was still crying. I put the money on the table. She looked up and smiled weakly. She could not believe that I had found her money. She could not believe that anyone would return one thousand rubles. Gradually, her smile returned to her face. It was like the smile of Heaven. I felt so good at that moment. I knew that my life would never change. I knew that my children would always wear used clothing. I knew that there would never be enough food on our table. But I knew how good it felt to be a Jew. My friends are making a party in my honor. They are celebrating how good it feels to listen to God's voice.

Rebbe Mendele Sokolover joined the shoemakers, the tailors, and the water carriers in their celebration. He knew he had found a real Jew. He told the story of Moshele the water carrier, the real Jew, each year on his *yahrzeit,* the anniversary of his death.

Let's Go Right

As a young man, Yechiel Mayer[1] arose early each morning to begin his day with prayer and study. He prayed with special *tefillin* (phylacteries) and *tallis* (prayer shawl) that were gifts from the parents of his bride, and he cherished them with all his might. After he finished his prayers, he carefully rewound the *tefillin* and placed them in their special sack. He folded the *tallis*, placed it in its special sack, and laid them on a nearby table. Then he commenced studying, remaining in the study hall most of the day. He never deviated, and by mid-morning, he was usually deeply immersed in *Torah* thought.

One day near noontime, he was interrupted by a stranger, a man named Rebbe Mayer Kvaller, who hastened breathlessly into the study hall, demanding to borrow Yechiel Mayer's *tallis* and *tefillin*. Yechiel Mayer was aghast and blurted out, "What kind of Jew are you? How is it possible that you have not yet prayed your morning prayers when the day is more than half over?"

[1]Yechiel Mayer became the rebbe of Gustinin. He was called "Hayehude Hatov," the Good Jew.

Rebbe Mayer Kvaller did not want to argue with Yechiel Mayer. He only wanted to use his *tallis* and *tefillin*, so instead of confronting him with a provocative answer, he pleaded, "Please, I'll explain the whole thing to you later. For now, let me borrow your *tallis* and *tefillin*."

Yechiel Mayer thought, "Maybe this stranger was involved in some sort of emergency and didn't have time to pray. Maybe there is something special I can learn from this man who prays so late in the day."

Reluctantly, Yechiel Mayer lifted his *tallis* and *tefillin* from the table and gave them to Rebbe Mayer Kvaller. He watched as Rebbe Mayer Kvaller prepared himself for prayer. It was clear that there was nothing unusual about his manner. Wrapped in *tallis* and *tefillin*, Rebbe Mayer Kvaller walked over to the window of the study hall, looked out, paced back and forth across the floor, returned to the window, and looked out again.

In the courtyard below, Russian soldiers were being trained to follow the marching commands of their officer. Rebbe Mayer Kvaller stood near the window and stared at the soldiers.

Yechiel Mayer was irritated. He thought, "I lent this stranger my *tallis* and *tefillin* because he wanted to pray so desperately. Now he stands by the window and looks down at the courtyard as the officer puts the soldiers through their paces. He is supposed to be praying, not staring out the window."

Rebbe Mayer Kvaller continued to alternately stare and pace back and forth across the study hall floor, always keeping his field of vision fixed on the sight beneath him.

Yechiel Mayer's anger was aroused. He felt that he was about to explode. He was outraged at Rebbe Mayer Kvaller's disrespect. He stood up and ran over to the stranger, determined to grab his precious *tallis* and *tefillin* from him.

In his anger, Yechiel Mayer had not noticed how Rebbe Mayer Kvaller had been shivering and shaking under his *tallis*. When he reached to grab it from his shoulders, he stopped dead in his tracks. The *tallis* was soaking wet.

Yechiel Mayer was even more incensed when he felt his new *tallis*, but when he saw the tears streaming down Rebbe Mayer Kvaller's cheeks, he calmed himself and said gently, "I don't understand what made you cry so bitterly. You stormed in here and demanded to use my *tallis* and *tefillin* to pray. You have not stopped looking out that window. Neither have you stopped pacing the floor. I lent you my *tallis* and *tefillin* because I thought that, since you wanted to pray so desperately, I would learn something from the intensity or manner in which you prayed."

Yechiel Mayer stopped, unable to continue speaking. Rebbe Mayer Kvaller extended his arm and placed it around Yechiel Mayer's shoulders. "Let me explain something to you," he said. "Look out this window. I want you to see what I see." The two of them watched the sight below for a long time. Then Rebbe Mayer Kvaller asked Yechiel Mayer, "What do you see in the courtyard below?"

Yechiel Mayer answered, "I see soldiers going through their paces."

Then Rebbe Mayer Kvaller continued. "There is much more to these maneuvers. There is much more than meets the eye. When the captain shouts right, all the soldiers turn right. When the captain shouts left, all the soldiers turn left. When the captain confuses the orders, and the soldiers could possibly trip over their steps, they still obey orders. The soldiers are terrified of disobeying a human commander. Just imagine what happens when generals assert their authority over captains and when the Tzar asserts his authority over the generals. The commander may be drunk, the orders ridiculous, but the soldiers would not dare disobey. I am trying to make a point. Please listen carefully. We Jewish people are the soldiers of the Almighty. In His Infinite Wisdom, He has given us marching orders that guide us through life. His marching orders are sensible. Not one of us has yet tripped by following His orders. Not one of us ever will. Yet, we do not follow His orders as carefully as the Russian soldiers follow the order of their commanding officer. The Almighty tells us to go right, and we go left. He tells us to go left, and we go right."

Yechiel Mayer understood what the stranger was trying to teach him. He was glad he had lent him his *tallis* and *tefillin*. He knew the *tallis* would dry, but he hoped that he would feel the tears every time he wrapped himself in that special *tallis*.

Sweet *Torah* Study

Rebbe Sholom ben Eliezer Rokeach of Belz was the scion of a distinguished rabbinical family. He was raised and educated in inner chasidic circles and was influenced by their leaders. He was known as a great scholar, both in the realm of the revealed *Torah* and the mystical writings.

He taught his followers about the simple things in life. He shunned the frills. When his followers watched him pray with intense devotion, they discovered the meaning of communication with God.

As his reputation spread throughout Galicia, tens of thousands of Jews sought his advice. He directed the erection of a magnificent synagogue in Belz, forty miles north of Lemberg, thereby setting the foundation for the modern Belz dynasty.[1]

Once he had to travel to Vienna. His son, Rebbe Yehoshua, accompanied him. They arrived around noon on Friday, and they made arrangements to stay in an inn for *Shabbos*. The

---

[1]The buildings of the European Belz dynasty were destroyed during the Holocaust, but the survivors are reconstructing the magnificent synagogue in Jerusalem.

innkeeper had heard of his honored guest's reputation, so he arranged to invite some of his friends to join the rebbe at his *Shabbos tish* (table). He wanted the rebbe to feel at home.

Rebbe Sholom conducted his *tish* just as he was accustomed to do in Belz. The studying and the singing continued late into the night. The innkeeper's guests had never experienced a chasidic *tish* before.

Rebbe Yehoshua excused himself before the *tish* was over. He was weary from the long journey. As he walked from the dining room along the long path connecting the rooms of the inn, he was attracted to the sound of a sweet melody. He hurried along, drawing nearer and nearer to the sound, bypassing his room, continuing onward to the end of the path. He stopped in front of the door where the melody was most intense and noticed that the room glowed in soft candlelight. He peered through the window, trying to make out the figure that was sitting at the table, chanting the sweet melody, pouring intently over a folio of Talmud. Surprised, he realized that the figure was dressed in the uniform of a Russian soldier. He stood outside, enchanted, watching for a long time. He had never seen such intensity, such devotion to studying in all his years in Belz.

The soldier was unaware that Rebbe Yehoshua was watching him. Finally, not wanting to disturb the soldier, but curious to know who he was, Rebbe Yehoshua knocked gently on the door, turned the knob, peeked into the room, and asked if he might enter. The soldier lifted his head from the page of Talmud that he was studying, smiled wanly, and motioned to the stranger to enter.

"I am sorry to disturb you," Rebbe Yehoshua began, "but I was very surprised to hear your chanting. I followed the sound of your voice. I have been standing outside your window watching you for a long time. I am curious to know what a soldier of the Tzar is doing in an inn in Vienna studying Talmud? If you don't think I am intruding on your privacy, I would like to hear your story. If you don't want to tell me, I shall leave now."

The soldier did not seem perturbed. He said, "Please sit down," pointing to an empty chair by the table.

I will be happy to tell you my story. You see, Jews living in Russia have been treated with great hostility for years. Tzar Nicholas I decreed a law conscripting Jewish children into the army for a period of twenty-five years. Parents were frightened lest their children be lost to Judaism. Many children were kidnapped from their villages soon after their twelfth birthdays, some even earlier if the quota was not met. I was a bit luckier than other Jewish children. I remained in my village until I was eighteen, and then I was conscripted. I had an opportunity to learn for many years after my *bar mitzvah*. Once I was in the army, I did not stop praying to the Almighty. I had only one prayer, "Please, never let me desecrate the *Shabbos*."

I prayed this prayer all the time. Fortunately, my prayer was answered, for I was placed in the battalion of a very considerate general. He seemed to take a liking to me. He treated me with great kindness. I was very surprised because most generals had horrible reputations. I knew that the Almighty had answered my prayer. The general wanted me to become his personal attendant. I felt confident in our relationship, so I asked the general if he would agree to permit me to rest one day each week.

"Yes," he said after thinking over my request carefully. "You may have one day a week for rest on the condition that you serve me faithfully the remainder of the week."

I do my best to please the general for six days each week, and I set aside *Shabbos* to serve God and study His *Torah*. Usually, I arrange to stay for *Shabbos* in an inn, in whatever area the battalion is camped.

The soldier's voice trailed off. He was anxious to return to his studies.

Rebbe Yehoshua was stunned by the soldier's story. He felt a need to respond. "I want to introduce myself," he began. "My name is Yehoshua. My father, who is the Belzer rebbe, and I are staying in this inn for *Shabbos*. I'm sure you have heard that the level of *Torah* learning in Belz is very high, yet I want you to know that I have never met anyone who has studied with such intent and with such devotion as I have heard you study tonight. The intensity of your studying *Torah* has the power to delay the redemption of the Jewish people, for 'the study of *Torah* is more precious to the Almighty than the offering of sacrifices in the Holy Temple.'[2] If the Holy Temple were rebuilt tomorrow, I know no one who could possibly serve God in a sweeter way than you. Your study is so sweet, so magnificent before the Almighty. I imagine the Almighty probably says, 'I would rather have that soldier's studying than any other offering My children might bring before Me.' "

Yehoshua blessed the soldier, wished him "Good *Shabbos*," and returned to his room. The next morning, he shared his experience with his father.

Rebbe Sholom Belzer lived to a ripe old age; his son, Yehoshua, succeeded him. In an attempt to inspire his students, he often repeated the soldier's story. He usually concluded by saying, "Never, never, have I heard the sweetness and the love with which that soldier studied *Torah*."

---

[2]*Avos D'Rabbi Nasan* 4:1.

Ayshes Chayil:
A Woman of Valor

"I remember my mother,"[1] mused Rabbi Aryeh Layb ben Rabbi Yisrael Mayer Hakohen (the Chofetz Chaim). "She was not a *Torah* scholar, but she epitomized the *Torah* way of life.

"When she passed away, my father eulogized her in a broken voice. 'For the little learning in *Torah* that I achieved. . . I have to thank her. In the beginning of our married life, she worked very hard to earn a livelihood. We lived humbly and meagerly. She never disturbed me from my *Torah* studies. She never asked for anything, even if she had to eat dry bread. She never demanded luxurious clothing or fancy houses. She was a merciful mother to those who knew her. No one was untouched by her acts of kindness.'

"Sometimes I reminisce about the past. I recall that general store," continued Rabbi Aryeh Layb. "It was stocked with fabric, leather, iron goods (hardware), oil, kerosene, herring, salt. . . most of the necessities for living in a *shtetl.* I can still see my mother's concern for her customers: she was obsessed with hon-

---

[1]Frayda bas Reb Shimon of Radin.

est business dealings. She recognized her limited skills in arithmetic, so she always insisted my father check her bookkeeping records after he returned from long days in the *yeshivah*.

"As I was growing up, she sang this lullabye to me: 'The study of *Torah* is the best investment.'

"As I matured, she hummed the same melody constantly. From the urgency in her voice, I knew that she wanted to instill in me the value of a life guided by the study of *Torah* and lived according to its principles."

Let me tell you about her acts of kindness that are engraved in my heart. She used to walk around our *shtetl*, with a big sack slung over her shoulder, asking people to contribute food that was ready to serve. She distributed the food to the poor.

She managed the *kosher kessel* (kettle) whereby meals were served in the *yeshivah* for those students who had chosen to devote their days and nights to study *Torah*. She abhorred the system of farming out "her boys" to different homes for meals; she did not want them to depend on the hospitality of lay people.[2]

She was actively involved with every family in Radin; she helped the ill, she arranged dowries for brides, she lent money to people who passed through the *shtetl*, she arranged introductions for people to establish credit in order that they might open their own businesses, thereby giving them independence. Helping was the focal point of her entire life.

I have never forgotten the vivid memory of my mother caring for a strange three-month-old child. One night, when I returned home from the *yeshivah*, I saw my mother carrying a baby in her arms. She walked slowly back and forth across the room, trying to comfort the child. When I asked her whose child she was cradling, she said softly, "This little girl's father is one of the villagers. Yesterday, he was arrested and imprisoned by the government. Her mother died. There is no one to care for her. I

---

[2]Many *yeshivos* were unable to provide room and board for their out-of-town students, so a system was devised whereby people in the community took turns inviting them for meals. This system was known as *tag*, from the Yiddish word for day. It enabled a student to eat at a different home each day.

hired a nurse, but the nurse changed her mind. She left the child on our doorstep. I have not yet found a proper woman to care for her. Until I do, I will feed her and care for her myself. I will not abandon her."

My most precious memory of my mother is her confrontation with the *shtetl* tailor. You see, she had hired him to sew a new suit for me for my wedding. She accompanied me to the tailor's shop to try it on when it was ready. The tailor was very pleased with his work. Smiling, he looked over his handiwork. Then he looked at me. Finally, he cleared his throat, and proclaimed in a deep voice, "Aryeh Layb, I bless you to become very successful with this wedding suit; I bless you to become a wealthy merchant. May you earn a lot of money."

My mother was incensed! She raised her voice angrily and screamed at the tailor, "Who asked you for such a blessing? If you really wanted to bless my son, it would be more appropriate to bless him to be a great *Torah* scholar and a God-fearing Jew!"

I Was with the First Jew—
I Will Be with the Last Jew

The prophecy, "I am the first and I am the last, and except for Me, there is no other,"[1] has been interpreted in many different ways. One biblical commentator suggests that this verse means that the Almighty existed before the creation of the world and will exist even after its destruction.[2] Another biblical commentator suggests that this verse means that the Almighty will be recognized as the King of the World when the Jewish people are redeemed.[3] A commentator of the chasidic school of thought interprets this verse to mean that the Almighty will be with the first Jew and with the last Jew.[4]

Who was the first Jew? Will there ever be a last Jew? Let me tell you the story of the first Jew and the last Jew.

The first Jew was the *maggid* of Koshnitz. There was never a Jew, a real Jew like him. He lived to see the devastation of

[1]Isaiah 44:6.
[2]Rabbi David Altschuler and Rabbi Yechiel Hillel Altschuler, Metzudas David, eighteenth-century biblical commentators.
[3]Rabbi David Kimchi, Radak, French biblical exegete, 1160–1235.
[4]Rebbe Avraham ben Yitzchak Mattisyahu Weinberg, 1805–1885.

his people at the hands of the Nazis. He was there when they rounded up all his disciples: hundreds of *chasidim* were shoved, pushed, herded, kicked, whipped, crushed, all destined to die for the sanctification of His Holy Name.

He was their leader, their inspiration. They followed his example. He walked with pride and dignity to the town square at the command of the Nazi officers, and they followed him. He walked in a lilting rhythm, and they imitated. He walked with a smile on his face, and they tried to smile. They were brave and courageous, for they knew the fate that awaited them. One student could not conform. He shuffled along the line of people, despondent, tears flowing freely down his cheeks. The sound of the Nazi soldiers' whips crackled through the still air, forcing the doomed people forward. He could not control himself any longer. Finally he screamed, "Rebbe, why are you smiling as we are being led to our death?"

The *maggid* of Koshnitz turned to his anguished student and answered gently, "Today is a beautiful day. I saw the sun rise. I thanked the Almighty for restoring my soul, for creating me a Jew, for allowing me to pray one last time in *tallis* and *tefillin*. I know we are being led to our death, but do you think that this is really the end of the Jewish people? I don't know when this will end. I do know that somehow the Jewish people will survive. I also believe, with all my might, that our ashes, and the ashes of all those holy souls who preceded us in death, of all those holy souls who died to sanctify His Holy Name, one day will purify the world. Isn't this enough reason to smile?"

The *maggid* of Koshnitz believed that the ashes of the six million would purify the world, and therefore he was able to smile as he neared death. He was the first real Jew.

The last Jew was the Jewish-born mayor of Koshnitz who had converted to Christianity when he saw the sudden rise of the Nazis to power. The Jewish community rejected him; they thought he was a traitor.

The Nazis considered him a Jew. As the mayor, he was commanded to order every Jew in Koshnitz to come to the synagogue. His deputies and guards proceeded with the round-up. The Jews knew why they hated him; he was working for the Nazis. They huddled together, carrying the remnants of their few belongings in battered suitcases. Stormtroopers stood outside the synagogue, pointing their clubs toward the door, forcing them inside, waiting for the synagogue to fill up so they could set it afire.

The mayor stood, watching helplessly. The Jews cried and screamed. Shrill shrieks pierced the air.

A Nazi general goosestepped over to the mayor.

"Jew," he shouted, "say that the word of Moses is not true, and I will let you live. Otherwise, you will join your people inside that synagogue."

The mayor shook his head. "No," he said, "I will not say it."

The general smacked him soundly across the face. Blood spurted from his nose. Then he beckoned a soldier holding a whip to beat the mayor. The mayor stood his ground. The more the soldier beat, the more the mayor cried out, "I will not say it, I will not say it."

Seeing that he would not say the words he wanted to hear, the general rephrased his question. "I will go with you into that synagogue. I will take one of those parchment scrolls and throw it on the ground. If you will spit on it three times, I will let you live!"

The general waited for an answer. The mayor of Koshnitz shook his head again.

"No," he said, "I will not do it. I will not do it!"

The Nazi general could not understand why the mayor would not do his bidding to save his life.

"Push him in with his companions," he screamed. "He is one of them."

Two soldiers grabbed the mayor and shoved him into the synagogue. Then they bolted the door and set it ablaze.

The flames slowly crept up the sides of the synagogue. The Jews waited for the flames to engulf them. Some of them realized that their mayor had converted for political reasons. They knew that he had never renounced Judaism. They knew he was not a traitor. They wondered if there would ever be another Jew like him again, a Jew who was willing to die with his people when he could have saved his life.

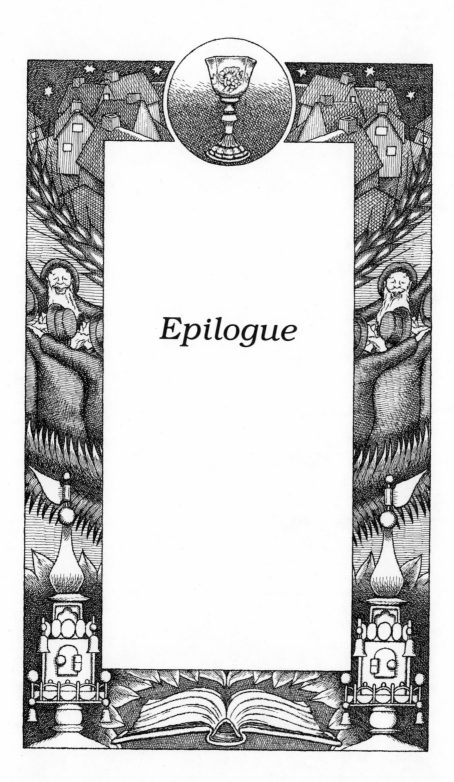

Epilogue

And We Are Still Waiting

Rebbe Moshe Teitelbaum, *der izeneh kop* (the child prodigy), was born in a small Galician *shtetl* in 1753. By the time he was seventeen years old, he was accepted by the Jewish community as an authority on Jewish law. Eventually, he settled in Oohel, Hungary, and attracted many followers. People from the surrounding area came to seek help and advice, to make requests, to complain of their lot in life. He listened to them all, comforted, encouraged, gently strengthening the weak, instilling new life into the broken-hearted.

In quiet solitary moments, he mourned over the destruction of Jerusalem and prayed for its rebuilding. He never permitted himself to forget the yearning in his soul for the coming of the Messiah, for the redemption of the Jewish people. Often, he repeated phrases from the prophecies of Jeremiah, at times mesmerizing those who heard him. He whispered, he sang, he preached, he prayed, "I will gather the remnant of My flock from all the lands of their dispersion (exile) and I will bring them back to their land, and they will multiply and be fruitful."[1] "There is

[1]Jeremiah 23:3.

hope (the conviction that *Zion* will be restored) for the future (of the Jewisl: people). . . . My children will return to their own borders."[2]

Jeremiah's prophetic verses swirled in his head continuously. His followers believed that his soul contained holy sparks from the prophet.

One day, three of his most outstanding students came to seek his advice. "Rebbe," they said, "if you had to choose two or three teachings that you want us to remember more than any other concepts that you taught us, which would you choose?"

For a long while, Rebbe Moshe was silent. He stroked his beard and furrowed his brow. It was apparent that he had difficulty answering their question. After a long while, he began to speak.

If I had to transmit to you only three of the most important concepts that I taught you, I would choose the following.

First, know that acts of kindness hasten the arrival of the Messianic Age. They are the keys, the means towards bringing people closer together. When people are brought closer together, they will be more apt to observe the *mitzvos*. When they observe the *mitzvos*, they will reach a high level of spiritual perfection. When a high level of spiritual perfection is reached, the Messiah will come to redeem us.

Second, the *mitzvos* in the *Torah* are God's advice on how to act when specific opportunities or situations present themselves. There is one dictum, however, which cannot wait for an opportunity. That dictum is, "Actively seek peace and pursue it."[3]

When we search for ways to bring peace between one human being and another in our world, we can demand of the Almighty that He make peace in His world, as we recite in one of the concluding verses of our daily prayers, "May He, who establishes peace in the Heavenly sphere, make peace for us and for all Israel."

[2]Jeremiah 31:16.
[3]Psalms 34:15.

Remember, when there is no peace between human beings, nothing else has purpose.

Last, I want to impress upon you that everything you acquire in the Diaspora is temporary, a material possession. That is why I live in this small, modest house. When the Messiah comes, I pray daily that I might be privileged to see him. Then I will return to the land of my fathers and buy a magnificent house near the rebuilt Holy Temple.

As Rebbe Moshe Teitelbaum grew older, he became more and more certain that the Messianic Age[4] was imminent.

Oftentimes, in the midst of his learning, he would stop singing the sing-song melody of the talmudic passages he always hummed. He would rise from his chair, walk over to the window, peer intently into the distance, stand silently for a few moments, shake his head, then return sadly to his seat.

His students swore they heard him muttering, "It was not him, it was not him. He has not yet arrived."

Sometimes he would walk over to the stove that heated his room, scoop up a handful of ashes, and rub them into his forehead as a sign of mourning over the destruction of Jerusalem.

If he heard an unusual commotion outside, he would send two students to investigate. He thought, "Maybe the bearer of good tidings, Elyahu Hanavi, the forerunner of the Messianic Age, is outside, waiting to be invited inside, into my study room."

When he retired for the night, he spread out his white holiday garment at the foot of his bed, along with his walking stick. He extracted a promise from the younger members of his family that, should they hear the blast of the *shofar* call of redemption

---

[4]The exact description of the Messianic Age has not been revealed to man: our sages have based their opinions on various biblical and talmudic passages. Some are of the opinion that the Messianic Age will be a time when the Jewish people, dispersed over all four corners of the world, will be redeemed and returned to their land. Others believe that the Messianic Age will bring an end to human suffering and an era of peace. Some promulgate the theory that a cataclysmic war will precede the Messianic Age. Others conclude that the prophet Elyahu will proclaim the arrival of the Messiah three days before redemption.

before him during the night, they would run to awaken him immediately.

Occasionally, he expressed concern that the delay of the Messianic Age was due to the fact that his people had grown complacent, too accustomed to the Diaspora, that they were not yearning sufficiently.

Yet he never lost hope. Redemption could come in an instant, in the blink of an eye.

Once, on the afternoon before the Passover *seder*, convinced that the celebration of the holiday of freedom would usher in the Messianic Age, he filled a basket with a silver goblet, wine, and *matzos*, dressed in his white holiday garments, and stood by the window in his study room for hours, awaiting the blast of the *shofar* call of redemption. He waited and waited in his study room, until two students came to escort him to the synagogue for the evening prayers. He was not disillusioned. All the way to the synagogue, he sang, "I believe with complete faith in the coming of the Messiah, and even though he may be delayed, nevertheless, I anticipate his arrival every day.[5] We will just have to wait a little longer," he told his escorts.

His hair thinned and turned white. His back became hunched. He could walk only with the support of two disciples holding him on either side. He worried that he would die before he met the Messiah. Two things comforted him: Jeremiah's prophecies and studying. He died on the 28th day of *Tammuz*, 1841, almost 150 years ago. Until his dying breath, he believed that he would live to greet the redeemer of Israel.

Since that time, profound changes have occurred in our world: the great Jewish migrations from Russia to *Eretz Yisrael* and America in the latter part of the nineteenth century, two cataclysmic world wars, the establishment of a political state in the land of our forefathers, increasing violence, the erosion of human freedom, the threat of nuclear extinction. And the Jewish

[5]Maimonides, The Thirteen Principles of Faith, found in Maimonides's introduction to the tenth chapter of the talmudic tractate *Sanhedrin* and in most prayer books.

people continue to yearn for redemption, daily reciting at the conclusion of our prayers, "I believe with complete faith in the coming of Messiah, and even though he may be delayed, nevertheless, I anticipate his arrival every day."[6]

And what must we do until that time?

We must continue telling stories!

[6]Maimonides, op. cit.

Glossary

aliyah: immigration to the land of Israel
aravos: willow branches
auto-da-fé: burning at the stake

baal teshuvah: one who returns to Judaism
bar mitzvah: age of religious responsibility for a young man, thirteen
    years old
batim: outer black boxes of the *tefillin*
bimah: pulpit of the synagogue
bris milah: circumcision ritual

challah, challos: twisted loaves of freshly baked bread
chametz: leaven
Chanukah menorah: candelabra that holds the *Chanukah* lights
chasidim: disciples of a rebbe
chol hamo'ed: intermediate days of *Pesach* and *Sukkos*
cholent: a mixture of meat, potatoes, beans, and barley that has been
    cooked from the eve of the Sabbath until the lunch meal on Saturday
chumash: Bible

daven: pray
Diaspora: exile
din torah: judgment

Elyahu Hanavi: Elijah, the prophet of peace and redemption
Eretz Yisrael: ancestral homeland of the Jewish people
esrog: citron

gabbai: appointment secretary to the rebbe, voluntary assistant to the
    shamish
gemar chasemah tovah: may you be inscribed and sealed for good
good yom tov: the traditional greeting for a holy day; literally, "a good
    day"
gragger: noisemaker used during the reading of the Scroll of Esther on
    Purim

hadas, hadasim: myrtle leaves
hagadah: booklet in which the exodus from Egypt is retold
hakafos: joyous processions with the Torah scrolls
havdalah: ritual separating the Sabbath from the weekdays, using
    wine, spices, and the light of a twisted, double-wicked candle
hoshanah: bundle of five willow branches

kaddish: a prayer exalting God, used to separate the parts of the prayer
    service and as a memorial for the deceased
kiddush: sanctification of wine
kiddush hachayim: sanctification of life
kiddush hashem: martyrdom for the sanctification of God's Holy Name
Kol Nidre: opening prayer of the *Yom Kippur* service, literally meaning
    "all the vows"

l'chayim: to life
lechem mishnah: two *challos* for the *Shabbos* meals
lulav: palm branch

ma'ariv: night prayer service
maggid: synonym for rebbe
ma'oz tzur: Chanukah song, *Rock of Ages*
matzah, matzos: unleavened bread
megillah, megillas Esther: Scroll of Esther

melave malkah: farewell feast to the *Shabbos* Queen

mezuzah: parchment scroll affixed to the doorposts of Jewish homes inscribed with the first two paragraphs of *Sh'ma* found in the *Torah* (Deuteronomy 6:4–8, 11:13–21)

midrash: legends and interpretations on verses in the *Torah*

mikveh: ritual bath

minchah: afternoon prayer service

minyan: quorum of ten adult males gathered for a prayer service

mitzvah, mitzvos: commandment(s), good deed(s)

mohel: ritual circumciser

na'aseh v'nishma: "we will do and we will listen," the oath of loyalty to *Torah* the Jewish people swore to uphold at Mount Sinai

Ne'ilah: closing prayer of the *Yom Kippur* service, literally meaning "closing the gates"

parsheyos: parchment upon which four sections of the *Torah* are inscribed and inserted into the black boxes of the *tefillin*

Pesach: Passover

pidyon haben: redemption ceremony of the first-born son

pittum: distinctive, knobbed stem of the *esrog*

poretz: landowner

rebbe: rabbi of a chasidic sect

rebbetzen: title for the rabbi's wife

rosh yeshivah: dean of a school of higher Jewish learning

seder: ceremonial and festival meal of the first two nights of *Pesach*

se'udah: festive meal celebrating a holy day or a religious ritual

Shabbat Hamalkah: the *Shabbos* Queen

shalach manos: sending two gifts of food to friends during *Purim*

shanah tovah: "a good year"

shalom aleichem: greetings of peace; hello; goodbye

shamash: candle used to light the other candles in the *Chanukah* menorah

shamish: beadle

Shavuos: Pentecost

shofar: ram's horn

sholosh seudos: third meal of *Shabbos*

Sh'ma: prayer affirming faith in One God

shtetl, shtetlach: village(s) in eastern Europe, almost entirely inhabited by Jews

shul: synagogue

siddur: prayer book

sukkah: temporary hut

Sukkos: Festival of Tabernacles

tallis: prayer shawl

tefillin: phylacteries

tish: table where the meals of holy days are eaten. A rebbe's *tish* is usually filled with guests, song, joy, and words of *Torah*

Tosafos: primary talmudic commentary printed on every page of Talmud

tzadik: righteous man

yahrzeit: anniversary of a death

yeshivah: school of higher *Torah* learning

yetzer hara: evil inclination

yishuv: Jewish settlement in the land of Israel, particularly in Jerusalem, around the turn of the twentieth century

yom tov: holy day, literally "a good day"

yoshev: perpetual student

Zohar: the mystical secrets of *Torah*

For Further Reading

Agnon, Shmuel Yosef. *Days of Awe*. New York: Schocken Books, 1948.
Ayger, Yehuda Layb, *Imray Emes*. Jerusalem, 1973.
_____ *Toras Emes*. Lublin, 1790 (reprinted B'nai B'rak, Israel: Hotza'as Yahadus, 1970).

Bekmeister, Yisrael. *Seepuray Nifla'ot Migedolay Yisrael*. Tel Aviv: Defus Ayshel, 1969.
Bromberg, Abraham Yitzchak. *Hayehude Hatov M'Gustinin*. Jerusalem: Hotza'as Bays Hillel, 1982.
Buber, Martin. *The Legend of the Baal Shem*. New York: Schocken Books, 1969.

Chagay Yisrael U'mo'adav. Kefar Chabad, Israel: Kehot Publishing Society.
Chanoch Henich Hakohen M'Aleksander. *Megelas Polin*. Yehudah Layb Levin, ed. Jerusalem: Defus Da'as, 1969.

Ellberg, Yehuda. *Ma'aseeyos*. Tel Aviv: I. L. Peretz Publishing House, 1980.

Gershon Chanoch M'Izbitza. *Hagadah. The First Night of Pesach.*

Getz, Menachem. *Yerushalayim Shel Ma'aloh.* Jerusalem: Hotza'as Haginzar Hacharayde, 1977.

Heschel M'Apt, Avraham Yehoshua. *Baal Ohev Yisrael.* Yitzchak Alfasi, ed. Jerusalem: Machon Sifsay Tzadikkim, 1981.

Holy Beggar's Gazette. San Francisco: House of Love and Prayer, Spring/Summer 1976.

Kahana, Avraham. *Sayfer Hachasedus.* Warsaw, 1863. (reprinted Tel Aviv, 1978).

Kalmish, Klonimous. *Derech Hamelech.* 1976.

Kasher, M., and Belchrovitz, Y. *Anshay Ma'aloh.* Jerusalem: Defus Ma'arav, 1974.

Kenig, Yosef. *Sepurim Nifla'im.* Jerusalem, 1967.

Ki Tov, Eliyahu. *Sayfer Haparsheyos. Devarim.* Jerusalem: Aleph Publishers, 1974.

Klapholtz, Yisrael. *Hachozrim B'teshuvah.* B'nai B'rak, Israel: Pa'er Hasayfer, 1981.

_____ *Sayfer Hachasedus.* Israel, 1965.

_____ *Sepuray Eliyahu Hanave.* Vol. 1. B'nai B'rak, Israel: Pa'er Hasayfer, 1977.

Labovitz, Annette. *Secrets of the Past, Bridges to the Future.* Miami: Central Agency for Jewish Education, 1984.

Lamishpacha.

Menachem Mendel. *Purim. Yom Tov Ertzellungen.* Jerusalem, 1981.

_____ *Shavuos. Yom Tov Ertzellungen.* Jerusalem, 1981.

Mordechai Yosef M'Izbitza. *Hagada Shel Pesach im Sefer Hazemanim.* New York: Bays Yaakov, Saphrograph Co., 1956.

Nachman of Bratslav. *M'kor Hasimchah.* Jerusalem: Mesifta Chaseday Bratslav, 1982.

Necht, Y, Epstein, Z., and Baruch, Y. *Hashabbos.* Tel Aviv: Oneg Shabbos (Ohel Shem) Society, 1952.

Rabinovitz, Yisrael Mordechai. *Sayfer Yeshuas Yisrael.* Brooklyn, 1985.

Refael, Yitzchak. *Sayfer Hachasedus.* Tel Aviv: A. Tseyone Publishing House, 1955.

Rizhin, Yisrael Friedman. *Ner Yisrael.* Vol. II. B'nai B'rak, Israel, 1978.

Rosman, Shlomo. *Roshay Golat Are-ayl.* New York: Zichron Kedoshim Press, 1975.

Segel, Gedalyah. *Pardes Hagadah Hashalaym.* Jerusalem, 1972.

Weberman, Pinchas David. *Sayfer Ma'aseh Tzadikim im Divray Tzadikim.* Jerusalem: Defus Techeya, 1962.

Weinberg, Avraham. *Bays Avraham.* Jerusalem, 1979.

Yaakov Yitzchak M'Biala. *Toldot Adam.* Jerusalem: Kollel Biala, 1975.

Zevin, S. Y. *Sepuray Chassidim.* Tel Aviv: Hotza'as Seforim Avraham Tzeyone, 1959.

About the Authors

Annette and Eugene Labovitz are known professionally throughout the storytelling world as The Legendary Maggidim, a title reminiscent of the itinerant preachers who wandered from *shtetl* to *shtetl*, inspiring, teaching, guiding, and encouraging. They have traveled extensively throughout the United States, Europe, and Israel, lecturing and gathering material for their stories. Annette Labovitz is the coordinator of the Jewish Educational Resource Center and the Holocaust Learning Center of the Office of Jewish Education, Jewish Federation of South Broward, Hollywood, Florida. Eugene Labovitz has been rabbi of Temple Ner Tamid in Miami Beach, Florida, for the past thirty-two years. They are the authors of *A Touch of Heaven: Eternal Stories for Jewish Living.*